MW00805681

DISCARDED

Hats Off

HATS OFF

Headdress of the U.S. Army
1872-1912

John P. Langellier

Schiffer Military History
Atglen, PA

DEDICATED TO

WES CLARK and GLEN SWANSON
for their many contributions to this publication

"You're not properly uniformed Captain, nor are your men. You look like scratch dirt farmers on market day. Your hat should be creased fore and aft like a fedora...."

Lieutenant Colonel Owen Thursday (Henry Fonda)
Fort Apache (RKO) 1948

Book Design by Ian Robertson.

Published by Schiffer Publishing Ltd.
4880 Lower Valley Road
Atglen, PA 19310
Phone: (610) 593-1777
FAX: (610) 593-2002
E-mail: Schifferbk@aol.com.
Visit our web site at: www.schifferbooks.com
Please write for a free catalog.
This book may be purchased from the publisher.
Please include $3.95 postage.
Try your bookstore first.

In Europe, Schiffer books are distributed by:
Bushwood Books
6 Marksbury Road
Kew Gardens
Surrey TW9 4JF
England
Phone: 44 (0)181 392-8585
FAX: 44 (0)181 392-9876
E-mail: Bushwd@aol.com.

Try your bookstore first.

CONTENTS

PREFACE AND ACKNOWLEDGMENTS

This publication was inspired by a number of pervious works, which were produced by the Smithsonian Institution's Museum of American History, the Arizona Historical Society, and the Wyoming State Museum.[1] While these titles provided excellent details relative to the matter of U.S. Army headdress, especially for the years after the American Civil War, they relied upon black and white illustrations. Although of high caliber, these images could not convey certain particulars concerning color. Further, since the appearance of these monographs, additional information has been forthcoming to add to the previous body of knowledge.

It is for these reasons that I set out to provide *Hats Off* as a complementary publication that not only would make the information found in earlier titles available to a new generation of collectors, curators, and historians, but also provide information and illustrations not included in these earlier efforts, particualrly items adopted at the beginning of the twentieth century.

As such, *Hats Off* traces the many changes that occurred in U.S. Army headgear from the immediate post-Civil War era, when the American martial establishment was little more than a frontier constabulary, to the early 1900s—a time when the American soldier began to emerge as a major player in international relations. During the years charted in this work, headgear was but one outward sign of this evolution.

Early on, military uniforms tended to emulate European fashion trends. With the passage of time, however, the U.S. Army began to adopt its own distinct look, including articles that were created in response to the varied environments where American troops served.

In addition to developing headgear that responded to climate, not a few officers and men alike modified their issue items, both to improve upon what Uncle Sam provided, and at times, to customize their kit as a means of establishing individuality. Unlike conscript armies of foreign monarchs, the American soldier was the swordbearer of a democracy. As such, his headgear often took on a non-regulation shape or nuance corresponding to the spirit of individuality, a characteristic often associated with the people of the United States.

Whatever the motivation behind opting for one style of headdress over another, chronicling these variations on a theme proved intriguing. In order to assemble adequate representations of many types of headgear to illustrate this study, assistance had to be obtained from several institutions and individuals.

First of all, it was Wes Clark who planted the seed for *Hats Off*, and then kindly supplied many extraordinary items from his personal collection to illustrate this work. So did Glen Swanson, who additionally photographed many superb pieces from his collection. Jack Blades, Robert G. Borrell, Sr., Dr. James Brusk, Dr. Edward Burka, Mark Cassel, Chuck Fowler, Jerome Greene, George Langellier, Jr., Dr. Michael McAfee, Joe Parr, Hayes Otoupalik, and Walt Redling all permitted me to utilize materials from their fine collections.

Preface and Acknowledgments

Institutional assistance for this project included the Museum of American History, where Dr. Lonnie Bunch, Ms. Jennifer Locke, and curator emeritus of the military history collections, Donald Kloster, aided in many ways. At the former Wyoming Archives, Museums, and Historical Department, Paula Chovoya and Tom Lindmier always were ready to respond to requests for support. Michael Winey and Randy Hackenberg of the U.S. Army Military History Institute at Carlisle Barracks, Pennsylvania, are due thanks. Clif Chappell of the U.S. Army Engineer Historical Holding at Fort Belvoir, Virginia, Terry VanMeter of the U.S. Cavalry Museum, Fort Riley, Kansas, and Luther Hansen of the U.S. Army Quartermaster Museum, Fort Lee, Virginia, contributed to this project, too. Kevin Mulroy, director of the Autry Museum of Western Heritage's research center, also facilitated my research, as did his colleague Marva Felchin. Likewise, staffs of the Kansas State Historical Society, the North Dakota Historical Society, the National Archives and Records Administration in both Washington, D.C., and College Park, Maryland, along with the Library of Congress, all rendered professional services.

Dr. Vincent Transano, the U.S. Naval Facilities Engineering Command Historian, patiently read drafts of the manuscript and offered valuable comments on the text. Finally, Gordon Chappell provided extensive photographic support and expert advice, while Kurt Cox likewise lent his photographic skills. To these individuals and many others, I offer my sincere thanks.

NOTES

[1] These titles were Edgar M. Howell, *United States Army Headgear 1855-1902: Catalog of United States Army Uniforms in the Collections of the Smithsonian Institution*, II (Washington DC: U.S. Government Printing Office, 1975); Sidney B. Brinckerhoff, *Military Headgear in the Southwest, 1846-1890* (Tucson: Arizona Pioneers' Historical Society, n.d.); and two works by Gordon Chappell, *Brass Spikes and Horsehair Plumes: A Study of U.S. Army Dress Helmets, 1872-1903* (Tucson: Arizona Pioneers' Historical Society, 1966), and *Summer Helmets of the U.S. Army, 1875-1910* (Cheyenne: Wyoming State Museum, 1967).

LIST OF ABBREVIATIONS

Pictorial Sources

AHS	Arizona Historical Society, Tucson, AZ
AMWH	Autry Museum of Western Heritage, Los Angeles, CA
CBF	Christian Barthelmess Family Collection, Miles City, MT
CECSM	CEC and Seabee Museum, Port Hueneme, CA
CF	Chuck Fowler
CSPM	Colorado Springs Pioneer Museum, Colorado Springs, CO
DJB	Dr. James Brust
EB	Dr. Edward R. Burka, MD
FAM	Frontier Army Museum, Ft. Leavenworth, KS
FSHM	Fort Sam Houston Museum, Ft. Sam Houston, TX
GC	Gordon Chappell
GGNRA	Golden Gate National Recreation Area, San Francisco, CA
GL	George Langellier, Jr.
GS	Glen Swanson
HO	Hayes Outopolik
JB	Jack Blades
JG	Jerome Greene
JP	Joe Parr, Historic Framing and Collectibles, Ellicott City, MD
KC	Kurt Cox
KSHS	Kansas State Historical Society, Topeka, KS
LBBNM	Little Big Horn Battlefield National Monument, Crow Agency, MT
LC	Library of Congress, Washington, DC
LF	Dr. Lawrence Frost
MC	Mark Cassel
MM	Dr. Michael J. McAfee.
NA	National Archives, College Park, MD
NSHS	Nebraska State Historical Society, Lincoln, NE
RB	Robert Borrell, Sr.

SHSND	State Historical Society of North Dakota, Bismark, ND
SHSW	State Historical Society of Wisconsin, Madison, WI
SI	Smithsonian Institution, Museum of American History, Armed Forces Collection, Washington, DC
T&L	Turner and Laughlin, Tucson, AZ
UKL	University of Kansas Spencer Library, Kansas Collections Lawrence, KS
USAMHI	US Army Military History Institute, Carlisle Barracks, PA
USAPAM	US Army (former Presidio Army Museum Collection) Presidio of San Francisco, CA
USAQM	US Army Quartermaster Museum, Ft. Lee, VA
USCM	US Cavalry Museum, Ft. Riley, KS
WSA	Wyoming State Archives, Cheyenne, WY
WSUL	Washington State University Library, Pullman, WA
WR	Walt Redling
WC	Wes Clark
WCC	Western Costume Company, North Hollywood, CA

Abbreviations In Notes

AGO	Adjutant General's Office
A&NJ	Army *and Navy Journal*
ARSW	*Annual Report of the Secretary of War*
CCF	Consolidated Correspondence Files
GO	General Orders
HQA	Headquarters of the Army
LR	Letters Received
LS	Letters Sent
NA	National Archives
OQMG	Office of the Quartermaster General
RG	Record Group
SO	Special Orders
WD	War Department

Seventh U.S. Cavalry Lieutenant Charles Braden purchased an 1872-folding hat that differed from the enlisted version in having even a larger brim. Note also that he wears the hat from side to side rather than fore and aft as was more typical, at least for enlisted men. USAMHI

1

THE THIN BLUE LINE,
1872-1880

While William T. Sherman traveled abroad in Europe, in April 1872, many of the general's former Civil War compatriots received a tasking from the secretary of war. A group of officers was called upon to form a board of review for U.S. Army regulations. They ultimately were instructed to consider the matter of the army's clothing, as well. From May though June 21, 1872, these men pondered the subject, then adjourned soon thereafter.[1] In the process this body ignored Quartermaster General Montgomery Meigs and his department, the officials charged with outfitting the army. In fact, the prototypes of uniform components the board inspected as part of its deliberations were obtained without calling upon the quartermaster or his subordinates for assistance.

This situation probably did not escape Meigs, because word soon spread that Colonel Randolph Marcy, the inspector general of the army, was heading the effort to obtain samples of uniforms, and report on new styles that might be adopted.[2] This included a hat that was described by the *Army and Navy Journal* as "a sombrero which can be looped up at the sides so as to resemble a chapeau."[3]

This item was the folding hat reviewed by an 1868 board and also featured in a study prepared for the surgeon general's office by a member of the Medical Department, Assistant Surgeon Alfred Alexander Woodhull. Among other things, this so-called "Woodhull Report" treated the clothing of the army. While there is no direct evidence to support the fact that the members of an 1872 Board had a copy of this document, its text was not unknown, having been reprinted years earlier in the *Army and Navy Journal*. Thus, there is little doubt that some if not all of the 1872 Board were aware of Woodhull's findings and the illustrations which accompanied his work. Additionally, these men reviewed the discussions of an 1862 board, and would draw from this prior effort concerning the uniform. In fact, these sources and many ideas found elsewhere were evident in the 1872 Board's decision-making process.

In July the secretary of war related that President Ulysses S. Grant had approved the new uniform recommended by the board, and it was to be adopted as of December 1872.[4] Soon the board's new outfit appeared on July 29, 1872, as General Orders No. 76, Adjutant General's

The enlisted version of the 1872-pattern campaign hat as issued, open and folded. Photograph by Gordon Chappell. USAPAM

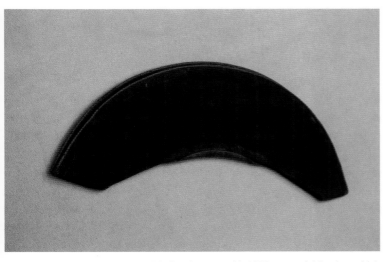

Captain Fredric Benteen, Seventh U.S. Cavalry, wore this 1872-pattern folding hat, which had tape sewn around the outer edge of the brim and a shape that differed considerably from the enlisted model. The hat is in the folded position. Photograph by Glen Swanson. GS

Comparison of the 1872-pattern and 1876-pattern campaign hats. Photograph by Glen Swanson. GS

Office. Subsequently, the order was published by the government with color plates featuring headgear, coats, jackets, dress belts, and shoulder knots for officers. After that an identical text, without lithographs, was released as General Orders No. 92, War Department, October 26, 1872.

The illustrations from the earlier version of the orders especially would prove useful for those interested in manufacturing uniform components for officers, as well as for those in the Quartermaster Department required to oversee compliance to the regulations adopted by these orders. These images were based upon photographs taken of the prototypes for the forage cap made by the military supply house of Warnock and the dress helmet fabricated by Horstmann (a Philadelphia-based firm), two changes having been made from the board specimens. One was the removal of ornamental trim from the forage cap, and the other was the reduction of the diameter of the helmet braid that was draped on the front and back of the headdress. The idea was to reduce this decorative element by one-third.[5]

Meigs estimated that the first order for helmets should provide for approximately 9,600 cavalry models and 400 light artillery.[6] Inquiries were sent on to prospective suppliers.[7] Horstmann, the firm that had delivered the board sample for $59.60, received the contract to furnish 9,000 helmets (8,700 cavalry and 300 light artillery), at a cost of $5.46 each complete, being more than sufficient to allow one helmet per eligible soldier for the first and third year of his five year enlistment.[8]

While this helmet could be construed as taking its basic inspiration from European military modes, its origins cannot be attributed directly to one foreign military power only. Indeed, even though Americans had more than ample evi-

RIGHT: Sergeant Charles N. Loynes of Company I, Seventh U.S. Infantry, added worsted sky-blue hat cords and brass infantry insignia of the 1875-pattern to his hat. Typically campaign hats of the 1870s and 1880s were worn without insignia. WSUL

Lieutenant Colonel George A. Custer's 1872-pattern helmet had the tassel attached to the bands on the right side, which was typical of officers' helmets of the period. SI

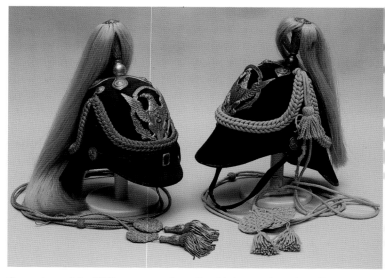

Comparison of the 1872-pattern cavalry enlisted helmet and cavalry officer's helmet. Among other things, officers had a gold cord, gilt fittings, and a silver regimental numeral on the front of the plate, while enlisted men had no numeral and their cords were yellow worsted for cavalry and scarlet worsted for artillery. Photograph by Glen Swanson. GS

dence of European helmet styles to study, at least from illustrations in circa 1860 advertisements from such military suppliers as Robert Weir, a Boston military costumer; as well as from a trio of military outfitters—Horstmann Brothers & Allien; John A. Baker; and Schuyler, Hartley & Graham. The 1872-pattern was not akin to anything in the Old World lexicon.[9] In fact, all four firms depicted a Prussian "Pickle Haube" of leather as available for purchase, thus indicating the Germanic dominance that began to influence martial wear even before the Franco Prussian War. Yet the style adopted by the United States Army

was not of the versions found in Germany in the strictest sense when the types are compared.[10]

In fact, the 1872-pattern is a hybrid of European models at best, especially in that the helmets worn across the Atlantic regularly were of leather or metal, or a combination of these two materials, rather than "black felt," which was the one adopted in the United States by General Orders No. 92.[11] Furthermore, the helmet cord and bands, that could be traced to as early as 1833 for U.S. dragoons and subsequently to light artillery batteries, generally were not used in tandem with European helmets.[12]

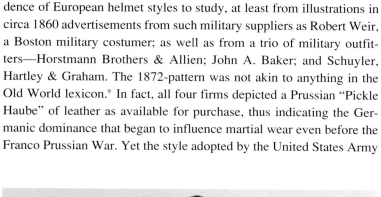

The enlisted 1872-pattern cavalry dress helmet had yellow cords and a yellow horsetail plume, while those for light artillerymen were to have scarlet and signalmen orange cords and plumes respectively. Photograph by Gordon Chappell.

Light artillery enlisted 1872-pattern helmets were distinguished by scarlet bands, cords, and plume, and side buttons that bore crossed cannons. Photograph by Glen Swanson. GS

Side view of the official pattern of an 1872 officer's helmet, in this case for light artillery because of the crossed cannon devices on the side buttons. The side buttons also have horizontal lines instead of stippling usually found on enlisted helmets. Also, the gold cords festooned to the front and back of the helmet are separate from the breast cord, another difference from enlisted helmets. The tassel is separate here as well, an uncommon feature in most surviving examples. Moreover, the cords are hung from scroll and rings found on enlisted helmets rather than the scroll and hook more commonly used on officers' models. NA

Regardless of this divergence from European modes, a few years after the U.S. helmet was adopted Colonel H.J. Hunt, a member of the 1872 board, recalled "the model was that of the English horseguards."[13] Hunt went on to comment:

> The helmet is not according to the model selected by the Board.... The visor is unnecessarily large and awkward, and has not the military style of the model, the horse hair plume is unnecessarily large, awkward, heavy and long—one third the amount of horse hair and of shorter length would answer the purpose much better than the present pattern. The model was more erect and the plume sat better than the one actually issued.[14]

Whether quartermaster officials made more changes than just the diameter of the helmet braid, or in fact Hunt's memory was faulty, can-

An official quartermaster photograph showing the front view of the prototype or approved pattern for the dress helmet adopted in 1872 for officers of light artillery and for cavalry officers. The plume was to be scarlet for artillery and yellow for cavalry. The socket that held the plume has been removed from this photograph. Upon careful examination it can be seen that the "helmet plate" was rendered in paper for this official photograph taken for the Quartermaster Department, perhaps because no specimen of the brass or gilt plate was available at that time. NA

not be determined. The latter case seems somewhat more likely, in that Meigs evidently had the Horstmann sample held in Washington until Marcy could pass judgment on the proposed pattern.[15] This he did in 1873, writing that it "seemed to conform to the requirements of Genl. Order No. 92."[16]

All this not withstanding, production of the helmet moved forward. The quartermaster officer charged with the production even revealed:

Comparison of the original type of officers' breast cord worn with the 1872-pattern dress helmet (right) and the style of cords produced later for wear with the 1881-pattern officers' dress helmet (left). Note the separate tassel that could be attached to the helmet by a gold loop when the cord was disconnected. Small clips commonly were used on both types of cords to allow detachment. GS

Detail of First Lieutenant William W. Cooke, Seventh U.S. Cavalry's 1872-pattern dress helmet showing the scroll and hook most commonly found on officers' helmet to keep the gold cord in place. Note the screen ventilator that also forms part of officers' helmet. CSPM

Captain James Jackson, First U.S. Cavalry, has detached the breast cord from his top-heavy 1872-pattern helmet with steep rear visor. The plume is yellow horsehair and the cords on the helmet and his chest are of metallic gold thread. The gilt eagle device on the front of the helmet bears a silver number "1" to indicate his regiment. NA

"It is the most sightly head-gear I have ever seen...."[17] Despite this praise, he added some short-comings would have to be rectified later. He specifically indicated the fur felt of the shell was "almost too light; the disk on the crown should be broader to bear the strain of the spear, plume, and socket, and the binding should be heavier and broader."[18]

Even before these comments, the color of the plume came into question. Obtaining a uniform shade of yellow posed a difficult problem that experts had no solution for save leaving the color as natural white.[19] No authority existed to depart from the yellow plume set forth in the general orders. Further, Horstmann representatives assured Meigs that it could produce a permanent yellow dye, although it was understood that over time, exposure to the elements would tend to fade the hue, as it would do on the facings for the uniform coat. As such, retaining the yellow plume was recommended and approved.[20]

The same fugitive dye problem affected the helmet cords as well, or so Horstmann Brothers contended. For this reason they produced cords that were darker than the sealed samples (they had an orange cast).[21] The company had manufactured some 200 cords by this point, enough

to complete the first small lot of helmets, that of 228 that were being made.[22] Horstmann spokespersons defended the firm's actions by stating: "The color used is the same as we have used for the Army since 1851—and it was adopted on account of its durability, being not likely to fade—and a medium between an orange and a yellow."[23] The firm then concluded with the question as to whether they should produce a lighter color.

The answer was to the affirmative.[24] Horstmann representatives responded that delivery would be delayed if new ones had to be made up, while the firm also would lose money.[25]

While it is unclear what the final outcome was about the color of cords, one other matter related to these adornments would be considered. How were these cords to be worn? The light artillery cap had no such provisions. Surviving photographs depict a number of options. This same latitude was not to continue with the new uniform, in that GO No. 67, War Department, June 25, 1873 read:

The helmet cords will be attached to the left side of the helmet, and come down to the left shoulder, where they are held together

An unidentified field grade officer of the First U.S. Artillery has kept the breast cord attached to the helmet, despite the fact he has removed his headgear for this portrait. The plume was to be scarlet for artillery officers and men alike. GS

Seventh U.S. Cavalry Second Lieutenant Ezra Fuller opted for the model of the 1872-pattern helmet made by Baker and McKenney, with its distinct cruciform rather than "X" style plume holder base and slightly abbreviated front and rear visors. GS

by a slide; one cord then passes to the front and the other to the rear of the neck, crossing upon the right shoulder and passing separately around to the front and rear of the right arm, where they are again united and held together by a slide under the arm; the united cords then cross the breast, and are looped up to the upper button on the left side of the coat.

This prescription essentially coincided with the issuing of the first 194 helmets, but did not address the cumbersome matter of a soldier extracting himself from the tangle of cords when he needed to remove his helmet.[26] In due course, certain enterprising individuals cut their cords, often near the tassel on the helmet band, and improvised an attachment scheme, such as a hook and eye or a brass spring clip, much as had been provided for officers' helmet cords. For the remainder of the decades during which the dress helmet was issued, the government failed to make a similar adjustment, thereafter providing cords of one piece instead of taking this more practical approach.[27]

The matter of altering the cords stemmed from individual initiative, but the shape of the 1872-helmet itself was based on contractors or suppliers, who were to follow certain guidelines set forth for the helmet by the Quartermaster Department. These were as follows:

To be made of felt composed of one part each of Russia, best coney-back, muskrat, extra coney, and a half part of wash-blow. The body approaches in shape the helmets as seen in antique Greek sculpture—top spherical, sides vertical, front and back gently sloping outward to the point where the helmet is to rest on the head; thence, in a more diverging line extending in front to a vizor, in the back to a cape for the protection of the neck. From center of top along the side to lower edge about eight (8) inches, to extreme point of vizor eleven and one-half (11 1/2) inches, to extreme point of back eleven (11) inches.

Vizor is gradually narrowing, and rounded at front; length about three and one-half (3) inches, width across, the forehead about twelve (12) to twelve and one-fourth (12 1/4) inches, across the front (one inch above the extreme point) about five (5) inches.

The neck-cape is about seven and one-fourth (7 1/4) inches wide, three and one-fourth (3 1/4) inches long, corners rounded.

This Fifth U.S. Cavalry officer's 1872-pattern helmet with the less drastic front and rear visors was one of the variations available for purchase by officers from military suppliers, in this case the New York firm of Baker and McKenney. HO

Side buttons for the 1872-pattern helmet were to display crossed sabers for cavalry troopers and signalmen and crossed cannons for light artillerymen. LBBNM

The edge of the helmet, vizor, and cape is bound with fine enameled leather. On either side, about three and one-half inches (3 1/2) inches above the lower edge, is a ventilator.

At the lower edge, on either side, is a button-fastening for chin-strap.

The latter consists of two parts, made of enameled leather, five-eighths 5/8 of an inch wide, each about nine and one-half (9 1/2) inches long. These parts are united, and can be lengthened or short-ened by means of a loop (same material as strap) at the end of one, and a brass bar-buckle one (1) by three-fourth (3/4) of an inch at the end of the other part. From one side button to the other, straight across the front, is another strap of enameled leather, five-eighths (5/8) of an inch wide, stitched on the body of the helmet.

Sweat-leather two and one-half (2 1/2) inches wide of Bel-gium [sic] sheepskin.

The helmet is ornamented with eagle, top piece, and plume socket, scrolls and rings, and side buttons, and is trimmed with hair plume and cords and bands.

Helmet ornaments are made of sheet-brass, No. 24.

Hair Plumes for Helmets: Made of good horse-hair, dyed. To droop from top of socket over back and sides of helmet.

The hairs are woven and sewed together at one end, giving the latter the form of a flattened knob about one and five-eighths (1 5/8) inch diameter, with star-shaped brass eyelet in center to admit the pen of the top piece. Length of plume from eyelet to end, four-teen (14) inches.

Cords and Bands for Helmets: Made of worsted, No. 26, and machined cord. The bands are loop-plaited, fastened to the scroll-rings, and festooned on front and back of helmet, the festoons reach-ing in front to the upper edge of chin-strap, and approaching the lower edge of back within two (2) inches.

The loop-plaiting is about one (1) inch wide, and ends under scrolls on the left side in a tassel of sixty (60) to seventy (70) fringes one and three-fourths (1 3/4) inch long. Through the braided head, about three-fourths (3/4) inch diameter, passes the continuation of the bands in the form of two cords, each five (5) feet eight (8) inches long, with two (2) slides netted over a fuller's board three-fourth (3/4) inch in diameter, five-eighths (5/8) of an inch high. Three

Rear view of Sergeant William Williams' 1872-pattern dress helmet. Williams was a non-commissioned officer in the Seventh U.S. Cavalry who survived the ill-fated Little Bighorn engagement. Photograph by Gordon Chappell. LBBNM

Interior with contractor's label of Sergeant Williams' 1872-pattern cavalry helmet. Note the small wedges of leather that were used to hold the rings of the plume base in place. Photograph by Gordon Chappell. LBBNM

inches from the lower end the cords are fastened together by a braided knot hold a loop about two and three-fourths (2 3/4) inches long. At the end of each cord is also a small braided knot and aiguillette, plaited flat in three strands of smaller cord, in oval shape, two and three-eighths (2 3/8) inches long, two and three-fourths (2 3/4) inches wide. From the lower end of each aiguillette is suspended another tassel of from sixty (60) to seventy (70) fringes one and three-fourths (1 3/4) inch long, with braided head three-eighths (3/8) of an inch high, three-fourth (3/4) inch diameter.[28]

The helmet's trimmings likewise were detailed. They were to be:

Eagles for helmet.—made of sheet-brass No. 24, of the shape of the eagle in the coat of arms of the United States, with a national shield on the breast, head surmounted by a scroll with the motto "E pluribus unum"; scroll extending downward and meeting olive branch and arrows in the talons of the eagle. Whole height, four an one-half (4) inches; greatest width between tips of wings, three and seven-eighths (3 7/8) to four (4) inches. Two loops of strong wire soldered on the back to fasten to helmet by means of two small pieces of leather.

Side Buttons for Helmet.—One on each side, a little above lower edge of helmet.

They are to be one (1) inch diameter, edge beveled and grooved, surface slightly convex, and chased.

They are secured to the helmet by two double brass-wire loops, as the scrolls are.

Design for Cavalry and Signal Service: Two crossed sabers, hilts downward and outward [the Signal Service would not have its own side buttons specified until the 1881-pattern helmet was introduced]. For Light Artillery: Two cannon crossed at trunnions.

Plume-Sockets for Helmet.—A crossed shaped foot, with convex bend, to fit exactly the surface of the helmet top.

Each leaf-shaped point of the cross is fastened by means of an ornamented button with stem of two thin wires.

Length of cross between alternate points, five and a quarter (5) inches; each leaf one and a quarter (1) inch at widest, three-quarters (3/4) of an inch at narrowest part; edge beveled and grooved.

On the center of the cross rest a sphere one (1) inch in diameter, surmounted by a short neck with ring, the former one-half (1/2), the latter five-eighths (5/8) of an inch diameter, combined about

RIGHT: Detail of the worsted bands for the enlisted 1872-pattern mounted dress helmet and the japanned pinwheel side ventilator. LBBNM

The plates of enlisted 1872-pattern helmets were devoid of regimental numerals, and were of sheet brass without gold plating unlike those worn by officers. LBBNM

Signal Corps enlisted men's 1872-pattern mounted helmets were to have orange horsetail plumes and orange worsted cords as worn by Signal Private Will C. Barnes. Private Barnes likewise seems to have modified his bands so that he could remove his helmet without undoing the breast cord. NA

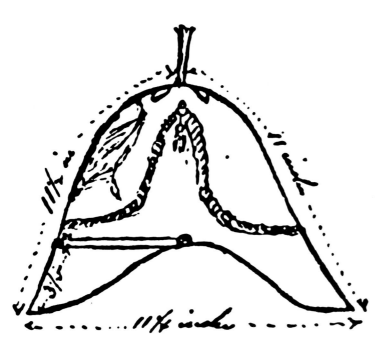

Military Storekeeper Rodgers made this rough sketch of the 1872-pattern mounted dress helmet with the dimensions indicated, as part of his analysis of this type of headgear's design in the early 1870s. NA

one-half (1/2) inch high, from which arises an inverted conical tube, fluted, ornamented by an heraldic eagle with star above his head.

The top of the tube ends in four triangular points. Width of tube across top, one (1) inch. The plume is fastened to the top of this socket by means of a brass pin one-fourth (1/4) of an inch thick, four and three-quarters (4 3/4) inches long, with ornamented button at upper and screw-thread at lower end.

The latter enters through the socket and helmet, and is fastened at the inside by means of a brass washer one and seven-eighths (1 7/8) inch diameter, and a thumb-nut. The plume is held in a drooping position by the head of the above-mentioned brass pin and a brass disk, one and one-fourth (1 1/4) inch diameter, laid under the woven top part of the plume and resting on the points of the socket.

Scrolls and Rings for Helmet.—One on each side, between leaf-shaped points of the top piece, its lower edge one-half (1/2) inch below these points.

The scroll is three-quarters (3/4) inch in diameter, ornamented to correspond with the fasting top piece.

The worsted bands and cords of enlisted 1872-pattern dress helmet were formed of one piece of material. A number of enlisted men cut the cords and modified them in many different ways in order to make it possible to remove the helmet but retain the breast cord, as officers could do because their helmets were constructed in this way by the supplier. This private of the Fourth Cavalry has cut his cords below the sliding tassel, thereby making it possible for him to take off his helmet and place it on the stand next to him (see inset, which also shows the chinstrap placed under the eagle's wings) in this circa 1875 photograph taken at Ft. Sill, Indian Territory. Two other photographs are known that depict another private and a first sergeant from the Fourth Cavalry. Their helmet cords are altered in the same manner. AMWH

The pronounced profile of Seventh U.S. Cavalry Private William Crisfield's 1872-pattern enlisted mounted dress helmet is evident in this c. 1875 picture. So, too, is the fact that he has not cut his cords, but retained them as issued in one piece. LBBNM

On the top of the scroll, in the center, is an eye of thin wire three-sixteenth (3/16) of an inch high, holding a thin brass ring one-half (1/2) inch in diameter, to keep cords and bands in position.

The stem of scroll is formed of two pieces of thin brass wire to fasten it at the inside of helmet.[29]

The helmet worn by officers also was delineated in some detail, although in point of fact a number of variations came into being, in that certain military suppliers deviated from the specifications as provided, which were:

...heavy body of fur bound in fine patent leather; measurements as indicated on cuts [see figure drawn by Military Store Keeper John Frederick Rodgers, p. 18]; patent-leather chin-strap 5/8 of an inch wide with gilt slide; patent-leather vizor-strap folded 3/8 of an inch wide, double stitched, connecting chin-strap buttons; goat-skin sweat-leather.

Ornaments as follows:

Eagle.—Of yellow metal, gilt; pattern same as in coat of arms of the United States, national shield on breast; head surmounted by scroll with motto "E Pluribus Unum in relief letters, scroll extending downward and outward and joining olive branch and arrows in talons of eagle; whole height, 4 inches; greatest width between tips of wings, 4 inches; secured to helmet by wire stems.

Top piece and plume-socket.—Of yellow metal, gilt; base of foot a cross-piece made convex to fit top of helmet; ends of arms mitre-shaped and fastened to helmet by ornamental buttons; length between points of opposite arms, 5 inches; arms at widest part 1 inches, edges grooved and beveled; sphere one inch in diameter, on base surmounted by a short neck with ring, (neck inch, ring 5/8 inch diameter,) from which is raised an inverted conical tube representing rays and displaying on front an heraldic eagle, the head of which is surmounted by a star, in relief; diameter of tube at top one inch; height, (including sphere at bottom,) three inches; the plume held in position at top of socket by a brass pin 4 1/2 inches long, having ornamental head, and a small brass disk; this pin enters through the socket top piece; the shell of helmet and concave brass disk, (1 7/8 inches in diameter,) on the inside, and is secured by a brass thumb-nut.

Scrolls and rings.—Of yellow metal, gilt, placed at sides near top, between the arms of the top piece; the scroll, (or button,) is ornamented to correspond with the fastenings of top piece, and in 3/4 of an inch in diameter; small eye and ring, (inch in diameter,) in center, to hold cords and bands; stem to enter shell of helmet and fasten on the inside.

Side or chin-strap buttons.—Of yellow metal, gilt, 7/8 of an inch in diameter, according to arm of service [crossed sabers for cavalry and crossed cannons for light artillery]; edges beveled and grooved, surface slightly convex and chased; secured to helmet as scrolls are.

Plumes.—According to arm of service. [yellow for cavalry and scarlet for light artillery]

Cords and bands or braids.—Of gold-thread cord. 2 lines; the bands loop plaited and fastened to rings and scrolls at sides and festooned on front and back of helmet; the front festoon falls to the upper edge of vizor and the rear one to a corresponding depth be-

Private George Walker, Seventh U.S. Cavalry holds his 1872-pattern dress helmet with its steep front visor and unaltered yellow worsted cords. GS

hind; the loop plaiting is about 3/4 of an inch wide; at left ring and scroll a pendant tassel of sixty or seventy fringes where the cords are fastened; gilt cords about 5 feet 8 inches long with two netted slides of about 3/4 inch diameter; flat braided ornament 2 3/4 inches in diameter and tassels at each end of cord.[30]

This attention to detail as to how the helmet would appear became moot when Congress disapproved further funds to continue making the components adopted by General orders No. 92. As Meigs pointed out: "In obedience to this law, you will make no further issue of the new uniform corresponding with that above named [hats, uniform caps, forage caps, uniform coats, uniform jackets, flannel sack coats, and unlined coats], including campaign hats with the exception of the helmets of light artillery. There being none of the old dress caps for that branch of service on hand, the helmets will be supplied to the light artillery."[31]

In the conclusion to his statement Meigs could have indicated that one of the reasons for the need for the new headgear for horse artillerymen stemmed from sales of many items of the old pattern before Congress halted momentum with its restrictions. In fact, the old light artillery caps were among the first items placed on the open market.[32] Some

60,000 uniform hats, forage caps, sack coats, and enlisted frock coats followed, but did not deplete supplies to the degree that would have made it necessary to procure the new patterns for some time.[33] Indeed, many items, particularly Civil War vintage "bummer's caps" were worn well into the mid-1870s, as were 1858-pattern hats with the black ostrich plume and insignia for enlisted men on dress occasions, and devoid of such adornment for field purposes.

As such, only the light artillerymen would continue for the moment to receive their horsetail plumes.[34] The foot soldier fared no better, however, because as one of Meigs' subordinates replied when a request came for this new headgear: "the caps are not supplied at present."[35]

This news impacted foot troops and officers of infantry and heavy artillery who were to have a distinctive cap that drew from a number of European antecedents, including the circa 1840 French *casquette d'Afriqué*. The British adapted a version of the cap from the French.[36] Her Majesty's officers had shakos both of the 1860-1869-pattern and its 1869-1878 replacement, that were much like those of their sometimes rivals across the Channel.[37] Indeed, military dealers in the United

In 1875, Horstmann Bros. received a contract for 3,125 enlisted dress caps. The interior of this Horstmann-made dress cap shows the ventilator as well as the thread that held the outer mohair lace to the body of the cap. The leather rectangle and thong were fastened inside to keep the pompon in position and to hold the sheet brass arms of the United States in place on the cap's front. JG

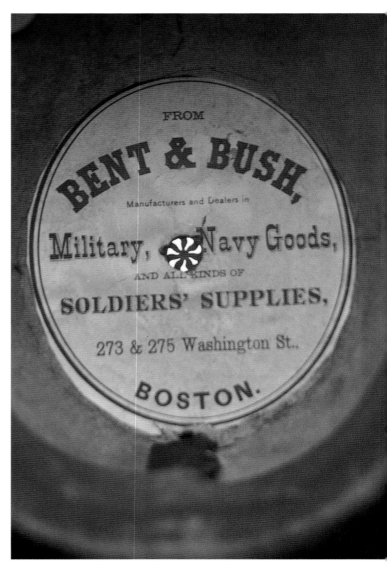

In 1872 Bent and Bush was awarded a contract for 18,000 1872-pattern enlisted dress caps. Two years later the firm was to deliver another 10,800. This is an example of the label found in the inside top of such caps. CF

States had carried similar designs in the 1860s, while the dress cap worn by the U.S. Marine Corps, since 1859, and that of cadets at the U.S. Military Academy, starting prior to the Civil War, were also along comparable lines.[38] Further, the Woodhull report had depicted headdress that was akin to the 1872-pattern dress cap.

Although not identical to counterparts from across the Atlantic, the cap had a distinctive European flavor. Horstmann Brothers and Allien of New York furnished the prototype officer's cap for the board's review, and at some point made two enlisted samples, as well.[39] The main enlisted model for the board, however, was from Warnock, also the maker of the pattern campaign hat.[40]

A stiff fur felt body covered with fine material, trimmed in gold lace was the basic element of the sample officer's cap. Surmounting this was a white cock feather hackle plume, and on the front appeared an embroidered bugle device that completed the model. The plume was retained briefly by the Quartermaster Department as an example, after the officers and enlisted caps were sent back to Horstmann.[41]

This particular ornament caught Meigs' attention. He wanted to have the color changed. While remembering, "the ballad on the white plume of Henry of Navarre," he nonetheless was repulsed by the idea of "any officer of the United States Army being made liable to the state joke of 'showing the white plume.'"[42] Although he made this point, the white cock feathers remained regulation for infantry officers, while the

Paper contract label for an enlisted 1872-pattern helmet produced by G. Davis & Co. in 1876. A portion of the helmet's leather sweatband is evident. AHS

Front, side, and rear view of the 1872-pattern enlisted dress cap. The 1872-pattern enlisted infantry cap bore a bugle device through 1875 for all enlisted men. This headdress resembled the "stiff cap" discussed in the Woodhull Report. CF

Pompons made of dyed worsted wool strips, which were tightly wrapped around a cloth covered wood core. They topped the enlisted 1872-pattern dress cap, in this case for heavy artillery as determined by the scarlet color. Infantrymen had white ones, hospital stewards green versions, commissary sergeants cadet gray pompons, and engineers scarlet upper and white lower examples. These decorative items averaged three inches in height and measured approximately 1 5/8 inches at their widest part near the base. A heavy 2 inch long brass wire loop and a stamped brass cap at the bottom completed the pompon. RB

1872-pattern enlisted heavy artillery cap. RB

Closeup of the rear of the japanned ventilator that was inserted in the top of 1872-pattern dismounted enlisted dress caps and both sides of the 1872-pattern mounted enlisted dress helmet.

heavy artillery at least could avoid being the butt of humor with their scarlet versions. Despite this objection, the white cock feather remained as the crowning glory of the officer's cap for infantrymen, while scarlet ones were called for in the case of artillerymen.

Another matter of concern to some resulted from the lack of precise information available as to the exact pattern of the hat. This meant various military suppliers provided officers with caps that varied one from another.[43] In this light, the quartermaster general's office eventually provided specifications for the headpiece as follows:

...felt shell, covered with indigo-blue cloth; 3 inch high in front; 4 high on sides; 6 inches high over the swell at the back; crown 5 inches long by 5 inches wide; revolving ventilator in crown; gold-wire braid 1/8 of an inch wide around the lower edge and around the crown at top, also, from top to bottom, at each side and back; patent leather vizor unbound; patent leather chin-strap of an inch wide with gilt slide; gilt side or chin strap buttons, vest size, according to arm of service [I for infantry and A for artillery in center of shield respectively]; japanned or goatskin sweat-leather, silk lining; plume-socket of leather on inside at front with metallic guard at opening at top and front edge of crown; gold-embroidered eagle with shield on breast, surmounted by thirteen stars in silver; length from top of stars to end of tail, 1 3/8 inches; width from tip to tip of wings, 1 inches; tips of wings joined by an arc of rays; embroidered badge of arm or corps in front; bottom of badge to be even with top of chin strap.[44]

This last mentioned bit of ornamentation consisted of the by now traditional embroidered crossed cannon in gold with the silver regimental numeral at the intersection for artillery officers, and a gold hunting horn device with a silver regimental numeral in the center of the circular crook for infantry officer. General Orders No. 96, War Department, Adjutant General's Office, November 19, 1875, however, provided that infantry officers were to sport a new device, crossed rifles, in lieu of the long-standing hunting horn insignia.[45]

Enlisted men were to receive a similar dress cap to that set forth for heavy artillery and infantry officers, but the pattern for the other ranks was to be trimmed in worsted braid to match facings on the coat, such as sky-blue for infantry, scarlet for artillery, crimson for ordnance, and so forth. Similarly, the "pear-shaped" (somewhat more like an unopened pine cone) woolen pompon matched the trim, except for infantrymen, who had white pompons to coincide with the cock feather plumes of their officers, and engineers, who had a red pompon with the upper half in white.

Distributing these caps to the rank and file, Meigs acknowledged, presented a considerable obstacle. He wrote the secretary of war that just as it was impossible to obtain regulation ostrich feathers (about 3,000,000) for every man in the Union Army because not that many were available in "the markets of the world, or in the accessible wilds of Africa," so, too, might Warnock face a problem in procuring the right kind of furs to make the cap formula.[46] He seemed confident that the contractors would find a way to deal with this situation when it came time to respond to bids.[47] Evidently he was correct, although Warnock did not obtain the order. It was Bent and Bush, who were to deliver 18,000 caps complete with trimmings at $2.49 each.

1872-pattern enlisted engineer cap was identical to the heavy artillery cap, only the trim differed. Originally the letters "CE" were to appear on the cap for Corps of Engineers prior to a change to the brass castle. This example bears a German silver insignia, contrary to regulations. SI

The 1872-pattern pompons for 1872-pattern engineer dress caps had an upper white portion and a lower scarlet segment, an arrangement that was unique to Engineer Corps enlisted personnel. The insignia was a stampted sheet brass castle worn below the eagle device. USAQM

These were to be as the sealed samples except that they "should contain two ounces of Double Ring Russia" [a type of fur commonly used by hatters of the era] and one half ounce of Coney [hare] each."[48] In this instance, Meigs' supposition as to some means being found to provide the cap resulted in an allowed change from the original specification.[49]

Thereafter, the cap, once issued, was "admitted on all sides to be a vast improvement on the old unshapely and unserviceable thing which was dignified with the name of a dress hat."[50] But praise was not universal. An infantry officer soon asked for the chapeau as a substitute. In his estimation the cap was so small it had the tendency to blow off of the head when officers were mounted.[51] One other infantry officer made a different comment. Captain Charles Wheaton of the Twenty-third Infantry reported: "...the dress caps, nearly all of them new of the largest sizes," were so enormous "that the men now wear them with capes inside the linings to make them fit."[52]

A more positive endorsement of the cap came from an army surgeon, J. Frazer Boughter, who served in the Southwest. He indicated: "The new shako is certainly a great improvement over the old dress hat, it is light, weighs but seven and one-half (7) ounces, has sufficient height above the hair and is ventilated by openings at the top, its peak is horizontal, a moderate curve would perhaps be better to shade the eyes; it is liked by the men very much."[53]

Lieutenant Colonel Joseph Whistler, in command of Fort Riley, Kansas, agreed the cap was a decided improvement over the "Hardee" hat.[54] Colonel George Andrews commented that it was suitable for its purpose.[55] The Tenth Infantry's commanding colonel, Henry Clitz, was

LEFT: Private J.M. McDougal, Eleventh U.S. Infantry wears the 1872-pattern infantry enlisted cap with hunting horn device but no company or regimental insignia. Early regulations for the wear of numbers and letters were somewhat confusing or vague when the dress cap was first issued, and had to be clarified by subsequent orders. JB
BELOW: Enlisted men of Company G, Nineteenth U.S. Infantry at Jackson Barracks, Louisiana, commanded by Captain J.H. Bradford, all wear the 1872-pattern dress uniform with dress cap having the white pompon and sky-blue worsted trim. USAMHI

Ordnance sergeant in the 1872-pattern dress cap. USAQM

Official quartermaster photograph depicting a commissary sergeant's dress uniform, including cap, as prescribed in 1873. USAQM

The 1872-pattern ordnance enlisted dress cap was to bear the shell and flame insignia of stamped sheet brass, although originally the letters "OD" were selected as the insignia. SI

A green pompon, sheet brass eagle, and a gilt wreath with silver "U.S." was to adorn the 1872-pattern dress cap of hospital stewards, these details relative to cap insignia being spelled out shortly after the new uniform regulations were released. SI

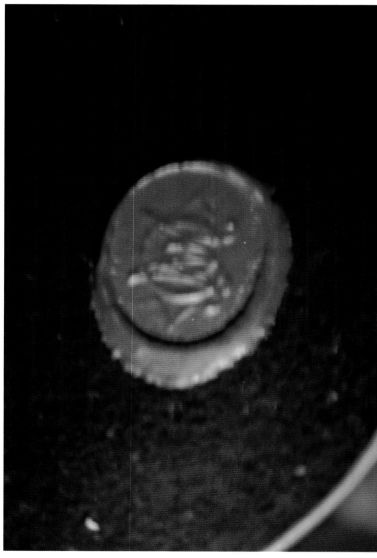

In 1873 commissary sergeants were added to the U.S. Army's rolls. Their 1872-pattern caps were to have gray mohair lace and a matching gray pompon. A brass crescent appears on the front of the standard pattern cap below the arms of the United States device, although it seems that white metal crescents actually were issued to commissary sergeants. The pompon is removed to depict the wax seal that indicates this was the official pattern sample. SI

A wax seal affixed to a commissary sergeant's 1872-pattern dress cap displays the letters "QMD" (Quartermaster Department) to indicate that this was an official pattern "sealed" sample. SI

Most probably the 1872-pattern dress cap for commissary sergeants bore the German silver crescent rather than the brass insignia affixed to the official sample. Also note this version of the cap made by Horstmann had a bound visor unlike most other contract examples that had an unbound visor. JG

more demonstrative, maintaining it was "well made, durable, light, and comfortable."[56]

Others qualified their support for this headdress. Captain C.E. Morse, although he indicated the color, durability, and quality all were positive attributes, found the pompon, while excellent, required cleaning. He wanted instructions to be provided to make it possible for the men to keep this woolen top piece in good appearance.[57]

Assistant Surgeon Clarence Ewen remarked the top ventilator was worthless. It made more sense to him for troops at his station, Baton Rouge Barracks, to have a summer helmet with an interior ring to promote circulation of air.[58]

Nonetheless, Captain Loyd Wheaton, in command of a company of the Twentieth Infantry at Fort Pembina, Dakota Territory, also thought the dress cap an improvement over the 1858-pattern hat. The new style was both "serviceable and appropriate for full dress, excepting during the winter in this latitude." Moreover, Wheaton concluded the forage cap was "of good material, a neat and comfortable headdress for a mild climate and ordinary wear." Some of the caps, however, had visors that were of insufficiently thick leather. Further, it was pointed out that "In this latitude (49°), it is not practical to wear in the field, during winter, any of the headdress issued. The men all wear fur or woolen caps purchased from traders or made by themselves."[59]

Another item of headdress from the 1872 board had its share of difficulties as well. Based on the Mexican War era Andrew's hat that had been revisited by the 1868 board and the surgeon general's report, the folding campaign hat was adopted. The prototype selected by the 1872 board was made by R. Warnock & Co., but others bid on the contract to provide the 10,000 hats called for by the quartermaster.[60] In the meantime, Philadelphia hatter P. Herst had furnished Langdon C. Easton, the chief quartermaster officer at the depot in that city, with a sample hat, which was then sent along to Meigs. Meigs examined the Warnock and Herst prototypes and pronounced the pattern on hand from the board as "plain" in comparison to the Herst sample, which he described as having a "velvet" finish.[61] Nevertheless, Meigs confessed he was not a

Regimental band members had latitude in the matter of uniform components, including custom headgear, as these infantry musicians exhibit at Ft. Rice, Dakota Territory c. 1875. SHSND

Stamped sheet brass crossed rifles with separately applied stamped sheet brass regimental numerals above the rifles and the company letter below the rifles, with the exception of regimental staff NCOs who wore the numeral only, became the norm in 1875 for infantrymen. This example was worn by Private Frank Drew of the Fourteenth U.S. Infantry. Drew ultimately deserted from this unit, but inexplicably, his 1872-pattern dress cap survived. JG

RIGHT: Second Lieutenant Charles Andrews Williams joined the Twenty-first U.S. Infantry upon graduation from West Point in 1874. His 1872-pattern officers' dress cap with white cock feathers sits on the table next to him in this portrait taken about 1877. USAMHI

hat expert, and while he thought the Herst example was "better finished and likely to keep cleaner than the Board hat, and I think it may be received, so far as appearance goes, as fully equal," he still was not convinced as to "the important question of durability and wear." Consequently, he recommended that Easton "get the best expert advice and aid in inspection" before selecting the best choice between the two hats.[62]

Perhaps Easton followed this prescription, because a contract was not issued for nearly a month. When it was made, the award went to Herst, who bid $2.83 for each hat with cords and tassels.[63] Just after this agreement, however, the contractor discovered he could not obtain cords on the open market for the hat as supposed, artillery ones being the only ones that had been released as surplus in quantities.[64] This finding was minor, in that sufficient quantities were in stock at the depots to make delivery without cords acceptable, although the ones for infantry tended to be very faded, a factor that seemed of little consequence, because the hats were "only to be worn on fatigue duty and on campaign or marches."[65] Herst thus received an order for 10,000 hats without cords at $2.80 each.[66]

Some derogatory comments accompanied the introduction of another of the 1872-pattern pieces of headgear, the low-crowned forage cap of the type previously popular with officers and those enlisted per-

sonnel inclined to purchase it.[67] Now it was to be worn by everyone. Warnock & Co. also produced the sample for the board. As noted, the prototype had braid on it, but the trim was to be removed before the cap was adopted and the first contract sent to Bent and Bush of Boston, for 28,000 caps.[68]

Likewise, 30,000 cap covers conforming to the shape of the sloping crown were to be issued to render this headgear more serviceable in foul weather.[69] These were similar to the covers that had been issued with the 1851-cap and provided for earlier forage caps by the Civil War in that black treated material was used as a water repellent. Although the concept was utilitarian, the execution evidently met with little favor. It seems many enlisted men did not draw them at all, and if they did, the covers were disposed of or not used, thereby resulting in their discontinuance as an item of issue by 1877.[70] Despite the lack of appeal to the rank and file for the waterproof cap cover, Meigs intended for these items to be issued by July 1, 1873, along with the new forage caps, dress caps, campaign hats, Berlin gloves, mounted helmets, and dismounted dress caps.[71]

Marcy, as president of the board, must have been pleased with this goal, albeit would soon learn that the progress toward this end would be short-lived. As a major proponent of change, though, he relished the original speed in which the 1872 clothing items were being sought by the Quartermaster Department. He based his wishes on the following rationale:

The inspection reports for several years past have shown that the issues from the clothing remaining on hand after the rebellion which as a measure of economy have been considered unavoidable, have caused considerable dissatisfaction among the enlisted men; for the reason that this clothing is made from material inferior in quality and cut so badly that the soldier generally has been obliged, at his own expense, to have his coat and trousers made over again.[72]

Other general officers supported Marcy, at least in terms of the uniform with chapeau, epaulets, and sash that they were to wear for formal occasions.[73] The 1872 regulations likewise called for all other officers of the staff corps, as well as engineers and signal officers, to don the chapeau, too. A subsequent addition to the General Orders No. 92 even went on to indicate how this traditional headdress was supposed to "be worn with the front peak turned slightly to the left, showing the gilt ornaments upon the right side."[74]

But headgear for generals and staff officers were not the only ones to be refined as the 1872-pattern continued. One of the first additions to be considered came as a result of the 1873 creation of a new non-commissioned specialty—the post commissary sergeant. This required a cap with cadet gray worsted trim and pompon to be made, and a cap insignia consisting of a white metal crescent with the points in a vertical line to be worn on dress caps and forage caps.[75]

The dress caps for hospital stewards also had to be clarified. Was it to have a green pompon and worsted braid of that color? The response from the inspector general through the quartermaster general was in the affirmative.[76] Further, the insignia was to be the same as that worn during the Civil War, to wit, "of white metal, chased: Roman capitals one-half (1/2) inch high, to be placed within the wreath. To have wire loops

Side view of official pattern of the 1872 officers' cap for infantry and heavy artillery. NA

soldered on the back to fasten to cap." In turn, the wreath was to be, "of dead or unburnished gilt-metal, representing two olive branches, held at the bottom by a loop and a knot, turning upward and bending in an oval shape, approaching each other at the top." The height was given as 1 1/2 inches with the width at the greatest point between the outer edges set at 2 5/8-inches. The branches were five-eighths of an inch and the whole wreath was held by a pair of brass wires on the back.[77]

Some years later exact details of the cap's composition were published as Quartermaster Specification 3, as approved on May 31, 1876. The cap was to be:

Thirteenth U.S. Infantry officers pose with their colonel, French born Philip Regis de Trobriand (center front with white beard and hair) all holding their 1872-pattern infantry officers' dress caps. USAMHI

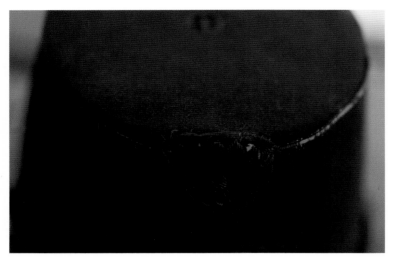

Colonel Nelson A. Miles' Fifth U.S. Infantry 1872-pattern officer's dress cap with white cock feathers removed to show the bugle insignia. WC

Rear view of Colonel Miles' 1872-pattern infantry officer's dress cap. WC

The body or shell is made of felt composed of equal parts of Russia, best coney-backs, muskrat, extra coney, and one-half (1/2) part of washblow. It weights, uncovered, two and three-fourths (2 3/4) to three (3) ounces, according to size. Front vertical about three and one-half (3 1/2) inches high; back five and one-half (5) inches long, rises upward and forward in a convex sweep, and meets the crown at a point one and one-eighth (1/8) to one and one-fourth (1/ 4) inch higher that the point where it meets the upper edge of the front.

The crown is slightly oval, five and one-fourth (5) inches in diameter from front to back, four and one-half (4) inches across. Ventilator in center of crown. At the front edge is an opening, bound with thin strap of enameled metal, to admit the stem of the pom-pon, which is also held in position by a small leather socket sewed to the inside of the cap-front, about one-half (1/2) inch below the crown.

The body is covered with fine wool-dyed indigo-blue cloth, braided around the upper edge immediately below the crown, around the lower edge one-fourth (1/4) to five-sixteenths (5/16) of an inch above the latter: also straight down the back, and in a straight slant-ing line on both sides, equidistant from back and front seam. This

braiding is worsted three-sixteenth (3/16) of an inch wide, and of the following colors: for infantry, sky-blue; engineers and artillery, scarlet; ordnance, crimson; commissary sergeants, gray; hospital stewards, green. A visor of heavy enameled leather, straight and horizontal, front edge slightly convex, sides straight, corners rounded, inner edge following the shape of the cap on both sided, ending in a point about five (5) inches from the seam.

On each side, immediately behind the end of visor, is a small regulation brass button for chin-strap.

The latter is made of thin enameled leather five-eighths (5/8) of an inch wide, in two parts, eight and one-half (8 1/2) to nine (9) inches each, and arranged to be lengthened and shortened, as de-scribed for helmet chin-strap. Sweat-leather, one and three-fourths (1 3/4) to two (2) inches wide of Belgium leather. In front, immedi-ately below the crown, is a brass eagle, and below the latter the badge of the corps or arm of services.

As for pompons, they were to be "of fine worsted, firmly made on a woodblock." Further, the pompons were to have:

Nap well raised and close. To be pear shaped, three (3) inches long, one and three-fourths (1 3/4) inch in diameter at the bottom, and one inch (1) at top. Under the center, of the bottom is a brass

Side views of Colonel Miles' Fifth U.S. Infantry 1872-pattern officer's dress cap show the flat gold cord that trimmed the cap and the leather chin strap, along with small gilt infantry officer's eagle button, two of which were used to secure the strap to the cap. WC

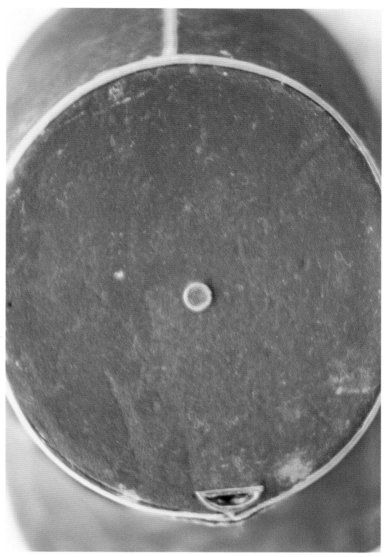

It seems many makers of the 1872-pattern foot officer's cap replaced the regulation Brasher device with other types of ventilators, including a simple black japanned metal stamped "pinwheel" as Colonel Nelson A. Miles' cap, which was worn from 1872 through 1875 (left), exhibits. A small gauze screen served the same purpose in the cap Miles obtained from R. Ackerman & Son in 1875, or shortly thereafter (right). Note also that Miles' earlier cap had a sheet brass reinforcement where the cock feathers were inserted, per official specifications, while the cap obtained in the mid-1870s had a small japanned half-circle for this same purpose. WC

half sphere about eleven sixteenths (11/16) of an inch in diameter, from which protrudes a stem three (3) inches long, made of strong copper wire.

Color of pompons for infantry, white; artillery, scarlet; engineers, lower half scarlet, upper half white; ordnance, crimson; commissary sergeants, gray; hospital stewards, green.

Marcy also noted in his endorsement that ordnance and engineer soldiers would have the same wreath but white Roman letters "O.D." and "E.C." were to be substituted for the "U.S."[78] Several months later a general order rescinded the ordnance and engineer designs and replaced them with a brass shell and flame device and a brass castle with company letter respectively.[79] Although a number of caps had been made up with the wreath and E.C., they were refitted with the castle before being issued to enlisted engineers.[80]

On a related subject, the military storekeeper at the Philadelphia Depot, John F. Rodgers, thought the ordnance shell and flame device for the collar too small for the cap, while the larger version was too great in size that the chin-strap covered the lower portion of the insig-

nia.[81] He suggested the wreath be retained, sufficient numbers of these already being on hand from the previous order, and used in tandem with the smaller ordnance bomb.[82] This recommendation was disapproved.[83] Thus, a second sample was sent for the inspector general to examine and approve, this one being of a lesser size and having a back filed with solder and a loop for attachment on the rear.[84]

The inspector general once again ultimately was contacted, because the old 5/8-inch size brass hat numbers were adequate for the regimental designation on the dress coat but too large for dress caps and forage caps. What is more, the larger sizes were being sold as surplus.[85] Marcy concurred that 1/2-inch brass should be procured for caps.[86] Prior to this, Meigs had permitted 1/2-inch numbers to be procured in limited quantities. He further took it upon himself to speculate that the general orders incorrectly had called for the badge of the corps or letter of the company to be worn on caps.[87] Meigs indicated that the wording should have permitted both devices to be used.[88] Marcy thought that the change of adding the company letter rather than a regimental numeral on the forage cap should be adopted for artillery, cavalry, engineer, and infan try troops, but not ordnance, nor would this be necessary for commissary sergeants.[89] No such statement was made in regard to the dress cap, although it seems that a similar method was employed regularly, with the company letter and badge being used together, in the case of infantry and artillery troops at least. It would take another four years for this arrangement finally to be spelled out in detail.[90]

General Order No. 96, War Department, Adjutant General's Office, November 19, 1875, settled this confusion, as well as was the same directive that changed the enlisted insignia for infantry to sheet brass stamped crossed rifles, except for musicians who were to retain the traditional hunting horn. In all instances save for musicians, General Orders No. 96, indicated the number of the regiment was to go above the crossed sabers, rifles, or crossed cannon insignia and letter of the company or battery below the insignia. Field musicians and bandsmen were to bear the number of the regiment in the crook of the bugle and the company letter above the crook.[91] Further, engineer rank and file were to display the company letter above the brass castle.

Indeed, prior to 1875, regulations for insignia on the dress caps for infantry, artillery, and engineer troops did not mention regimental or company identification. It also should be noted that all the insignia were to be of stamped sheet brass, with the exception of the white metal "US" that was enclosed by a brass or gilt wreath, and the crescents for commissary sergeants that likewise were to be of white metal, and worn with "the points in a vertical line, on dress and forage caps." Previously the sample pattern had included a sheet brass crescent worn points up. In practice it appears that at least the manner of wearing the device in a horizontal fashion continued, despite orders to the contrary.

Quartermaster Specification No. 8, adopted on May 31, 1876, further clarified the appearance of these insignia as:

Cap Bugles: an old-style bugle with circular crook, and a cord slung three fold around the lower part, terminating in two tassels on one and one tassel on the other side. Height across crook 1/2 inch; width from mouth piece to outer edge of bowl, 2 inches.

Castle for Cap: an ancient caste with three towers; height of center tower 7/8 inch; of side towers; inch; of battlements between towers, 5/8 inches; width at base 1 7/8 inch.

Crescents for Caps: width from point to point, 1 5/8 inch, greatest width in center 1/2 inch.

The 1872-dress cap worn by Captain Malcolm McArthur displays no reinforcement for the cock feather holder, while the brass gauze ventilator is a larger version than on the Miles' 1875 cap. In fact, the McArthur cap ventilator is the essentially the type found on 1872-pattern Horstmann-made dress helmets. GS

The "Brasher" patent ventilator, although primarily associated the with 1876-pattern campaign hat, was at first called for in official specifications of the foot officer's dress hat to be inserted in the center of the top to promote air circulation. JG

Crossed Cannon: two cannon crossing each other at the trunnions, muzzles upward; length 2 1/8 inches; breadth at breeches 2 inches; at muzzles, 1 7/8.

Crossed Rifles: two rifles crossing each other at a point equidistant from butt and muzzle; muzzles pointing upward and outward, hammers upward, their position crossed making the upper space form an angle of 137°; length of rifle, 2 5/8 inches; the whole ornament occupying a rectangular space about 2 7/16 inches wide by 1 3/8 inches high.

Eagles for Cap: To be worn on caps of all arms of the service; an eagle with national shield on breast, head surmounted by a scroll bearing the motto "E pluribus unum," extending downward and meeting olive branch and arrows in talons of eagle; height 1/2 inch; greatest width between tips of wings, 1/2 inch.

Shells and Flames for Cap: diameter of shell, 3/4 inch; height of flame from upper edge of shell, 7/8 inch; greatest width of flame. 1/8 inch.

Wreath for Hospital Stewards Cap: two olive branches held together at the bottom by a loop and knot, turning upwards and bending in an oval shape, approaching each other at the top; height inch; greatest distance between outer edges, 2 5/8 inches; greatest width of single branch 5/8 inch.

Brass Letters for Cap: 'A' to 'M'; Roman capitals 5/8 inch long; edges beveled.

Letters 'U.S': of white metal, chased; Roman capitals 1/2 inch high; to be placed within wreath.

Numbers for Cap: Nos. '1' to '0" inclusive; 5/8 inch long, edges beveled.

It should be noted that the eagle described in this list of insignia was solely for the dress cap, and not the forage cap. This point seemed clear from the outset, and was but one of many issues that had to be addressed before the first 1872-pattern uniform items were made available.[92] Further, the eagle's design virtually was identical to the one provided for the mounted helmet, but of a considerably smaller size.

One such subject of discussion from the field was the infantry insignia adopted in 1875. It proved not to everyone's liking. A veteran perhaps responded for others when he penned his discontent about "The time honored bugle" that was "to be done away with. Now we have 'crossed rifles without bayonets.'" "Yes but that is so much more appropriate for infantry. That's so, and by the same token let's give the engineers crossed quills, nibs upward, or if they prefer, a pick and a spade. For what do they have to do with castles, unless they are in the air?"[93]

Other aspects related to the headgear prescribed after 1872 received varied reviews, too. Again, Acting Assistant Surgeon J. Frazer Boughter voiced his opinion, and gave a clean bill of health to the forage cap, writing:

Front view of Colonel Miles' 1872-pattern infantry officer's cap with cock feathers in place. Photography by Glen Swanson. WC

Second Lieutenant Daniel Morgan Taylor of the First U.S. Artillery wears the 1872-pattern heavy artillery officers' cap. GS

"The forage cap is in every respect a great and marked improvement over the old and miserable cap heretofore issued, the new one has all the requisites of a good cap, the material (dark blue), is good, the cap does not touch the hair; it would perhaps be an advantage in this climate to have the cap perforated on the top with several small openings, before being issued" (a suggestion that was not implemented although non-Regular Army specimens exist with a Japanned vent in the crown). The forage cap covers also were described as good.[94]

It should be noted that a few minor improvements were made even before these affirmative reports reached officials in Washington.[95] For the most part, the cap remained virtually unchanged from the specifications published in 1876 and retained until 1895, when a new piece of headgear was ushered into service.[96] The description as of 1876 was as follows:

> Made of best wool-dyed indigo-blue cloth. Band about one and one-fourth (1 1/4) inch wide, strengthened by a strip of strong leather of the same width, sewed in between the cloth and the sweat-leather. The front rises straight and vertical one and one-half (1 1/2) to one and five-eighths (1 5/8) inch above the band, side straight and slightly converging toward the crown. The back, about five (5)

1872-pattern heavy artillery officer's dress cap with scarlet cock feathers removed to illustrate the Second U.S. Artillery insignia of gold embroidery with silver regimental numeral where the cannons intersect. RB

inches long, rises from the band forward at an angle of 45 degrees, slightly convex.

The front of the 1872-pattern heavy artillery officer's cap obscured by the cock feathers. JG

Detail of typical "tulip" or socket that held the cock feathers on the 1872-pattern officer's cap in place, in this case for heavy artillery because of the scarlet cock feathers. JG

Colonel Miles kept the cock feathers for his dress cap stored in japanned tin carrying cases when the plumes were not in use. WC

Detail of white cock feathers worn on Miles' c. 1875 dress cap, including the large size tulip that held the feathers in place. This holder essentially was a modified plume staff from the 1872-pattern mounted helmet. WC

small brass ring was inset into the top of the cock feathers for Miles' c. 1875 cap. Its urpose is not entirely clear. WC

The crown is circular, about four and three-fourths (4 3/4) inches in diameter, made upon strong "tarred board." The shape of the cap would thus give an incline to the crown of one (1) to one and one-fourth (1 1/4) inch from rear to front.

A straight horizontal vizor of patent enameled leather, about three-sixteenths (3/16) of an inch thick, shaped as described for dress-caps. A small brass regulation button on each side, immediately behind the end of the vizor, for chin-strap.

The latter is made in two parts, of fine enameled leather about one-half (1/2) inch wide, each part about nine (9) inches long, and arranged, as on dress-cap, to be lengthened or shortened at will.

Sweat-leather of Belgium leather, one and one-half (1 1/2) inch wide.

Lining of glazed muslin, fastened by its lower edge gathered with strong thread.

While enlisted men tended to wear the caps as prescribed, with little variation save for insignia, this was not to be the case for officers. For one thing, the height of the cap ranged from medium to a very low crown from one officer to the next, as did the type of insignia. Most individuals had the insignia embroidered to the cap's front, but some wore separately applied embroidered insignia, or in at least one case even pin-on metallic devices. Additionally, most officers seemed to have patent leather chin-straps similar to those worn by enlisted men, while others opted for gold cords of various types, or dispensed with chin-straps altogether.

Although officer's models ran the gamut, at least the brass had this headgear, while its issue to the men was spotty for a while. The congressional mandate to continue issue of existing stocks once more meant

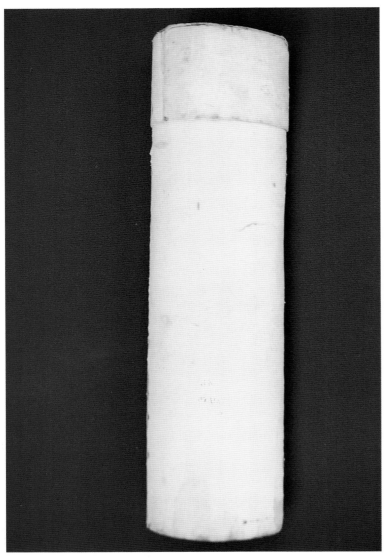

Lieutenant Colonel Frederick Dent (President U.S. Grant's brother-in-law) kept his artillery cap feathers in a cylinder made of stout cardboard. JG

Colonel Miles maintained his dress caps in japanned tin carrying cases. WC

old patterns, in this case Civil War vintage forage caps, were being sent when requests came from the field for supplies to the troops.[97]

On the other hand, news that yet another 1872-pattern piece of head-gear had to be held back came as a mixed blessing. This was the folding campaign hat. Even loyal quartermaster officer John Rodgers proposed an abbreviated brim. He observed the standard hat, after wear in the field, became very pliable. Then, because of the weight associated with the broad brim it tended to droop "down in an uncomfortable and un-sightly manner over the neck and face of the wearer."[98] Easton then forwarded an improved model for Meigs to examine.[99] This was the beginning of several years of deliberation on this matter that led to the adoption of a new pattern in 1876.[100]

William O. Taylor, a Seventh Cavalry trooper who had to wear this hat on rugged campaign service, summed up the reason why this head-piece ultimately was replaced. Taylor rightly recollected the old black campaign hat had:

> a very wide brim that had hooks and eyes on it, front and rear
> so that it might be made to appear in shape at least like a chapeau of
> a Major General, but the handling that it got and the rain and wind
> gave it an appearance unlike anything I ever saw on the head of a

man. Some of the Companies like L, F, and C, refused to wear them and purchased out of private funds, a hat of much better shape and quality. Owing to the cheap material and its great width the brim of my hat had become separated from the crown for nearly one half the way round, and in consequence I was sometimes look-ing over the brim and sometimes, under it.[101]

n 1875, the gold embroidered hunting horn device on the front of the infantry officer's dress cap was replaced by crossed rifles with regimental numeral in silver embroidery above, in this case for the Seventeenth U.S. Infantry in which the cap's original owner, Malcolm McArthur, served as a company grade officer. GS

Front of Colonel Nelson Miles' dress cap with the 1875-pattern crossed rifles. WC

nterior of Miles' 1872 dress cap. WC

Interior of Colonel Miles' c.1875 dress cap made by J.R. Ackerman & Son. WC

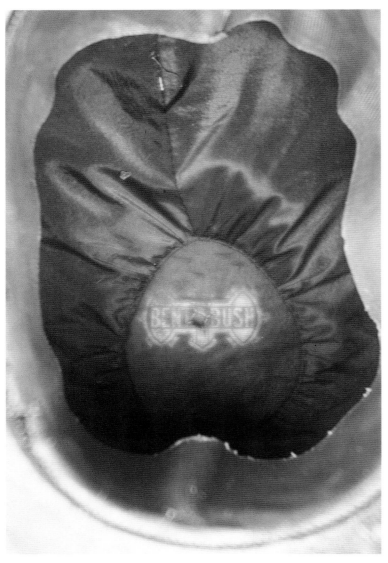

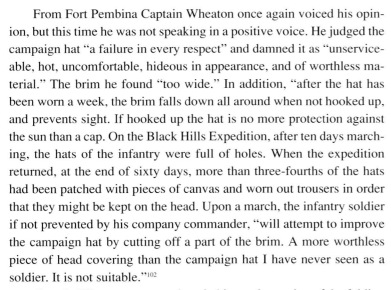

Interior of Captain Malcolm McArthur's c.1875 dress cap. GS

Variant of the 1872-pattern infantry officers' dress cap with sloping visor. Because officers purchased all uniform items from diverse sources, numerous departures from regulation patterns existed. AHS

From Fort Pembina Captain Wheaton once again voiced his opinion, but this time he was not speaking in a positive voice. He judged the campaign hat "a failure in every respect" and damned it as "unserviceable, hot, uncomfortable, hideous in appearance, and of worthless material." The brim he found "too wide." In addition, "after the hat has been worn a week, the brim falls down all around when not hooked up, and prevents sight. If hooked up the hat is no more protection against the sun than a cap. On the Black Hills Expedition, after ten days marching, the hats of the infantry were full of holes. When the expedition returned, at the end of sixty days, more than three-fourths of the hats had been patched with pieces of canvas and worn out trousers in order that they might be kept on the head. Upon a march, the infantry soldier if not prevented by his company commander, "will attempt to improve the campaign hat by cutting off a part of the brim. A more worthless piece of head covering than the campaign hat I have never seen as a soldier. It is not suitable."[102]

Captain Wheaton was not alone in his condemnation of the folding hat. For instance, Surgeon Thomas Andrew McParlin wrote to the colonel of Fifth Infantry, Nelson Miles: "The campaign hat also soon wore

out, and fell to pieces; attempts were made to patch or sew the parts together again, but the material was very poor, easily torn, and insusceptible of any proper repairs. In such a state of affairs, the men would soon be without any protection to the head, against the solar heat, or the elements generally." The doctor preferred gray soft felt campaign hats or "Glengarry Scotch" caps with "ear flaps and a waterproof falling flap behind" to the folding hat.[103]

From another Kansas source, Major C.E. Compton, who commanded Fort Dodge, Kansas, came a report from yet one more member of the Fifth Infantry, Captain E. Butler. The captain again presented a familiar scenario—the issue hats were not durable. Compton sent this complaint on to Rodgers, the military storekeeper at Philadelphia. Rodgers rebutted that the hats furnished to the men of the Fifth Infantry met government standards, and that there should be no grounds for dissatisfaction. He, therefore, suggested that some of the supposedly faulty hats be sent to Philadelphia for examination by experts.

Butler complied, as well as furnished an affidavit from eight of his men indicating that the hats became unserviceable after only 120 hours of wear. Rodgers and his experts could not accept this, and retorted that it was not possible for the headgear to degenerate after such a brief period. Thus, he dismissed the whole matter as "groundless."

Not to be put off, Butler secured forty-four testimonials from enlisted men and several from officers at his post backing up the discontent with the hat based upon poor serviceability.[104] By this point the secretary of war entered the picture with a directive that all commanding officers furnish responses to the adequacy of the uniform items being issued, including the campaign hat.[105]

Once more Surgeon Boughter expressed his views, this time in regard to the campaign hat, which he indicated was:

> ...for the purpose designed very serviceable, but for New Mexico, where the heat of the summer is excessive, it would certainly be better to have the color a gray or light drab, as next to white, grey gives the greatest protection from the direct solar rays, and black the least. The cost of this hat complete ($2.64) is high but it must be considered that the material from which it is manufactured is excellent.[106]

Assistant Surgeon W.F. Buchanan at Fort Brown, Texas, echoed discontent, as did the majority of other respondents. He felt: "The present style of head covering is in my opinion, entirely unfit for this climate and would recommend a straw or felt hat of light texture and color."[107]

Colonel J.H. Potter, the commander at Fort Brown, also found: "The campaign hat objectionable in many respects and...entirely unsuited to this climate. I am of the opinion that this article of clothing should not be issued in this climate or any other. I would recommend a straw or felt hat for summer and the forage cap for winter wear in this section of the country."[108]

Similarly, from Fort Quitman, Texas, Acting Assistant Surgeon B. Alexander prescribed a straw hat for wear during the "summer months in all Southern climates."[109] From Fort Craig, New Mexico, Captain George Shorkley flatly stated: "The Campaign hat I find no real use for in the present shape on account of its being too large and heavy, the men often narrow the rim to moderate the size and make it more convenient, a smaller and cheaper hat would be preferable."[110]

Yet one more medical officer stationed in Texas, this time at Fort Richardson, made another damning diagnosis. The hat did not even warrant "the redeeming quality of durability or usefulness to offset its horrid ugliness."[111] At distant Fort Buford, Dakota Territory, First Lieutenant William H.H. Crowell provided corresponding observations. He found the hat "of such poor quality, that the broad brim when not hooked up—particularly in bad weather—breaks and falls down over the eyes making it necessary either to narrow the brim, or wear it always hooked up."[112] Another individual recalled that the poor material soon caused the brim to drop down "like a pair of elephant ears" around the wearer's face.[113]

Few commentators made positive statements regarding the campaign hat. At least one writer did sing its praises as being "made of first class material, and its proportions are so generous that, when unhooked and let down it altogether dispenses with the necessity of an umbrella, and enables its happy possessor to utterly defy and spit upon 'Old Sol.'"

Artillery officers with their red cock feathers atop the 1872-pattern dress cap and the post surgeon in his chapeau de bras stand for a group portrait at Jackson Barracks, Florida. This image was taken about 1875.

A first lieutenant of the Engineer Corps poses in the regulation 1872-pattern company grade staff officer's dress uniform, its most noteworthy feature being the chapeau de bras that was to be worn by all officers except those for the artillery, cavalry, and infantry. The profile of the chapeau adopted after the Civil War was lower than its predecessors. GS

This portrait of Second Lieutenant Orin Mitcham of the Fourth U.S. Artillery provides a profile of the 1872-pattern officer's forage cap, which was the French-inspired, low-crowned chasseur style that many individuals and some volunteer and militia units favored during the Civil War. GS

A Second Lieutenant of the Third U.S. Cavalry wearing the 1872-pattern officer's forage cap with insignia embroidered directly to the body. GS

The conclusion was: "To cavalry especially the campaign hat will prove an inestimable blessing, and many a poor trooper, sitting wearily on his horse in the blinding sun of Colorado or New Mexico will from his heart thank the man who invented the hat."[114]

Such support was rare, though. For the most part overwhelmingly reactions to "the campaign-hat" were adverse, and this headdress was "universally condemned because of its poor material"[115] In the face of such criticism Rodgers still did not relent. He contended the shape of the hat, not the materials used to make it, was the problem. To rectify the situation the original makers of the standard hat, Warnock and Company, were to examine the matter once again in theory to secure "as durable a hat as possible."[116]

Consequently, in 1875, the deputy quartermaster general, Lieutenant Colonel J.D. Bingham, announced: "steps are now being taken to procure hats satisfactory to the Army."[117] Meigs himself pursued one of the paths to reach this goal when he requested assistance from Sir Edward Thornton, England's Minister to the United States, in obtaining "samples of cloth-covered cork helmets worn by Her Britannic Majesty's troops in tropical climates such as India."[118]

Securing samples of foreign patterns was by no means a new concept, nor was the quest for a cooler version of headgear for summer months. Previously, however, the solution to beat the heat often was a civilian straw hat, or boater, as had been the case at the Fort Monroe Artillery School in the late 1850s, and by orders in the Department of Texas and much farther north in the Department of the Platte, both in the early 1870s.[119] While straw hats continued to be sanctioned as optional for hot climates for years to come, the English-inspired cork helmet constituted a parallel effort that indicated a continued dual track of reliance on foreign models of headgear versus homegrown American solutions.[120]

Indeed, Secretary of War William Belknap ultimately permitted the purchase of 100 British imports complete with *puggree* (cloth band) for experimental issue to troops in the Arizona Territory, although previously he had declined such a request by Meigs. After the Medical Department supported the concept, Belknap made a favorable ruling, and sanctioned the purchase of the experimental helmets.[121]

These items, replete with puggree, cost $3.50. They were received in San Francisco, and distributed to certain troops in Southern Califor

The first version of the 1872-pattern forage cap for infantry officers bore a gold embroidered bugle with the regimental number in silver appearing in the crook, as Second Lieutenant Frank Baker of the Thirteenth Infantry wore for this photograph that was taken sometime after his graduation from West Point in June 1872. GS

First Lieutenant Frank Edmunds of the First U.S. Infantry wears the gold embroidered crossed rifle insignia with silver regimental numeral adopted in 1875 for officers' forage caps and dress caps. FAM

nia and Arizona.[122] After a suitable period, responses proved less than enthusiastic—the verdict, the helmets were too heavy and insufficiently ventilated.[123]

Despite this criticism the quest for a summer helmet did not end there. Such a piece of headgear going back as early as the "Ventilated or Eastern Hat" discussed and illustrated in the Woodhull Report found continued advocates. This meant that West Point cadets would be provided with a version of the helmet produced by the New York firm of Henry V. Allien, in compliance with General Orders No. 121, War Department, December 22, 1877.[124] By the following year, 100 similar helmets were sent to Ninth Cavalry troopers for trial in Texas, while similarly Fort Monroe's garrison was to be receive 250 helmets.[125]

While the summer helmet did not end with this preliminary issue, the matter became a sidebar compared to the quest for a better campaign hat. Even while the first summer helmets were being tested, Warnock personnel had revisited the content of the folding hat and re-

ported that a different formula should be used, one that would be more expensive, but in theory more substantial. Both Warnock and P. Herst made up samples using the new specifications. Meigs thought the latter firm produced a better version, the former contractor turning out what he considered an ungainly, stiff rendition. Consequently, he opted for the Herst hat, and requested a tandem trial of 100 of these items be made for field study alongside the summer helmets sent to the Department of Arizona—a move that was approved on September 18, 1875.[126]

While efforts to improve the folding hat ran concurrently with trials for a cork helmet, Quartermaster General Meigs sought another course of action. In October 1875 one of his subordinates requested that a board be convened to deliberate over some key matters of uniform issue, including "the best pattern of a campaign hat for the Army."[127] This suggestion was carried out through Special Order No. 264, War Department, December 27, 1875, with Brevet Major General D.H. Rucker presiding.[128]

Lieutenant Colonel George Forsyth had a miniature pin-backed pair of crossed sabers in silver and gilt as a forage cap device in lieu of the usual embroidered type. The back was inscribed. KSHS

Front view of an 1872-pattern infantry officer's forage cap with the crossed rifles insignia adopted per General Orders No. 96, November 19, 1875. This example was worn by an officer of the Twenty-fifth U.S. Infantry. JB

Side view of an 1872-pattern officer's forage cap worn by Major Marcus A. Reno, Seventh U.S. Cavalry. GS

Even while the members met, Meigs informed the group that 100 experimental hats of a new model had been sent to Arizona for field tests.[129] This effort proved of no consequence, however, because the board never received information about the hat's performance during their session.[130] Nevertheless, the group launched into the subject in depth, submitting a report that presented their findings:

> The board is of the opinion that the Campaign Hat for the Army should be soft, pliable, of light-weight, firm texture and the greatest possible durability that can be obtained for a reasonable price.

> With this view the Board has procured information from all available sources in regard to the manufacture and component ma-

terials of the various hats of the character named fabricated for Army and commercial purposes. Experts in the manufacture of hats of all kinds have been examined and their opinions obtained.

> There appear to be two distinct kinds or classes of felt hats:— one made from fur and one made from wool.

> Those manufactured from fur are of a vast variety of qualities ranging from very low to very high prices according to the quality and kind of material. It is, however, generally conceded that no fur hat, that will give good service, can be manufactured, except for the better quality of furs and at a price varying from 2.50/100 to $3.00/100 each. If from the best quality of furs, the prices would range much higher.

Front and side views of the enlisted 1872-pattern forage cap. Per General Orders No. 67, War Department, June 25, 1873, the branch insignia and company letter were to be worn with the cap for cavalry, artillery, and infantry enlisted men, as shown here. This order, however, did not specify whether the letter went above or below the branch device, or in the crook of the horn in the case of infantry. JG

Interior of an 1872-pattern enlisted forage cap. JG

In 1878, P. Herst, the original supplier of the folding campaign hat, likewise received a contract for 6,000 enlisted forage caps as indicated in the stamp that appeared in the leather sweatband. JG

Whether made from fur or from wool, no inspection can exactly determine the particular material or materials from which made, so that in any case, much reliance must be placed on the integrity of the manufacturer. No positive test can be applied save actual wear.

It is, however, thought by the Board that there will be less opportunity for imposition in the manufacture of wool hats, while the cost of the material being much less, there will be less inducement in that direction.

From all the information the Board has been able to obtain, wool hats of the best grade will give equal service with the best grade of fur hats. This has been attested, even by prominent hatters engaged exclusively in the manufacture of fur hats. Severe tests were also instituted by the Board with satisfactory results.

In view of all these facts, and the greatly decreased cost to the soldier, together with the large saving to the government, the Board is induced to recommend felt hats made of wool for issue to the enlisted men of the Army.

The pattern recommended for adoption, has been sent to the office of the Quartermaster General, duly sealed for identification.

It is a plain black, velvet finished, hat. similar to the fatigue hat worn by officers during the late war; with crown 5 inches high, and brim 248 inches wide, for medium sized hats, the edge of the brim turned over and stitched, without biding; with a revolving ventilator in each side 3 inches above the brim; and with japanned sweat leather.

For all purposes of the service it is believed that black is the most desirable color.

It is further recommended that the campaign hat for officers be of the same color and pattern as that for enlisted men, either fur or wool as may be preferred by the individual officer. If of fur, the brim need not be turned over or bound. A sample hat of fur, duly sealed, has also been sent to the Quartermaster General's Office.[131]

The board's wishes were to be carried out, although it is somewhat of a puzzle why a challenge did not arise about the color.[132] Many officers of the era had sought a light colored or drab hat.[133] Clearly the board championed black, perhaps under the false assumption that the ventilator fans, a feature previously called for in the case of the 1872-pattern infantry and heavy artillery officer's dress caps, would address that need.

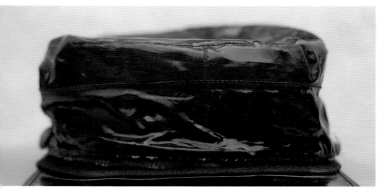

Front, side, and rear views of the oilcloth cover for the 1872-pattern enlisted forage cap. CF

Wasting little time, specifications were approved on June 14, 1876, for the board's proposed campaign hat.[134] These were to be:

Mixture.—To be clean wool, of fine grade, equal in quality to XXX Ohio fleece. No waste or shoddy to be used in mixture.

Weight.—Hat bodies to be weighed out, five and one-half (5 1/2) ounces heavy, of clean wool.

Shape.—The 7 1/8-size to be six (6) inches deep to center of tip, and five and one-half (5 1/2) inches deep at front and rear. Other sizes in proportion, varying one-sixteenth (1/16) of an inch to each size.

Brim.—Edge of brim to be turned over three-eights (3/8) of an inch on the upper side, and stitched down with two (2) rows of stitching, and to measure two and one-half (2 1/2) inches in front and rear and two and five-eights (2 5/8) inches in width at sides.

Trimming.—Trimmed with eight (8) ligne Union braid, same quality as on sample hat; to be sewed on by sewing machine. Sweat to be of brown Japanned leather, turned on top, one and three-quarters (1 3/4) inch wide, and sewed in hat by sewing machine. Two "Brashers' Patent Ventilators," one on each side of crown, three and one-half (3 1/2) inches from brim.

The hat to be velvet finished, soft and pliable, same as standard sample.

No more than six (6) hats to be packed in each bandbox.[135]

Once again, the hat's actual issue lagged behind its official adoption. Not until April 1877 did the first disbursement take place.[136] Even then it was made clear that hats only were to be "supplied to troops in the field or on the frontier, as required by existing numbers."[137] In all other cases, the folding hat continued to be offered, in the main to officers, but also even to military prisoners, a group that continued to be so supplied until 1881.[138] These were to be altered by cutting down the

An unknown soldier wears the 1872-pattern forage cap at a rakish angle. The first insignia allowed for the cap was a company letter, although some men did not follow this directive, and wore their caps without devices, or conversely added other badges such as crossed sabers for cavalry, crossed cannons for artillery, and the like. JB

An Engineer Corps company musician in the 1872-pattern enlisted forage cap with proper gilt castle device and company letter. JG

The wreath for hospital steward's 1872-pattern forage caps was to be of white metal as were the letters "US" within the wreath. In 1882, a German silver caduceus of the type that served as the overlay on the dress helmet was to replace the traditional US, although the older device evidently continued for some time in that this image was taken about 1885. NA

For decades the U.S. Army did not provide adequate winter headgear, thereby forcing officers and men alike to purchase whatever type of fur headdress they wished. This is evident in a photograph of officers taken along the Tongue River in Montana during the winter of 1877-78, when the temperatures dropped to 20° below zero! The man in the center of the group is Colonel Nelson A. Miles. NA

This privately procured fur cap, shown in front, side, and interior views, was worn by Colonel Miles on campaign. WC

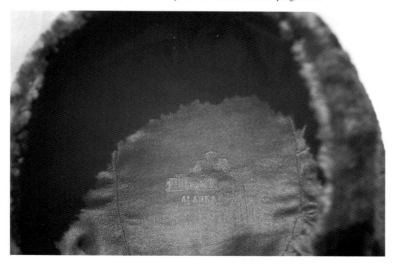

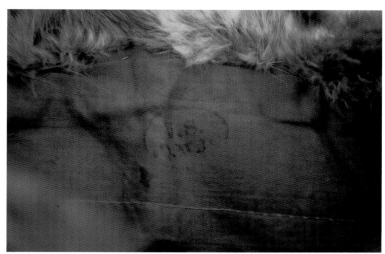

As of 1879 the Quartermaster Department adopted a standard fur cap for issue to troops in extremely cold climates. The specifications were simple: "To be made according to standard sample, of muskrat skin, with ear-flaps, cape, and visor, according to pattern." Lining of brown chintz, padded with cotton wadding." JG

Portion of the interior lining of the issue winter muskrat cap. JG

large brim and reblocking the crown in such a manner as to approximate the 1876-pattern hat.[139] As time passed, the reworked hats and those that remained as first made in the early 1870s were removed from the inventory and provided for sale to various entities, including the "extra Inauguration Police" in Washington, DC, and military surplus dealers of the era.[140]

In addition to the new campaign hat adopted at the board's behest, this same group considered the topic of the summer helmet, and also the long-standing requirement for issue winter headgear.[141] In the latter instance, they recommended a sealskin cap, a prescription that likewise was heeded and made official on May 23, 1876. These were: "To be of the 'wool seal' skin, with ear flaps, cape, and visor, according to pattern. [Unfortunately, the pattern piece evidently did not survive.] Lining of Turkey-red chintz, padded with cotton wadding."[142] On June 22, 1876, the Quartermaster Department's clothing bureau let a prelimi-

nary contract for 2,000 of these caps. The award went to Edmund R. Lyon of Philadelphia. The following year another purchase was made for an additional 6,158.[143] Some of these were to be supplied to troops taking to the field against the Plains Indians in the wake of the ill-fated Custer fight of the previous summer. Many of the men did not receive these much needed articles.[144] Those who did were at least grateful to learn that they would not be charged for the caps and the gloves that accompanied them, but the men were to turn them in when no longer needed.[145]

After more than 6,000 of these caps went to the field, it was determined that they became stiff upon becoming wet and then drying out. This prompted a rethinking of the situation that soon led to adoption of a muskrat version of the cap. In September 1878, another Philadelphia firm, that of Edward S. Mawson & Son, received the contract for 2,500 muskrat caps for $.84 each, versus the $2.78 that the soldier was charged

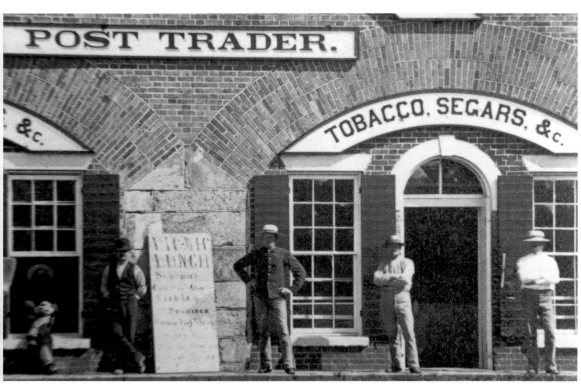

Straw hats continued to be worn by enlisted men in a number of areas during the hot season, including Ft. Monroe, Virginia where this c. 1880 photograph was taken. USAMHI

In 1868, the Woodhull Report called for "solar helmets" similar to this example, for wear in extremely hot climates. JG

for the previous sealskin model.[146] While the price and material changed, it seems that the basic design remained essentially as it had been for the 1876 style. The specifications called for ear-flaps, cape, visor, and chintz lining or silesia, padded with cotton wadding. The lining color, however, was to be brown rather than Turkey-red.[147]

This was the cap that remained in use for years to come. Before the final decision in favor of muskrat headgear, however, some thought was given to the use of other fur.[148]

That short-lived effort ended quickly, and while the switch to muskrat for winter caps was in the offing, another board was called into session by Special Orders No. 244, War Department, November, 11, 1878. Colonel Nelson A. Miles, a Civil War volunteer officer who eventually

was to receive the Medal of Honor for his actions at Chancellorsville, was the senior officer for this group that had been called together to consider entrenching tools specifically, as well as "the equipment of troops in general." After Miles and his comrades gathered in 1879, they took their mandate to an even broader level. As such, they included a number of recommendations for changes or additions to the uniform, including several items of headdress.[149]

One of the items of headgear was for the summer uniform—a white covered cork helmet. Those for officers were to have "a ventilator-button and spike (both detachable), and chin chain to be attached to the left side and to pass diagonally up across the front of the helmet and be secured at the back." In like manner, "the helmet for enlisted men" was "to be the same as that prescribed for officers, without the spike and chin-chain, which may be replaced by a strap of russet-leather...."[150]

The army's senior officer, William Sherman, disagreed with many of these findings. For one thing, he rebutted: "I prefer that commanding officers of posts be authorized to allow in hot weather, their officers and men to buy white pants, using their present uniform blue flannel sack coat and a straw hat."[151]

While a number of the 1879 Board's recommendations were disallowed or tabled, the concept of the summer helmet was revived. This was in keeping with a group of advocates for this British-influenced style. One proponent probably spoke for several others when he wrote:

When commanding officers of posts give a tardy permission for the sweltering portion of humanity subject to their will to wear white trousers and straw hats, the permission, as a rule, only extends to 'off duty.' Now the summer uniform of white sack coat and white trousers, and either straw hat or white cork helmet, is an absolute necessity in Texas, where the mercury will register 109

Ft. Monroe was one of the garrisons where the summer helmet was issued first, as indicated by these regimental bandsmen who have gathered on the parade ground. USAMHI

deg. in the shade at more than one post in July. The helmet would be the most soldierly looking, as every one who has taken the trouble to notice it, knows that after the men have worn straw hats a short time the hat looks dirty and slouchy, and military commanders have a special aversion to 'slouchy' looking men.[152]

This type of commentary evidently made an impact. In short order Meigs instructed Rodgers to "take up and consider the subject of the cork helmet as soon as possible, with a possibility of obtaining a substitute for the white facing cloth, which has heretofore been used to cover them." Early helmets previously procured for the Artillery School and West Point had been covered with facing material, which was "considered too expensive for helmets issued to troops." Meigs further directed "The covering material should be of some light color for the sake of coolness, a light grey probably, which will not soil or become shabby as soon as white...." Meigs further contemplated a cover which could be removed, "if possible, in order that it may be taken off and be washed when soiled."[153] Later the quartermaster general indicated what he considered were other important features of the helmet. First, he noted the top ventilator, which was "part of the pattern...is thought essential in hot climates, though I think the free ventilation around and outside of [the] sweatband will in time be determined to make the crown ventilator superfluous." Further, General Meigs postulated, that the eventual

discontinuance of the ventilator would make it possible "to take a helmet full of water to a wounded man on the battlefield as has been done in old history."[154]

While the grey shade, removable cover, and water carrying properties never were adopted, white drill did become the material of choice. So it was on May 5, 1880, the secretary of war approved specifications for the summer helmet.[155] For the most part these particulars were to remain unaltered for decades from the following original:

Shape and weight.—To be in shape according to standard sealed sample, and weight about seven and one-fourth (7 1/4) ounces when finished; reasonable variations (from this weight) due to sizes to be allowed.

Material &c.—The shell to be composed of two thicknesses of the best quality of cork, laminated or scarf-seamed, and securely cemented together with shellac. The linings to be firmly shellacked to the inside of shell; that for the dome to be slated-colored drilling, and that for the visor or shade to be of emerald-green merino or cashmere. Sweat-leather to be of frame or hoop as in sample, well separated from shell (for ventilation) by ten (10) small cork studs securely fastened; sweat to be about one and three-eighths (1 3/8) inches deep, and to be provided with a drawing string. Outside covering to be of the best quality of bleached cotton drilling, in four (4)

 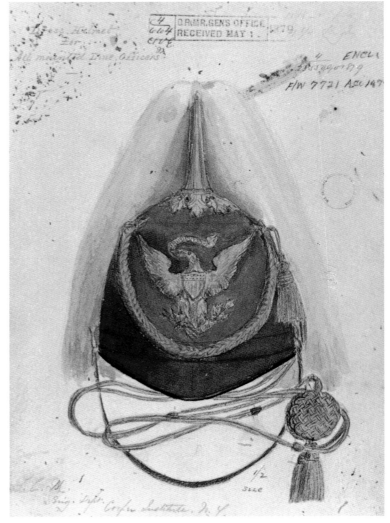

Watercolors rendered for the 1878-79 Miles Board showing front views of the proposed helmets for officers commanding foot troops with spike (left) and for officers when mounted, with plume (right). NA

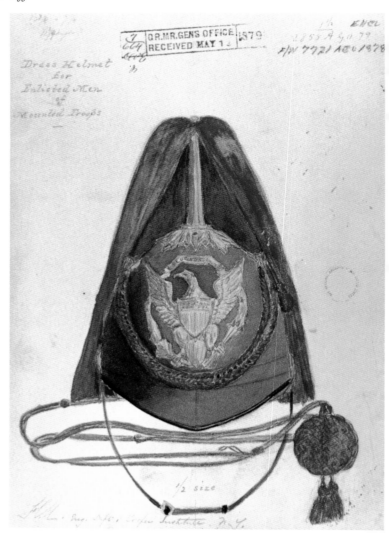

Front and side views of the proposed enlisted foot helmet also were depicted in watercolors for the Miles Board. NA

An artist conception of the mounted enlisted man's helmet, in this case for horse artillery, was provided for the board. NA

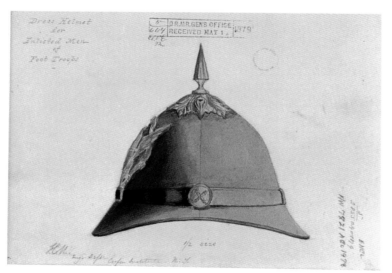

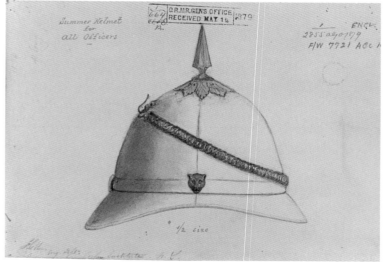

Side view of the proposed officer's summer helmet covered in white facing material with detachable chin chain, spike, spike base, and lion's side buttons as provided for the Miles Board. NA

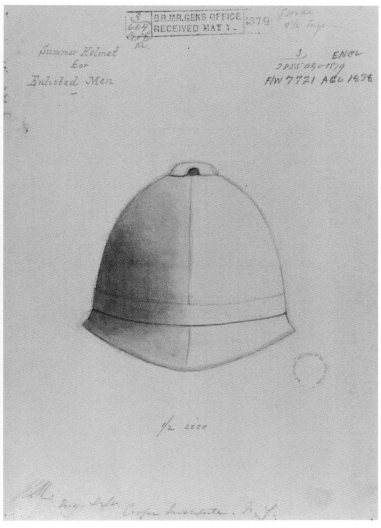

Front view of the enlisted summer helmet covered in drilling as considered by the Miles Board. NA

sections, welt seamed and secured with shellac. Band of same material, about three-fourths (3/4) of an inch deep. Edge to be bound with stout bleached stay binding. Adjustable ventilator top as in sample. Chin-strap of white enameled leather, and brass hooks for same, as sample.[156]

There were some second thoughts about then proper composition of the summer helmet body, with Captain Rodgers suggesting a change to the specifications. To this Meigs replied: "It appears to me the best and cheapest material offered was the compressed and cemented pulverized cork between two layers of linen or cotton as the body of the helmet." Thus, Meigs asked: "Why is it now proposed to reject this?" He went on to state: "If it proves not to be the best or cheapest, and a contract is awarded for another material or sample, that contract should specify precisely what is to be furnished by it, and not the general specifications given to inform all bidders." The quartermaster general displayed flexibility in the matter, when he opined: "We may perhaps find it well to buy felt helmets for one climate and pulverized cork for another." Even in this circumstance he directed: "Each contractor however is to be bound in his contract" as to the material being required.[157]

The matter of changing body composition from cork never resurfaced, however, and as of June 1880, the department let a contract to Horstmann Brothers for the production of helmets, of which some 6,000

copies were made in due course for distribution "to troops serving in extremely hot climates...in lieu of campaign hats."[158] This first procurement had to last for some time, in that follow up funds for more orders were not forthcoming for nearly a year, thereby necessitating judicious issue to the field on a limited basis.[159] In turn, officers bought them, albeit covered in the finer facing material, as they saw the fit. Not every one of them obtained this optional headdress, however, which in the case of officers included a chinchain, along with a spike and base as a substitute, if desired for more formal wear, in place of the ventilator.[160]

The summer helmet's appearance was but the first of the seeds planted by the 1879 Board, in terms of headdress, that would come into being. Soon, another proposal from this body was to bear fruit as well. This was a replacement for the mounted dress helmet and for the cap worn by foot soldiers.

In the former instance, not long after the helmet had been issued, many objections were raised as to its shape and design. Typical of these negative comments, Assistant Surgeon John Vance Lauderdale wrote from Fort Wingate, New Mexico, "The helmets worn by the cavalry are too heavy for comfort...."[161] Eighth Cavalry officer, Captain George W. Chilson, added, "The helmets are unwieldy. A helmet after the style of the Prussian Helmet made with a skeleton of light spring steel and covered with some black water-proof material is recommended, the plume to be dispensed with and a spike substituted."[162]

A former dragoon officer and author of a number of important works related to U.S. Army history, Theophilus Rodenbough, chimed in with the judgment that the helmet was "exceedingly uncomfortable, much too heavy and, if worn under a hot sun, sure to cause headache, if nothing worse."[163] An 1875 circular from the surgeon general more or less repeated the same verdict, based upon dozens of reports from officers around the country who thought "The helmet furnished is too heavy, and has too steep a visor; there is general complaint that it causes headache."[164] As noted previously, even Captain Rodgers admitted that the headdress required redesign soon after its adoption.[165]

The Miles Board went a step further when it came to this piece of headgear and its counterpart for foot troops. The group insisted: "The present shako and helmet of Infantry, Cavalry, and Artillery are objectionable and cause great dissatisfaction. They are of poor material (felt), and badly shaped, and the Board accordingly recommends the adoption for all officers and men of the line of the Army of helmets of the pattern herein submitted...."[166]

These forenamed pieces were samples made up by Henry V. Allien's firm, a one-time partner with Horstmann, along with four prototypes furnished by Horstmann, as well. Watercolor renditions of some designs were included, too.[167] In short, the board envisioned adopting "A cork helmet covered with black cloth, with an eagle and chin-chain" and topped by a buffalo hair plume in the branch color was sought for "mounted officers of the line." For "dismounted officers of the line" a similar cork helmet "with spike and eagle and chin-chain" was submitted for consideration. The members of the Miles Board proposed enlisted men should be provided with a comparable helmet, horsehair plumes adorning cavalry and light artillery models, and spiked helmets for all other enlisted men. In so doing, the idea was to "reduce the first cost of the dress hat five dollars or more, and the weight of the hat for mounted troops six ounces."[168]

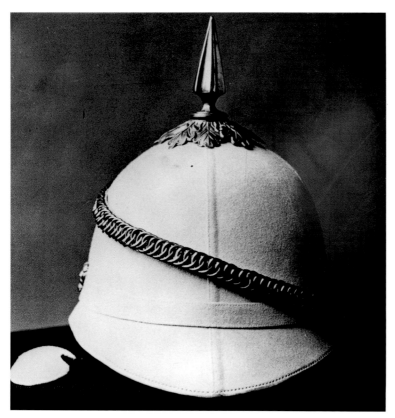

Front and side view of a prototype for the 1880-pattern officers' summer helmet prepared for Captain J. Rodgers by the firm of Henry V. Allien with lion's head side buttons. These were not adopted when the helmet actually was made official. Rather the side buttons for the 1881-pattern officers' spiked and plumed helmet were prescribed. Note the ventilator top that could be removed so the spike and base could be worn as an option. GC

It appears that the so-called "home service" helmet adopted earlier in 1878 by the British had inspired these proposals.[169] Regardless of the source, their vision was not shared by General Sherman, who vetoed the design, despite the fact that for once the quartermaster general showed an interest in a potential change of an issue item.[170]

Sherman's denial of this helmet and several other items proposed by the Miles Board provoked one commentator to send a letter to the editor of the *Army and Navy Journal* inquiring why the suggestions of

"young, energetic, and experienced officers" would be ignored by the general of the army who ordered "officers and soldiers to dress in old and obsolete styles" in lieu of "modern ideas of comfort and neatness...." He further asked: "Why are soldiers ordered to purchase their summer clothing and straw hats from traders when the Government contracts with the soldier to supply his clothing?"[171] These probing statements ultimately would be answered within a matter of a few years, when some of Sherman's objections were overturned.

Views of an 1880-pattern officer's helmet as actually adopted, in this case for infantry as indicated by the side buttons with crossed rifles. Note the optional spike and base have been replaced by the more commonly used detachable ventilator top that was covered in facing material to match the helmet. This version was manufactured by Allien of New York, a firm that produced summer helmets and dress helmets for officers with a visor that had a pronounced point at the front. CECSM

1880-pattern enlisted summer helmet with chinstrap. RB

1 Adjutant General to R.B. Marcy, April 25, 1872, Letters Received, Adjutant General's Office, Record Group 94, National Archives; Secretary of War to Adjutant General, June 26, 1872, ibid; and M.C. Meigs to Secretary of War, July 29, 1872, ibid. Hereinafter referred to as LR, AGO, RG94, NA.

2 Marcy seemed an appropriate choice to guide the revision of regulations because the Inspector General's Department served as the overseer of conformance to army regulations. Moreover, Marcy's political connections and enviable personal military record afforded him considerable clout. A West Point graduate, Class of 1832, Marcy boasted an impressive service record prior to the outbreak of the Civil War. Soon after the war erupted, he became inspector general under his son-in-law, George McClellan (his daughter also had been courted unsuccessfully by A.P. Hill). Marcy recorded much of his long and eventful career in three publications, *Prairie Traveler*, *Thirty Years of Army Life on the Border*, and *Border Reminiscences*, published in 1859, 1860, and 1871, respectively, works that brought him some degree of fame as well as favor. Mark M. Boatner III, *The Civil War Dictionary* (New York: David McKay Company, Inc., 1959), 512.

3 *Army and Navy Journal*, June 22, 1872, 720. Hereinafter referred to as *A&NJ*, with appropriate dates and pages. The article also noted Colonel Henry B. Clitz was to assist Marcy in "obtaining the samples and reporting upon the new styles to be adopted." ibid. This officer graduated with the Class of 1845. After West Point, he joined an infantry regiment as a second lieutenant. He later saw service in the Mexican War, for which he was breveted, then returned to the U.S. Military Academy to teach infantry tactics, "before going to the frontier." Soon after the Civil War he rose to major of the Twelfth Infantry, participated in a number of engagements, was captured and held at Libby Prison, then paroled to return to the banks of the Hudson as commandant of cadets. His Civil War service brought him a brevet as brigadier general in the U.S. Army. He retired in 1885 as the colonel of the Tenth Infantry. Ibid., 159.

4 Secretary of War to E.D. Townsend, July 29, 1872, LR, AGO, RG94, NA.

5 J.M. Lee to Quartermaster General, April 5, 1872, Consolidated Correspondence Files, Box 1170, Office of the Quartermaster General, RG92, NA, requested photographs to be taken of the articles the board was considering so that they might be used to illustrate the report expected to be made at the end of the deliberations. Hereafter referred to as CCF, OQMG, RG92, NA. See also M.C. Meigs to L.C. Easton, August 15, 1872, Letters Sent, Clothing & Supply Branch, Pt. 1, 1872, OQMG, RG92, NA, called for photographs of the cap and helmet and the changes required to bring them to final standards. Because of the several name changes for the Clothing and Equipment Branch or Clothing and Supplies Branch, for the sake of ease, all future references will be LS, Clothing Br., OQMG, RG92, NA.

6 M.C. Meigs to L.C. Easton, August 13, 1872, ibid.

7 M.C. Meigs to Warnock & Co., August 12, 1872, ibid.; and Horstmann Brothers & Co. to L.C. Easton, August 3, 1872, CCF, Box 1170, ibid., in which Horstmann originally estimated a cost of $4.50 to $5.00 per complete helmet.

8 M.C. Meigs to R.B. Marcy, June 28, 1872, LS, Clothing Br., Pt. 1, 1872; M.C. Meigs to R.B. Marcy, July 16, 1872; ibid; M.C. Meigs to L.C. Easton, August 9, 1872, ibid; M.C. Meigs to L.C. Easton, August 15, 1872, ibid.; M.C. Meigs to W.B. Baker, October 24, 1872, ibid.; and Contract in Branch E, Regular Supplies, Contracts, ibid.; General Orders No. 73, War Department, July 10, 1872; and General Orders No. 138, War Department, March 20, 1873. Hereinafter referred to as GO No., WD, date.

9 For reprints of several of these antebellum and slightly later advertisements see, Jacques Noel Jacobsen, Jr., *Regulations and Notes for the Uniform of the United States Army 1857* (Staten Island: Manor Publishing, 1973).

10 Jan K. Kube, *Militaria; A Study of German Helmets & Uniforms, 1729-1918* (West Chester, PA: Schiffer Military History, 1990); Heinrich Müller and Fritz Kunter, *Europäische Helme* (Berlin: Militarvelag der Deutchen Demokratischen Republik, 1971); Robert H. Rankin, *Helmets and Headdress of the Imperial German Army, 1870-1918* (New Milford, CT: N. Flayderman & Co., 1965); and Gerd M. Schultz,

    Helme und Mutzen der Armee, 1871-1945 (Munich: Jorg Minnergut, 1978), offer further information for comparisons.

11 One notable exception to this was the dark felt helmet with blue *puggree* worn by British officers in the Second Punjab Cavalry (Probyn's Horse). In the late 1840s, these helmets were used in India for parade, in which case they had white plumes, while in the field "a brass spike was substituted." Christopher Wilkinson-Latham, *The Indian Mutiny* (London: Osprey Publishing, 1991), 33 and Figure B1. Probably this helmet was unknown in the United States, however, and if anything was more a precursor to the 1878-pattern British home service helmet, examples of which appear in Robert H. Rankin, *Military Headdress: A Pictorial History of Military Headgear from 1660 to 1914* (London: Arms and Armour Press, 1976), 76 and 81.

12 Gordon Chappell, *Brass Spikes and Horsetail Plumes: A History of U.S. Army Dress Helmets, 1872-1904* (Gettysburg: Thomas Publications, 1997), 5-6, makes several insightful comments on the various European models that presaged the American helmet. He maintained: "...contemporary opinion attributed the helmet to Prussian origin. This seems essentially correct...." As evidence he cited an incident whereby Captain Anson Miles, during an 1878 visit to Paris, was taken for a German by the French, as he rode in a procession immediately behind the British. Chappell argued: "Had his American uniform imitated the British style, there would be no reason the French should have mistaken the Americans for Germans." He further concluded the helmet had been either "inspired by recent Prussian victories over the Danes, Austrians, and French," or was "filtered through nearly thirty years of English helmets whose original inspiration had been Prussian." Chappell rested his case with the statement: "Certainly it was the Prussians who popularized the style."
    A late nineteenth century observer made a similar comment writing about the 1881-pattern U.S. Army helmet: "Ours is commonly supposed to be the German helmet but it is as different as can be imagined. The English first corrupted the German Shape and we have made the matter worse both in shape and weight." Captain Theo A. Bingham, "Army Uniform," XX *Journal of the Military Service Institution* (1897): 292.

13 H.J. Hunt, to Adjutant General, March 13, 1875, LR, AGO, RG94, NA.

14 Ibid.

15 M.C. Meigs to Horstmann Brother & Co., October 1, 1872, LS, Clothing Br., Pt. 1, 1872, OQMG, RG92, NA.

16 M.C. Meigs to L.S. Easton, February 13, 1873, Book A, 1873, ibid.

17 *Annual Report of the Secretary of War, 1873*, Vol. I (Washington, DC: U.S. Government Printing Office, 1872), 152. Hereinafter referred to as *ARSW*, with year and pages.

18 Ibid.

19 Endorsement M.C Meigs to Secretary of War, August 26, 1872, LS, Clothing Br., Pt. 1, 1872, OQMG, RG92, NA.

20 M.C. Meigs to Secretary of War, September 12, 1872, Pt. 2, 1872, ibid.; M.C. Meigs to L.C. Easton, September 21, 1872, ibid; Horstmann & Brothers to M.C. Meigs, September 28, 1872, CCF, Box 1170, ibid.

21 M.C. Meigs to L.C Easton, December 10, 1872, LS, Clothing Br., Pt. 2, 1872, ibid.

22 J.D. Bingham to M.C. Meigs, December 17, 1872, CCF, Box 1170, ibid.; and *ARSW, 1873*, Vol. I, 60.

23 Horstmann & Brothers to L.C. Easton, December 12, 1872, LS, Clothing Br., Pt. 2, 1872, OQMG, RG92, NA.

24 R.B. Marcy to Secretary of War, December 16, 1872, ibid.; and M.C. Meigs to L.C. Easton, January 2, 1873, Book A, 1873, ibid.

25 Horstmann & Brothers to M.C. Meigs, December 23, 1872, Pt. 2, 1872, ibid.

26 *ARSW, 1873*, Vol. I, 60.

27 The author has examined at least a dozen Signal Corps examples, however, that had uniformly been made as separate breast cords with snap devices for attachment and which evidenced no cutting. Rather they were made as a single cord. No information as to why this batch was made or for whom, has been found.

28 Quartermaster Department Specification No. 1, May 31, 1872.

29 Quartermaster Department Specification No. 8, May 31, 1876.

30 John F. Rodgers, June 9, 1875, CCF (Hats), OQMG, RG92, NA.

31 M.C. Meigs to L.C. Easton, July 11, 1874, LS, Clothing Br., Book B, 1874, OQMG, RG92, NA. Authority continued for purchases of certain other items related to the dress helmet and dress cap, even while efforts to issue old pattern items were in place. For instance, according to J.D. Bingham to L.C. Easton, November 10, 1874, ibid., 150 red horsehair plumes, and a like number of light artillery cords, bands, top pieces, and sockets, plus 1,000 yellow cavalry plumes, 500 scrolls and rings, 500 eagles, 500 top pieces and sockets, 500 yellow cords and bands, 1000 side buttons, 1500 infantry pompons, and 500 heavy artillery pompons, were to be contracted for, indicating helmet and dress cap procurement had not ceased. Additionally, in 1874 Bent & Bush received contracts for 10,800 dress caps, 8,500 helmets, and 28,000 forage caps, while the next year Horstmann Bros. were to provide 3,125 dress caps, but only 160 helmets. With one exception, not until 1878, however, were other substantial helmet orders placed. Howell, *United States Army Headgear, 1855-1902*, 90. That exception was a contract let with Jas. G. Davis Co., of Philadelphia for 5,000 helmets, on May 19, 1876. Chappell, *Brass Spikes and Horsetail Plumes*, 95. Thus, given the size of the army at the time, ample helmets and dress caps were on hand to supply most of the troops, even in the face of congressional restrictions for other articles of the uniform.

32 M.C. Meigs to Secretary of War, April 9, 1873, LS, Clothing Br., Book A, 1873, OQMG, RG92, NA.

33 M.C. Meigs to C.H. Hoyt, August 16, 1872, Pt. 1, 1872, ibid.

34 It should be noted that ample helmets were in stock to permit the Fourteenth Infantry's regimental band to draw them in lieu of the dress cap that was regularly prescribed for infantry troops, this being allowed under the portion of army regulations that authorized regimental commanders to set the uniform for the band under their command. J.D. Bingham to D.A. Rucker, January 20, 1876, Book A, 1876, ibid. This may have set a precedent in that the band of the Twenty-fifth Infantry was photographed at Ft. Randall, Dakota Territory, wearing white plumed helmets with cords,. the copy right on the image is 1884, one year prior to authorization of this practice. The non-issue additions were permitted by regulations for bands and the cost of obtaining the items were borne by regimental funds, a sort of subscription drawn from the officers of the regiment and other non-appropriated source. The picture of the Twenty-fifth has been reproduced in many publications including, Chappell, *Brass Spikes and Horsetail Plumes*, 80.

35 J.D. Bingham to Captain Charles Alexander Alligood, July 9, 1874, LS, Clothing Br., Book B, 1874, OQMG, RG 92, NA.

36 John Mollo, *Military Fashion* (New York: G.P. Putnam's Sons, 1972), 160.

37 W.Y. Carmen, *British Military Uniforms from Contemporary Pictures, Henry VII to the Present Day* (London: Leonard Hill, Ltd., 1957), 141. For comparative images see, Rankin, *Military Headdress*, 38, 60, and 61.

38 *A&NJ*, February 20, 1869, and January 1, 1870, 316, carried advertisements from Bent and Bush for a hat of nearly identical appearance. Evidently the Boston firm offered these caps for sale to militia units.

39 J.D. Bingham (for Meigs) to Horstmann Bros. and Allien, November 29, 1872, LS, Clothing Br., Pt. 2, 1872, OQMG, RG92, NA.

40 M.C. Meigs to L.C. Easton, August 9, 1872, Pt. 1, 1872, ibid. Evidently this cap survives and is in the collections of Museum of American History, Smithsonian Institution. Howell, *United States Army Headgear, 1855-1902*, 37.

41 J.D. Bingham to Horstmann Brothers and Allien, November 29, 1872, LS, Clothing Br., Pt. 2, 1872, OQMG, RG92, NA. Earlier the firm had been told that some of the samples they supplied had to be held for a time for Marcy's review. M.C. Meigs to Horstmann, October 1, 1872, ibid.

42 M.C. Meigs to the Secretary of War, August 2, 1872, Pt. 1, 1872, ibid.

43 Colonel Richard Dodge to Adjutant General, October 19, 1874, CCF (Uniforms), OQMG, RG92, NA, and Adjutant General to Quartermaster General, October 24, 1874, and endorsements, LR, ibid.

44 *ARSW, 1876*, Vol. I, 120-21.

45 R. Ingalls to D.H. Rucker, January 24, 1876, LS, Clothing Br., Book A, 1876, OQMG, RG92, NA, noted crossed rifle samples were received and approved by the secretary of war, and a contract for 35,000 was approved for bids on the open market.

46 Endorsement M.C. Meigs to Secretary of War, September 14, 1872, Pt. 2, 1872, ibid.

47 M.C. Meigs to L.C. Easton, September 21, 1872, Pt. 2, 1872, ibid.

48 Executive Document #159, House, 43rd Cong., lst Sess.; October 30, 1872 Contract with Bent & Bush, QM Contracts, OQMG, RG92, NA; and M.C. Meigs to W.B. Baker, October 24, 1872, LS, Clothing Br., Pt. 1, 1872, ibid. Horstmann had estimated about $2.25 per cap, but that figure was not firm, and the company must have found it cost more to produce the headgear as evidenced by the fact that they did not receive the contract. Horstmann and Brothers to L.C. Easton, August 3, 1873, CCF, Box 1170, ibid. J.D. Bingham (for Meigs) to L.C. Easton, December 4, 1872, LS, Clothing Br., Pt. 2, 1872, ibid., indicated thirty-seven caps were sent to Fort Sullivan, Maine, Company K, Fifth Artillery. This appears to be one of the first issuances of the headpiece. Later, GO No. 38, WD, March 20, 1873, set the price of issuance to the enlisted men as $2.50 each with trimmings and brass ornaments. GO No. 73, WD, July 10, 1873, set the allowance at one cap for each year of enlistment. Later contracts for the cap included an October 12, 1874 purchase of 10,800 more pieces from Bent and Bush at $2.00 each. Exec. Doc. No. 111, House, 43rd Cong., 2nd Sess. Horstmann received a contract on June 21, 1875, for 3,125 caps at $1.96 each. Exec. Doc. No. 95, House, 44th Cong., 1st Sess. In part because of the congressional restrictions on purchase of new uniform items until exhaustion of old materials, a lull in contracting was experienced. Then, in 1878 a new round of contracts went to Charles F. Bush on February 11, 1878, for 1,540 caps at $1.59; on September 14, 1878 another 1,550 were ordered at $1.17 from Edmund R. Lyon; and a small lot was procured on June 12, 1878, for heavy artillery caps from J.H. Wilson for 150 caps at $1.47. Exec. Doc. No. 40, Senate, 45th Cong., 3rd Sess. The following year, some 500 heavy artillery dress caps were to be obtained and 2,000 infantry, all from J.H. Wilson for $1.16 each. Exec. Doc. No. 56, Senate, 46th Cong., 2nd Sess.

49 The composition of the fur felt bodies ultimately was essentially that of the helmet. See Quartermaster Department Specification Number 3, May 31, 1876.

50 *A&NJ*, October 4, 1873, 122.

51 J. Van Voast to Adjutant General, USA, October 1, 1872, LR, AGO, RG94, NA.

52 J.D. Bingham to L.C. Easton July 9, 1874 conveying "Abstract from Annual Report of Capt. Charles Wheaton, 23rd Inf. Ft. Yuma, CA June 22, 1874," LS, Clothing Br., Book B, 1874, OQMG, RG92, NA.

53 Acting Assistant Surgeon J. Frazer Boughter to Post Adjutant, Ft. Craig, New Mexico Territory, March 18, 1875, Microfilm Roll 436, LR, AGO Correspondence, February-March 1875, RG94, NA.

54 Lieutenant Colonel J.N.G. Whistler to Adjutant General, USA, March 1, 1875, ibid.

55 Colonel George Andrews to Adjutant General, USA, February 25, 1875, ibid.

56 Colonel Henry Clitz to Adjutant General, USA, March 5, 1875, ibid.

57 Captain C.E. Morse to Adjutant General, USA, March 15, 1875, ibid.

58 Assistant Surgeon C. Ewen to Adjutant General, USA, March 10, 1875, ibid.

59 Captain L. Wheaton, Ft. Pembina, Dakota Territory to Adjutant General, USA, March 10, 1875, ibid.

60 M.C. Meigs to L.C. Easton, August 9, 1872, and M.C. Meigs to D.H. Rucker, August 13, 1872, LS, Clothing Br., Pt. 1, 1872, OQMG, RG92, NA; Horstmann Brothers & Co. to L.C Easton, August 3, 1872, and P. Herst to L.C. Easton, August 5, 1872, CCF, Box 1170, ibid.

61 L.C. Easton to M.C. Meigs, September 16, 1872, LS, Clothing Branch, Pt. 2, 1872, ibid., and Endorsement M.C. Meigs, September 17, 1872, to ibid.

62 M.C. Meigs to L.C. Easton, September 18, 1872, Pt 1, 1872, ibid.

63 Contract with P. Herst, Phila., October 19, 1872, Quartermaster Contracts, ibid.

64 P. Herst to L.C. Easton, October 24, 1872, CCF, Box 1170, ibid.

65 L.C. Easton to Quartermaster General, November 1, 1872, ibid.; and J.D. Bingham to L.C. Easton, November 23, 1872, LS, Clothing Br., Pt. 2, 1872, ibid.

66 P. Herst to L.C. Easton, November 7, 1872, CCF, Box 1170, ibid.; and R. Allen to L.C. Easton, November 22, 1872, ibid.

67 *Circular No. 8, Report on Hygiene of the United States Army and Circular No. 9, Report to the Surgeon General on the Transport of Wounded by Pack Animals* (New York: Sol Lewis, 1974), l, (hereinafter referred to as Circular No. 8), contains a statement from Meigs that the cap underwent some modifications from that which originally was adopted on November 23, 1872. He indicated: "The quality and make of the cap have since been improved, and on November 9, 1872, a new standard was adopted to be used in making future contracts. It is believed that the new cap will give general satisfaction." Evidently that was the case because a new specification did not supersede the November 1874-pattern until May 31, 1876, which was little more than a reprint of the specification adopted two years before, as was Quartermaster Department Specification No. 143, April 3, 1885.

68 M.C. Meigs to L.C. Easton, August 15, 1872, LS, Clothing Br., Pt. 1, 1872, OQMG, RG92, NA; and Exec. Doc. No. 159, House, 43rd Cong., lst Sess.

69 J.D. Bingham (for Meigs) to L.C. Easton, February 3, 1873, and M.C. Meigs to L.C. Easton, July 12, 1873, LS, Clothing Br., Book A, 1873, OQMG, RG92, NA.

70 Howell, *United States Army Headgear, 1855-1902*, 52. The post commander of a fort in Texas was one who believed the cap cover was not necessary. He wrote, "In obedience to circular letter H:120 S. from your office, I have the honor to report that in my opinion, it would be very conducive to the comfort of the men and economical to the government to issue cotton trousers instead of Cap Covers, to enlisted men where the mercury in the sun rises to 165 F. (Solar heat.)" Post Commander, Ft. Concho, Texas to Assistant Adjutant General, USA, August 20, 1876, Post Returns, Ft. Concho, Texas, Records of United States Continental Commands, RG393, NA. Further, General George Crook to Quartermaster General, November 2, 1876, LR, AGO, RG94, NA, noted that the veteran field campaigner was one of those who also thought the cap covers could be discontinued. Several years later, all but 1 of the 16,449 forage cap covers stored by the Quartermaster Department were sold. Perhaps the single example was retained for the department's museum. *ARSW, 1882*, Vol. I, 306.

71 M.C. Meigs to D.H. Rucker, LS, Clothing Br., Book A, 1873, OQMG, RG92, NA.

72 R.B. Marcy to E.D. Townsend, October 10, 1872, LS, Office of the Inspector General, RG159, NA.

73 Telegrams from C.C. Augur, P.H. Sheridan, and G. Meade to W.T. Sherman, October 5, 1872, LR, AGO, RG94.

74 GO No. 67, WD, June 25, 1873.

75 GO No. 38, WD, AGO, March 20, 1873.

76 L.C. Easton to Quartermaster General, November 25, 1872, and L.C Easton to Quartermaster General, December 9, 1872, CCF, Box 1170, ibid; First Endorsement, M.C. Meigs, December 6, 1872, ibid.; and Second Endorsement, R.B. Marcy, December 10, 1872, which also noted the brass wreath and Roman "U.S." as proper insignia. See also, J.D. Bingham to M.C. Meigs, December 17, 1872, LS, Clothing Br., Pt. 2, 1872, ibid.

77 GO No. 107, AGO, December 14, 1872. Also see, *ARSW, 1877*, Vol. I, 266-7, for the first published specifications for this cap insignia.

78 Second Endorsement, R.B. Marcy, December 10, 1872, CCF, Box 1170, OQMG, RG92, NA; and GO No. 67, WD, June 25, 1873. Originally GO No. 92, WD, October 26, 1872, had called for the letters "C.E.", but GO No. 107, WD, December 14, 1872, had changed this to the long-used castle motif.

79 GO No. 67, WD, June 25, 1873. This same order changed the long-standing silver script U.S. in a gold wreath insignia for forage caps of officers of the Adjutant General's Department to a shield within a wreath. Returning to the matter of enlisted cap insignia, it had been noted that the old shell and flame insignia were too large for the dress cap adopted in 1872, and as such new, smaller versions would have to be designed and procured. Memoranda, J.D. Bingham, November 23, 1872, CCF, Box 1170, OQMG, RG92, NA; and L.C. Easton to Quartermaster General, November 23, 1872, Box 1172, ibid. M.C. Meigs to L.C. Easton, March 6, 1873, LS, Clothing Br., Book A, 1873, ibid., noted Marcy approved the castle as a replacement for the letters "CE". J.D. Bingham to Chief Quartermaster Department of the South, January 12, 1874, Book A, 1874, ibid., indicated that enlisted ordnance men now were to have the new shell and flame on their caps.

80 J.F. Rodgers to L.C. Easton, April 5, 1873, LR, Philadelphia Depot, Box 85, ibid.

81 Previously, the quartermaster general had inquired as to whether any of the old pattern uniform hat ornaments were on hand that might be used for the new caps. It seems that their size made this impractical. M.C. Meigs to L.C. Easton, August 12, 1872, LS, Clothing Br., Pt. 1, 1872, ibid.

82 J.F. Rodgers to L.C. Easton, September 6, 1873, LR, Philadelphia Depot, Box 76, ibid.

83 M.C. Meigs to L.C. Easton, March 31, 1873, LS, Clothing Br., Book A, 1873, ibid.

84 M.C. Meigs to Inspector General, April 8, 1873, Book, A, 1873, ibid.; and M.C. Meigs to L.C. Easton, June 10, 1873, ibid.

85 L.C. Easton to Quartermaster General, September 11, 1872; L.C. Easton to M.C. Meigs, September 19, 1872; L.C. Easton to Quartermaster General, December 21, 1872, CCF, Box 1170, ibid.

86 M.C. Meigs to L.C. Easton, March 31, 1873, LS, Clothing Br., Book A, 1873, ibid.

87 M.C. Meigs to L.C. Easton, September 21, 1872, Pt. 1, 1872, ibid.

88 M.C. Meigs endorsement to Adjutant General, January 3, 1873, ibid., and Adjutant General to Quartermaster General, January 15, 1873, CCF, Box 1170, ibid.

89 M.C. Meigs to R.B. Marcy, June 6, 1873, LS, Clothing Br., Book A, 1873, ibid.; M.C. Meigs to L.C. Easton, June 19, 1873, ibid; and Endorsement to D.H. Brotherton to Adjutant General, November 23, 1873, LR, Office of the Secretary of War, RG107, NA. M.C. Meigs to L.C. Easton, June 3, 1873, LS, Clothing Br., Book A, 1873, OQMG, RG92, NA, indicated Marcy had been sent cavalry crossed saber insignia and the commissary and ordnance insignia for his approval as well. Also see, GO No. 67, WD, June 25, 1873, for the company letter and badge combination being generally called for on the forage cap of enlisted men except for the Ordnance Department, the Signal Corps, as well as hospital stewards and commissary sergeants.

90 GO No. 8, WD, February 8, 1877, rendered a concise description for how the various forage cap and dress cap insignia was to be worn.

91 D.H. Rucker to Quartermaster General, March 9, 1876, LR, OQMG, RG92, NA, asked whether a recent request for bids to obtain 10,000 cap bugles was in error? Was the order not really for "cap eagles"? Likely it was because so large a quantity of musicians' devices would have been far beyond what was needed.

92 M.C. Meigs to D.H. Rucker, April 9, 1873, LS, Clothing Br., Book A, 1873, *ibid.*, indicated that after several obstacles, Meigs had not been able to meet the December 1, 1872 issuance of the uniform, but intended to begin issue by July 1, 1873, at the start of the new fiscal year. The idea was that all men would receive the cavalry and artillery helmets, dress caps, forage caps, and cap covers, berlin gloves, trousers, and coats with stripes attached, and troops in the West also would have their campaign hats. This goal was achieved according to *ARSW, 1873*, Vol. I, 120.

93 *A&NJ*, December 25, 1875, 322.

94 Acting Assistant Surgeon J. Frazer Boughter, Ft. Craig, New Mexico Territory to Post Adjutant March 18, 1875, Microfilm Roll 436, LR, February-March, 1875, AGO, RG94, NA.

95 It should be noted that the original 1872-pattern was adopted on November 23 of that year. It was to have a six inch diameter crown, measure 6 inches in the rear, and slope to a height of 3 3/4 inches at the front. The visor was to be two inches wide. Changes were made thereafter, which became the standard on November 9, 1874, and later published in 1876, as reprinted above. It was "believed the new caps will give general satisfaction." *Circular No. 8*, l. As noted previously, the elimination of braid from the cap was one of the first alterations to be made prior to issue of the piece.

96 Quartermaster Department Specification No. 5, May 31, 1876. Later specifications were published on April 15, 1886, January 5, 1889, and April 12, 1892, but are similar to the first cap. Some notable exceptions include the addition of black enameled leather binding on the visor (1889) and the substitution of black satin for glazed muslin as the lining. In addition, the caps tended to become slightly lower as time passed, the later versions measuring 1 1/8-inches from the band at the front and the back raising 4 inches from the band, whereas the pattern of the 1870s through mid-1880s was to be from 1 to 1 5/8-inches at the front and 5-inches at the back. In turn, the earlier bands were to be "about one and one-fourth (1 1/4) inch wide" while the later ones were to be "about one and three-eighths (1 3/8) inches wide." This meant the overall height was approximately the same, but the outline changed subtly. Furthermore, the 1876 specifications called for a 4 3/4-inch crown and the later specifications a slightly larger 5-inch diameter crown. Finally, the later specifications went into considerably more detail regarding the blue cloth that made up the cap's body.

97 Major Judson David Bingham to Lieutenant John Wesley Dillenback, First Artillery, Savannah, Georgia, July 9, 1874, LS, Clothing Br., Book B, 1874, OQMG, RG92, NA.

98 J.F. Rodgers to L.C. Easton, November 12, 1872, LR, Philadelphia Depot, Box 56, ibid.

99 Endorsement 1, L.C. Easton, November 14, 1873, Pt. 2, 1873, ibid.

100 James S. Hutchins, "The Army Campaign Hat of 1872," XVI *Military Collector and Historian* No. 3 (Fall 1964): 65-73, offers additional information on the hat's promises, pitfalls, and uses.

101 William O. Taylor, *With Custer on the Little Bighorn* (New York: Viking, 1996), 155. Previous to this time, however, Taylor's commanding officer, George Custer, ordered: "Felt hats differing in color or materially in shape from the regulation campaign hat, will not be worn by officers or men of this command." Circular No. 52, Headquarters Detachment 7th Cavalry, May 22, 1873, General and Special Orders and Circulars Issued by General Custer's Detachment, April 1873-September 1873, Vol. 2, Records of U.S. Army Mobile Units, 1821-1942, RG391, NA. This order was ignored by many, including Custer himself! Custer also dictated guard mount was to be performed in full dress, and without overcoats, while white berlin gloves or light colored gauntlets could be worn. In the latter instance, the gauntlets would have to be purchased by individuals because none were issued until the mid 1880s to the troops. Conversely, he prohibited top boots for officers and men on dismounted duty. Special Order No. 76, Headquarters Battalion 7th Cavalry, November 19, 1873, ibid.

102 Captain Loyd Wheaton, Fort Pembina, DT to Adjutant General, March 10, 1875, Microfilm 666, Roll 436, LR, AGO Correspondence, February-March 1875, RG94, NA.

103 Surgeon Thomas McParlin to Colonel Nelson A. Miles, Post Commander Ft. Leavenworth, KS, March 5, 1875, ibid.

104 Howell, *United States Army Headgear 1855-1902*, 55, summarizes this series of ex changes found in May 5, 1875, CCF (Proceedings) OQMG, RG92, NA. Also see J.D. Bingham to Captain S. Ovenshine, March 20, 1875, LS, Clothing Br., Book A, 1875, ibid., which indicated that the acting assistant quartermaster at the Cheyenne Agency likewise reported troops who received the campaign hat from him considered the headdress unsuited for the purpose intended. Of forty hats issued, within three weeks of field wear, only about a half dozen remained in good shape. In response, Bingham requested the deteriorated hats to be sent to the quartermaster general's office for inspection.

105 GO No. 6, WD, January 29, 1875. A summary of the responses was published in *Circular No. 8*, xlvii-liii. For complete copies of the replies from this extensive survey obtain, Microfilm 666, Rolls 435 and 436, LR, AGO Correspondence, February-March 1875, RG94, NA.

106 Acting Assistant Surgeon J. Frazer Boughter, Ft. Craig, New Mexico to Post Adjutant March 18, 1875, Roll 436, ibid.

107 Assistant Surgeon W.F. Buchanan to Post Adjutant Ft. Brown, Texas, February 24, 1875, ibid.

108 Colonel J.H. Potter, Twenty-fifth Infantry to Adjutant General, USA, March 15, 1875, ibid.

109 Acting Assistant Surgeon B. Alexander, Ft. Quitman, Texas to Captain Charles Bentzoni, March 15, 1875, ibid.

110 Captain George Shorkley to Adjutant General, USA, March 20, 1875, ibid.

111 Acting Assistant Surgeon William H. Forwood to Post Adjutant, April 1, 1875, ibid.

112 First Lieutenant William H.H. Crowell to Post Adjutant, March 14, 1875, ibid.

113 Ezra Fuller, "Recollections of an Old Cavalryman," XXVI *Journal of the United States Cavalry Association* No. 1 (January 1916): 417.

114 *A&NJ*, October 4, 1873, 122.

115 *Circular No. 8*, xlix.

116 Ibid., l.

117 *ARSW, 1875*, Vol. I, 230.

118 Gordon Chappell, *Summer Helmets of the U. S. Army, 1875-1910* (Cheyenne: Wyoming State Museum, 1967), 7. This monograph remains one of the most useful references on the topic of the summer helmet. For Meigs' letter requesting samples, see, M.C. Meigs to Sir Edward Thornton, March 6, 1875, LR, Microfilm 666, roll 440, AGO, RG94, NA.

119 Circular No. 10, Headquarters, Department of Texas, July 7, 1871. GO No. 30, Headquarters, Ft. Laramie, Wyoming Territory, June 18, 1872, authorized local commanders to allow their men to purchase straw hats, but this meant the soldier had to do so out of his meager pay. During the summer of 1876, Major Marcus Reno indicated that he and some other officers of the Seventh U.S. Cavalry bought broad-brimmed straw hats without bands from a trader who brought a supply with him via riverboat. These cost between \$.25 and \$.50 each, and provided "Very good shelter from the sun." W.A. Graham, ed., *Official Record of a Court of Inquiry convened...upon request of Major Marcus A. Reno...to investigate his conduct at...the Little Bighorn, June 25-26, 1876* (Pacific Palisades, CA: 1951), 509. Another Custer subordinate, Second Lieutenant Charles A. Varnum, supposedly saw a fellow officer who had a straw hat, presumably acquired from the same trader. John P. Everett, "Bullets, Boots, and Saddles. Being Personal Recollections of Men Who Took Part in the Battle of the Big Horn in Montana Territory June 25, 1876, as Told to John P. Everett," IX *The Sunshine Magazine* (September 1930), 5.

120 Light colored wool hats also were obtained by the men from their own funds. Perhaps the best known examples were those worn by the men who rode with Custer on the ill-fated 1876 summer campaign. Custer himself wore a broadbrimmed version, for instance. W.A. Graham, *The Custer Myth* (Mechanicsburg, PA: Stackpole Books, 1995), 346. Another individual recalled he saw "white hats, brown, hats, black hats, all kinds of hats except the Service hat." *A&NJ*, September 15, 1877, 90. Recollections from the same campaign recorded a white wool trooper's non-regulation hat being spotted near the Rosebud by some of Brigadier General George Crook's men that had crossed sabers and a brass "C" or had the saber insignia drawn on the front along with the Seventh Cavalry's numeral. Douglas McChristian, *The U.S. Army in the West, 1870-1880* (Norman: University of Oklahoma Press, 1994), 286, citing Walter Camp's field notes of the 1876 campaign.

121 Meigs had asked for the authority to procure 200 helmets for trial, and sent a sample to the secretary of war. At first, Secretary of War William Belknap declined the request because of fiscal constraints. Shortly thereafter, Meigs returned to the secretary with a second recommendation to have the surgeon general review the British model just received through Sir Edward Thorton, such a helmet being a possible substitute "in view of the failure of the campaign hat." See, M.C. Meigs to Secretary of War, March 13, 1875, LR, Microfilm 666, roll, 440, AGO, RG94, NA, and lst Endorsement, March 18, 1875, along with M.C. Meigs to Secretary of War, 1875, and Endorsements 2 and 3, June 1, 1875, and June 26, 1875, ibid.; and Rufus Ingalls to Colonel Robert Allen, June 28, 1875, LS, Clothing Br., Book B, 1875, OQMG, RG92, NA, which indicated 100 British style helmets were being sent to Arizona.

122 Colonel Rufus Ingalls to Colonel Robert Allen, June 28, 1875; Colonel Stewart Van Vliet to Quartermaster General, October 4, 1875 and 3rd Endorsement, ibid.

123 Howell, *U.S. Army Headgear, 1855-1902*, 73. It was noted that in October 1875, when the 100 summer helmets were sent for trial to Arizona, "some of the troops declined to receive them; others reported adversely on them." After that it appeared "these helmets" were "distributed to various posts of the Military Division of the Pacific, and you are now requested to collect them at the San Francisco Depot and report their condition...." M.C. Meigs to Chief Quartermaster, Military Division of Pacific, May 21, 1879, LS, Clothing Br., Book A, 1879, OQMG, RG92, NA.

124 Several years later Meigs was asked to comment on the cadet helmet in response to a request for them to be provided by the Quartermaster Department and likewise fitted out with spike and chinchain as officers' models were. He replied his department did not supply clothing to the corps of cadets. Additionally, he indicated there were no cadet helmets in the Quartermaster Department's stocks. Nonetheless, Meigs saw "no objection to the cadets wearing these trimmings on their white summer helmets. I think that on duty their use adds to the beauty of the uniform." But for "off duty", he encouraged, "They wear the helmets instead of forage cap as being cooler and safer in the hot midsummer air of West Point and without trimmings." M.C. Meigs to AGO, June 10, 1881, ibid.

125 Chappell, *Summer Helmets of the U.S. Army, 1875-1910*, 7.

126 Howell, *United States Army Headgear, 1855-1902*, 56.

127 Acting Quartermaster General to Adjutant General, October 2, 1875, CCF (Proceedings), OQMG, RG92, NA.

128 The other members were Lieutenant Colonel H.M. Black, Eighteenth Infantry; Lieutenant Colonel W.B. Royall, Third Cavalry; Captain A.C. Wildrick, Third Artillery; and Captain J.G.C. Lee, assistant quartermaster, who served as the Board's recorder.

129 R. Ingalls to D.H. Rucker, January 17, 1876, LS, Clothing Br., Book A, 1876, OQMG, RG92, NA.

130 Howell, *United States Army Headgear, 1855-1902*, 57.

131 D.H. Rucker to M.C. Meigs, with endorsements and enclosures, June 9, 1876, CCF (Proceedings), OQMG, RG92, NA.

132 Early in June, Major James Jackson Dana at the Philadelphia Depot asked for precise specifications for the hat. June 8, 1876, Register of LR, Philadelphia Depot, ibid. The firm of John T. Waring & Co. of Yonkers, NY, said they would furnish the required specifications along with samples and express them to Philadelphia. June 6, 1876, ibid. Ultimately this maker would receive the first contract for 15,000 hats at $1.25. Cords, which were in stock from the Civil War, would be charged at an additional $.07, when issued with the hat. M.C. Meigs to D.H. Rucker, June 20, 1876, LS, Clothing Br., Book A, 1976, ibid.

133 In one case a order even was placed for a white campaign hat, but Meigs made it known that none were furnished by the Quartermaster Department. Only the black regulation one was provided. M.C. Meigs to Chief Quartermaster, Military Division of the Missouri, June 26, 1879, Book A, 1879, ibid.

134 Once the specifications had been completed, the secretary of war approved them and the adoption of the hat. M.C. Meigs to J.A. Ekin, June 14, 1876, Book B, 1876, ibid. M.C. Meigs to D.A Rucker, June 14, 1876, ibid., repeated this message and returned the sample hat as the sealed pattern, along with another hat furnished by P. Herst & Son, that had been rejected.

135 *ARSW, 1877*, Vol. I, 265.

136 It appears the first 3,500 1876-pattern hats were sent to the Omaha Depot, presumably for issue to the troops serving on the Upper Missouri and the Great Plains. J.D. Bingham to D.A. Rucker, April 7, 1877, LS, Clothing Br., Book A, 1877, OQMG, RG92, NA.

137 M.C. Meigs to Lieutenant Charles Cresson, September 14, 1876; endorsement to letter to Chief Quartermaster, Department of Arizona to Chief Quartermaster, Military Division of Pacific, October 31, 1876, Book B, 1876; M.C. Meigs to Chief Quartermaster, Military Division of Missouri, October 31, 1876, Book B.; M.C. Meigs to D.H. Rucker, April 7, 1877, Book A, 1877; M.C. Meigs to Chief Quartermaster, Military Division of Pacific, June 2, 1877, Book A, 1877; all in LS, Clothing Br., ibid. When a question was asked from the garrison at Angel Island, California, if general prisoners were to receive the 1876-pattern campaign hat, the response was no. M.C. Meigs endorsement to Adjutant General, USA, January 3, 1876, Book A, 1876, ibid.

138 Assistant Adjutant General to the Commanding Officer, Ft. Sanders, Wyoming Territory, October 5, 1878, Ft. Sanders Document File, Continental Commands, RG393, NA; and J.D. Bingham to D.H. Rucker, September 25, 1879, LS, Clothing Br., Book B, 1879, OQMG RG92, NA, instructed that 700 campaign hats were to be altered for military prisoners at Ft. Leavenworth, Kansas. Also see, Howell, *United States Army Headgear, 1855-1902*, 59. According M.C. Meigs to D.H. Rucker, July 14, 1880, Book B, 1880, ibid. some 3,913 hats of the 1872-pattern were permitted to be altered at an estimated cost of $.15 each.

139 *ARSW, 1879*, Vol. I, 64.

140 J.D. Bingham to D.H. Rucker, September 25, 1879, Book B, 1879; and M.C. Meigs telegram to D.H. Rucker, February 26, 1881, Book A, 1881, both in LS, Clothing Br., OQMG, RG92, NA.

141 In regard to the summer helmet see, J.G.C. Lee to Quartermaster General, January 26, 1876, LR, ibid., which asked if any reports had been received from Arizona relative to the cork helmets and new hat design trial piece that had been sent for testing in that command. R. Ingalls to Captain J.G.C. Lee, January 27, 1876, LS, Clothing Br., Book A, 1876, ibid., noted the Board still had not received reports from Arizona relative to the trial campaign hats and cork helmets. Ingalls also wanted to know if Lee had received samples of a summer helmet submitted by F.A. Goodhue of New York, for the group's consideration. This question came in response to Goodhue's correspondence relative to the status of the helmets he previously had left with the quartermaster general's office. F.G. Goodhue to Quartermaster General, January 25, 1876, LR, OQMG, ibid. The Board also considered some other options, including a patented hat from John Case that had been passed to D.A. Rucker, who presided over the board. War Department to Quartermaster General, January 27, 1876, LR, ibid.

142 Quartermaster Department Specification No. 7, May 23, 1876. According to Register LR, Philadelphia Depot, March 23, 1876, File 579, ibid., these sealskin caps, along with gauntlets were approved for troops at northern posts.

143 *ARSW, 1877*, Vol. I, 77.

144 The officer in charge of the Philadelphia Depot indicated "that owing to urgent demands for seal skin caps for Tongue River and Omaha, Nebra. the 454 seal skin caps due on order from this office dated 18 Sept last have not been supplied." Because they were not going to reach their destination in time, the order was canceled—news that probably was not well received by the troops who faced a bleak Plains winter. J.D. Bingham to J.M. Marshall, February 7, 1877, LS, Clothing Br., Book A, 1877, OQMG, RG92, NA. Marshall was at Ft. Ellis, Montana Territory, a remote locale that sorely needed this winter gear.

145 M.C. Meigs endorsement to Adjutant General, USA, March 28, 1877, Book A, 1877, ibid.

146 Howell, *United States Army Headgear, 1855-1902*, 78.

147 Quartermaster Department Specification No. 6, March 12, 1879.

148 Specifically buffalo fur caps and gauntlets as well as woolen mittens were considered. In terms of the buffalo type of headgear trials indicated at least one officer, Captain George B. Davis, the Fifth U.S. Cavalry stationed at Ft. D.A. Russell, Wyoming Territory, thought the caps of this material were stronger and better than those of muskrat. S.B. Holabird to Chief Quartermaster Military Division of the Missouri, February 14, 1880, LS, Clothing Br., Book, A, 1880, OQMG, RG92, NA. Meigs was interested in the reaction of others and sent a telegram to one of his key subordinates in the Department of Missouri, who was charged with supplying troops in many of the northernmost posts, as to whether he wanted buffalo caps and gauntlets. He likewise asked if buffalo was preferred over muskrat, how many cold weather items of this material should be acquired for issue. M.C. Meigs to R. Ingalls, June 11, 1880, ibid.
Meigs also received and consolidated reports about the suitability of the buffalo caps and gauntlets. He shared this information with General Philip Sheridan, who at the time commanded the troops in the areas where such gear was needed. M.C. Meigs to Adjutant General Military Division of the Missouri, June 12, 1880, ibid. In the end, however, buffalo gauntlets were favored, but sealskin remained the material of choice for caps, an opinion relayed by the chief quartermaster of the Military Division of the Missouri. Meigs followed this advice, in part directing that gauntlets thereafter were to be of buffalo and caps of muskrat. M.C. Meigs to D.H. Rucker, June 18, 1880, ibid.

149 The Miles Board likewise spoke in favor of the muskrat winter cap over the sealskin. T.J. Sperry, "Winter Clothing on the Northern Plains," XLIV *Military Collector and Historian* No. 3 (Fall 1992): 116.

150 GO No. 76, HQA (Headquarters of the Army), November 4, 1880.

151 Ibid.

152 *A&NJ*, August 23, 1897, 23.

153 M.C. Meigs to J.F. Rodgers, March 4, 1879, LS, Clothing Br., Book A, 1879, OQMG, RG92, NA. Also see, M.C. Meigs to D.A. Rucker, March 15, 1879, ibid., for a similar directive. Despite this change in covering, when 145 helmets were to be ordered as a replacement for worn out ones at the Ft. Monroe's Artillery School with white drilling ala the British, so they would be washable or able to be "whitened with chalk rubber", instructions were forthcoming not to follow this route. Instead, the helmets were to be the "same as those purchased last year" which meant that they would be in facing material. M.C. Meigs to Secretary of War, July 16, 1879, and M.C. Meigs to D.H. Rucker, July 18, 1879, ibid. Later this decision may have been overturned because Meigs informed the commander of Ft. Monroe that a sample cork helmet with permanently attached white drill exterior had been sent to the secretary of war, at an estimated cost of $2.50 each versus the $3.41 expenditure for a model covered with facing. The letter went on to instruct that the British used drill. From this it may be inferred that subsequent supplies of the helmet to the Artillery School would likewise be covered in the more durable, less expensive material. M.C. Meigs to Colonel George Getty, August 20, 1879, ibid. According to S. Van Vliet to D.H. Rucker, May 15, 1880, CCF, Box 77, ibid., the secretary of war approved "the sample cork helmet, made to conform to the suggestions of Colonel Getty, as the standard for the Artillery School. Given that this letter directed the letting of an order for the new helmet within days after the adoption of a general standard for all helmets, it can be inferred that the drill covered helmet was the universal style thereafter.
M.C. Meigs to Quartermaster Military Division of the Atlantic, April 6, 1881, LS, Clothing Br., Book A, 1881, ibid., noted an error that occurred when the cork helmets were turned in to Philadelphia from the Artillery School under the mistaken idea that they could be recovered in canvas. Meigs indicated: "The helmets previously issued (those covered with white cloth) cannot be altered, and they differ but slightly from those of those of the new pattern." Because there were no cork helmets in stock and no funds to acquire new ones during fiscal year 1881, Meigs directed "the cork helmets now on hand should be re-issued." This was important in that Meigs foresaw that the appropriations for the next fiscal year would not include money for enlisted summer helmets, an opinion he voiced again in a later piece of correspondence concerning projections for clothing supply during fiscal year 1882. M.C. Meigs to Major R. Batchelder, April 4, 1881, ibid. In this light, the quartermaster general's office issued a directive for the eighty-two cloth covered helmets and ninety-seven linen covered helmets sent to Philadelphia from the Artillery School to be returned to Ft. Monroe. S.B. Holabird to Chief Quartermaster, Military Division of the Atlantic, April 26, 1881, ibid.

154 M.C. Meigs to J.F. Rodgers, March 21, 1881, Book A, 1881, ibid.

155 S. Van Vliet to D.H. Rucker, May 15, 1880, Box 77, CCF, ibid., passed on the information that the original specification for the helmet was that adopted for the Artillery School, although the same design ultimately would be available for the army in general. The secretary of war approved both the specifications and sample helmet, which was made to conform "to the suggestions of Colonel [George Washington] Getty,

who commanded the school, and which was sealed as the standard sample. Another identical model was to be made to demonstrate that the standard could be met and was understood. ibid. In June, Meigs directed a supply of 100 copies of the specifications to be sent to Colonel Rucker, and another fifty to be dispatched to J.A. Ekin. S.B. Holabird to D.H. Rucker, June 28, 1880, and S.B. Holabird to J.A. Ekin. June 28, 1880, LS, Clothing Br., Book A, 1880, ibid. Soon thereafter he sent a copy of the complete specifications to several key officers for their use in future inspections of summer helmet to make certain that they conformed to regulations. Letters from M.C. Meigs to D.H. Rucker, R. Ingalls, L.C. Easton, and S. VanVliet, June 29, 1880, all in ibid.

[156] Quartermaster Department Specification adopted May 5, 1880, as reprinted in *U.S. Army Uniforms and Equipment, 1889*, (Lincoln: University of Nebraska Press, 1986), 2.

[157] M.C. Meigs to D.H. Rucker, May 7, 1881, LS, Clothing Br., Book A, 1881, OQMG, RG92, NA. According to M.C. Meigs to J.F. Rodgers, March 21, 1881, ibid., Meigs favored the "cemented powdered cork" for the composition of the helmet body, a fact that caused one contractor to question whether bids for helmets made of this material would be entertained. S.B. Holabird to Apple & Co., March 21, 1881, ibid.

[158] GO No. 72, HQA, November 4, 1880, delineated who should receive the helmets, while *ARSW, 1881*, Vol. I, 285, evidenced the original order was for 6,000 to be issued. As to the summer helmet, the May 5, 1880 standard pattern originally was that approved for the Artillery School at Ft. Monroe, Virginia. Meigs thought it should be made the standard for the army as well. Because the weather was turning hot, he asked for authority to adopt the standard and procure helmets of that design, with the secretary's concurrence. He also asked whether he should obtain 500 helmets specifically earmarked for the First U.S. Infantry, which was bound for Texas. M.C. Meigs Endorsement to Secretary of War, May 24, 1880, LS, Clothing Br., Book. A, 1880, OQMG, RG92, NA.

[159] For example, according to S.B. Holabird to Chief Quartermaster Military Division of Missouri, June 2, 1881, Book A. 1881, ibid., requests for summer helmets for the Texas posts of Forts Davis, McKavitt, and Clark, were being rejected in that no more helmets were in stock and would not be until after the new fiscal year. Another communique indicated that 310 cork helmets for Fort Sill, Indian Territory, requested on May 14 could not be sent until after July 1, when new appropriations became available. It was pointed out that the prior fiscal year funding allowed for only 6,000 summer helmets, and these had to be shared with the Atlantic and Pacific Divisions, including 275 for West Point and 725 held for miscellaneous posts and divisions, along with 500 that were "expressly purchased by direction of the general of the Army for the lst Infantry" for shipment to Fort McKavitt, Texas. S.B. Holabird to Chief Quartermaster Military Division of Missouri, June 2, 1881, ibid. These helmets had been set aside earlier in the year, before Colonel William "Pecos Bill" Shafter took his First U.S. Infantry to Texas. M.C. Meigs to Secretary of War, January 28, 1881, ibid.
By careful budgeting the Quartermaster Department reviewed its remaining funds and Meigs wanted to apply some of this money to the purchase of cork helmets especially for troops at Fort Sill. M.C. Meigs to Secretary of War May 13, 1881, ibid. Further, S.B. Holabird to Chief Quartermaster Military Division of the Atlantic, May 26, 1881, ibid., conveyed "that a limited number of cork helmets is now being procured" for issue "to troops in extreme hot climates." While S.B. Holabird to Chief Quartermaster of Department of the South, June 10, 1881, ibid., pointed out the Department of the South would not obtain the helmets for that command immediately, but would receive the summer helmets after the new fiscal year's appropriations became available. As such, each post requiring them was to supply their estimates. This was followed by instructions to issue the cork helmets required at the various posts of the department. S.B. Holabird to J.F. Rodgers June 10, 1881, ibid. So, too, was a directive to supply cork helmets to posts in Arizona Territory and across the river in California to the following garrisons in quantities indicated in parentheses: Forts Apache (233), Bowie (150), McDowell (95), Verde (190), Whipple Barracks (126), Yuma, (48), Lowell (165), Grant (245) and Camps Thomas (210) and Huachuca (65). S.B. Holabird to J.F. Rodgers, June 13, 1881, ibid. This order for cork helmets was sent by express from St. Louis. Telegram from D.H. Rucker to Quartermaster General, July 19, 1881, Book B, 1881, ibid.

[160] One officer questioned when the helmet was to be worn. In the North was it permitted from June 1 to October 1, and in the South from May 1 to October 1? This interrogative indicated the seasonal nature of the headdress. Captain Constantine Chase to the Commanding General of the Army, February 2, 1881, Book A, 1881, ibid. Another matter which had to be clarified was whether or not staff officers, not just artillery, cavalry, and infantry officers, could obtain the helmet. General Sherman had no objection to this practice, but left approval up to local commanding officers. R.C. Drum to Commanding Officer, Department of the South, August 24, 1881, Book B, 1881, ibid.

[161] Assistant Surgeon John Vance Lauderdale to Commanding Officer Ft. Wingate, New Mexico Territory, March 15, 1875, Roll 436, LR, February-March 1875, AGO, RG94, NA.

[162] Captain George W. Chilson Eighth Cavalry to Adjutant General USA, April 22, 1875, Ft. Wingate, NM, ibid.

[163] Theo. F. Rodenbough, *From Everglade to CaÈon With the Second Dragoons* (New York: D. Van Nostrand, 1875), 425.

[164] *Circular No. 8*, xlix. For some reason the Miles Board left the forage cap in place with no mention of improvement or replacement, perhaps because there was not an overwhelming feeling against the item. That is not to say the subject went without notice. For instance, a first lieutenant with the Fourth Artillery, George Gordon Greenough, sent a proposed forage cap design to the Board's recorder, which the quartermaster general favored. Meigs wrote: "I think the cap a fair attempt at improvement." He went on to state: "The rear flap, improperly called vizor, would tend to prevent headaches and other, ill effects produced by the rays of the sun in very hot weather by shielding the back of the neck where the spinal cord is near the surface and not well protected by clothing." All this aside, Meigs made a rare confession about the introduction of new design for issue when he acknowledged: "But the feelings and tastes of the troops must be considered in all attempts to improve their clothing, and they are governed very much by prevailing fashions of the day." He went on to relay how: "The forage cap now uniform was adopted on the report of a Board of officers assembled to consider the clothing-1872-I presume that within a few years public opinion will demand another change." In this statement he also was correct. M.C. Meigs endorsement to Adjutant General, USA, August 8, 1879, LS, Clothing Br., Book B, 1879, OQMG, RG92, NA.

[165] *ARSW, 1873*, Vol. I, 152.

[166] GO No. 76, HQA, July 23, 1879.

[167] Chappell, *Brass Spikes*, 19-20. See ibid., 19-28, for a useful synopsis of the Miles Board relative to the evolution of the dress helmet.

[168] GO No. 76, HQA, July 23, 1879.

[169] For examples of British helmets that were in vogue at the time see Rankin, *Military Headdress*, 61, 65 and 67; and Wilkinson-Latham, *Collecting Militaria*, plates 5 and 7.

[170] As evidence of his personal involvement the quartermaster general informed Lieutenant General Sherman: "samples of helmets now in use in the German Army" had been procured, and "as the subject of adopting helmets for our Army is now under consideration, I would be glad to show them to you at my office, or I would send them to you, if you prefer. M.C. Meigs to W.T. Sherman, July 18, 1879, LS, Clothing Br., Book A, 1879, OQMG, RG92, NA. A letter making the same offer to the inspector general also was sent. M.C. Meigs to R.B. Marcy, July 18, 1879, Book B, 1879, ibid. Later Meigs sent off two Prussian helmets, one for dragoons and the other an artillery model, to Jeffersonville Depot's museum. M.C. Meigs to J.A. Ekin, July 24, 1879, Book B, 1879, ibid. On the same day he forwarded a guards dragoon helmet and a Prussian infantry helmet for the collection at Philadelphia, but noted he retained a cuirassier helmet at his office. Presumably, all these European examples were being examined as inspiration for an American helmet.
Six helmets rejected by the Miles Board, likewise went to the Philadelphia museum at a later date. So did two greatcoats, a uniform coat, two white blouses, two pairs of white trousers, a pair of canvas leggings, one wool blanket, a rubber overcoat, and four towels. H.C. Hodges to D.H. Rucker, October 29, 1879, ibid.

[171] *A&NJ*, November 8, 1879, 264.

2

FROM ARMY BLUE TO OLIVE DRAB, 1881-1912

The summer helmet was not the only recommendation to take root after the Miles Board adjourned. In 1880, one of the suggestions that originally had been made by this conclave, but which had been denied at first, was resurrected. This was a replacement for the 1872-pattern

mounted dress helmet, although the style eventually prescribed was in a different form than conceived of by the 1879 Board. In addition, a dismounted helmet was adopted, which soon would do away with the dress cap and pompon for all enlisted men, who prior to that time had been issued this type of headgear.[1] Likewise, a helmet for heavy artillery and infantry officers was to take the place of the cap with cock feathers inaugurated in 1872.

The first round toward switching to helmets had begun in 1880, when prototypes prepared for the Miles Board were reviewed. Meigs instructed one of his subordinates that of these samples, two were adopted, one for field grade officers and the other for summer helmets to be worn by all officers. In the former instance, the quartermaster general indicated the field grade helmet also would be "the pattern for mounted officers. All have gold cords." He went on to clarify that officers' plumes would "be in the color of the arm of the service. Orange for Signal Corps."[2]

The introduction of a new model of dress helmet spurred the Quartermaster Department to convert unissued 1872-pattern mounted helmets by cutting them down to approximately the same configuration of the later style as seen in this front and side view of a cavalry helmet. In many ways, these altered bodies resembled the watercolors prepared by the Miles Board. Helmet plates and other trimmings from the 1872-pattern were retained until new replacements of the 1881-pattern could be obtained. CF

Interior of an 1872-pattern helmet with its original label and the label for the modification contract let to Horstmann Bros. & Co. so that the old helmet could be made to conform more closely to the 1881-pattern. CF

Like the summer helmet, the existing model required modification. Meigs directed that the brim was to be 1/2 inch wider all around for the regulation version for officers.

There was one other refinement called for in terms of officers' helmets. The eagle was to "have a motto" overhead, this being "an essential part of the arms of the U.S." That detail was evident in photographs taken of the specimens. The helmets themselves, including one made for enlisted men, along with the photographs, were on hand to provide guidelines for future manufacture.[3]

Meigs also noted the views of the army's commanding general, William T. Sherman, who proclaimed:

The helmets for officers shall be either of cork or other suitable material, covered with black cloth, or entirely of felt. All he desires is uniformity in shape. The material is left entirely to the wishes of the officers.

With time, the latitude permitted by Sherman would be pushed to the limit, with numerous variations of officers' helmets coming into existence based upon individual means and the differences extant from one military supplier to another.[4] Regardless of what the future would bring, the new helmet started out as a fairly straight forward affair as it was announced in General Orders No. 4, Headquarters of the Army, January 7, 1881. This document, which bore the sanction of the secretary of war, mandated:

The dress cap for regimental officers and men will be discontinued and in lieu thereof the following adopted:

Helmets for field officers. According to pattern on hand in the office of the Quartermaster General. Body of cork or other suitable material covered with black cloth, or of felt at the option of the wearer. Trimmings: cords and tassels, top piece and plume socket, chain chin-strap and hooks, eagle with motto, crossed cannon, rifles or sabers, all gilt, with the number of the regiment on the shield in white; plume of buffalo-hair, white for infantry, yellow for cavalry, and red for artillery.

Helmets for other officers of mounted troops and of Signal Corps. Same as above, except the color of the plume shall be orange for Signal Corps.

Helmets for other officers of foot troops. Same as above, except that the trimmings are as follows: top piece, spike, chin-strap with hooks and side buttons, eagle with motto, crossed rifles or cannon, all gilt with the number of the regiment on the shield in white.

Helmets for mounted troops. Body: of black felt as per pattern in the office of the Quartermaster General, with leather chin-strap, large crossed cannon or sabers, letter of company and number of regiment, plain side buttons, top piece and plume-socket, all brass: horsehair plumes and cords, and band with rings of the color of the arm of service.

Helmets for all foot troops. Of same pattern and material as for mounted troops, with leather chin-strap; and plain side buttons, top piece and spike, of brass.

Trimmings. Commissary sergeants, a crescent of white metal; hospital stewards, a wreath of brass, with letters U.S. in white metal; engineers, a castle, with letter of company; ordnance, a shell and

Another example of a modified 1872-pattern cavalry helmet with the old plume holder and eagle in place. AHS

A private of the Signal Corps wears a remodeled 1872-helmet with the new 1881-pattern staff plate. Note the old 1872-pattern plume holder and base. The cords and plume were orange for Signal Corps and the overlay was to be crossed signal flags in German silver. Crossed flags were adopted as the motif for the side buttons as well. USAMHI

A Signal Corps enlisted helmet with all the insignia adopted in 1881, including the German silver crossed flags overlay on the eagle plate's shield. Photograph by Glen Swanson. GS

flame; artillery, crossed cannon; infantry, crossed rifles, and letter of company and number of regiment, all in brass.

General Orders No. 4 was to become effective for all but cavalry and light artillery troops on July 1, 1881, "or as soon thereafter as the supplies can be procured by the Quartermaster's Department; for cavalry and light batteries whenever the present stock of helmets is exhausted by issues." As such the quartermaster general "recommended the sale of all dress caps, metallic hat and cap trimmings rendered obsolete by the adoption of the new helmets." The secretary of war concurred. These items were disposed of at public auction.[5] Consequently, an announcement was made underscoring: "Dress caps are no longer articles of uniform, the helmets having taken their place."[6]

As far as cavalry and light artillery helmets, Meigs decided to retain these items after questioning whether "the old pattern top piece and plume socket for mounted troops" could be utilized, thereby requiring no new specifications or production. Furthermore, according to General Orders No. 4, helmets for enlisted men would not display the eagle, but rather employ the brass crossed cannon, rifles, or sabers with number and letter that adorned forage caps.[7] So it was that existing items could be redistributed, as was indicated in a letter stating: "A sufficient supply of cavalry and light artillery hair plumes, cords & bands, plume sockets & rings & side buttons are reported on hand; hence these trimming should not be supplied." Indeed, for the first few years or so, mounted troops tended to receive the old trimmings and cords, as well as 1872-pattern helmets, but with one difference.[8]

The idea was to convert the earlier helmets in the inventory into approximately the same configuration as the new headdress. This process entailed the modification of the helmet bodies to conform more closely to the 1881 style by reducing the visors, and achieve a somewhat similar appearance by reblocking. Meigs noted, however, the appropriations for the fiscal year were exhausted and "none of the old pattern helmets" could be so converted until appropriations for the next fiscal year become available. Further, Meigs indicated instructions which had been given "to alter 10,000 of the old pattern helmets," but this work could not be undertaken until the Quartermaster Department obtained funds for that purpose. In the meantime, Meigs suggested the

In this circa 1885 portrait a trooper of the Sixth U.S. Cavalry holds his converted 1872-pattern dress helmet. The plate may be an infantry plate, rather than a cavalry version because the latter items were not available immediately after the new helmet design was adopted. Note that the plume staff and base continue to be of the 1872-pattern. GC

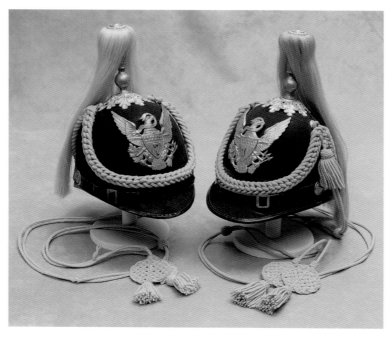

(Left) An 1881-pattern cavalry enlisted helmet with the new insignia including the regimental number on the helmet plate, albeit an incorrect officers' type which probably was applied to an unissued plate in recent times. Note the other enlisted cavalry helmet (right) is one that exhibits the darker yellow cords and plume authorized in 1887, in order to resolve the problem of fading of the lighter cords that had been issued since 1872. Photograph by Glen Swanson. GS

Side view of the 1881-pattern enlisted dress helmet. WR

In 1881 hospital stewards were to discontinue the cap with green pompon for a spiked helmet that bore a caduceus overlay on the helmet plate. WR

helmets at Jefferson Barracks should be recalled, if not needed, so that they ultimately could be remodeled at Philadelphia, once money was authorized by congress.[9] Eventually, money was forthcoming so that these reconfigured pieces of headgear could be provided to the troops.[10] In the meantime, old helmets continued to be issued to meet supply demands from the field.[11]

During this period, fine tuning of the proposed new version of the helmet was in progress, most notably in the matter of insignia. For one thing, there was some confusion over the term spike. At least one manufacturer had assumed this was the old plume socket, which it was not.[12] Another officer raised the issue as to the base for the spike. Illustrations for the foot officers' helmet depicted a British style, which was not unlike the old cruciform type used on some 1872-pattern officers' helmet, rather than the cluster of leaves that was the motif for field grade and mounted helmets, as well as for the new enlisted dismounted helmet. The writer, an artillery officer at Fort Monroe, Virginia, also queried as to the proper background material for the helmet chain. Was it to be in facing color or morocco, and how was the chain to be worn?[13]

Meigs responded by stating that the correct helmets for foot and mounted officers were illustrated in the *Army and Navy Journal*, and that so far as the chain was concerned, it would be looped from left to right. He then went on to underscore that everything had not been finalized at that time:

> There are several minor points which I scarcely think yet settled. The samples seen by the General of the Army, and adopted were made by various makers and are not the property of the Government. They declined to sell their models.
>
> I think the spike will start from a wreath of foliage and that the plume will be inserted in a socket like that of the cavalry; that all

soldiers will wear the eagle as well as the crossed cannons, rifles, sabers, &c&c. That it is better to have the flat chain naked and not complicated with a strap lining which adds to weight, cost and trouble of keeping neat.[14]

Meigs concluded his remarks with a projection that additional samples would be sent to the Headquarters of the Army for review, and that a more detailed general order probably would be the result of future deliberations. In this he was prophetic.

Indeed, as part of ongoing consideration of these particulars, in March 1881 the Quartermaster Department issued specifications, which indicated further evolution of thought on the matter. Many differences from the scheme first set forth in the general order were found in the specification that read:

Material: To be black. To be made of felt composed of one part each of Russia, best coney-back, muskrat, extra-coney, and one-part of wash-blow, or other suitable material, as determined from time to time upon bids received in response to advertisement.

Shape &ct: To be in shape according to standard sample. Black enameled-leather band about seven-eights (7/8") of an inch wide to surround the helmet at base of crown, and to have an adjustable chin-strap of same material, with brass sliding-buckle as on sample. The lower edge of helmet to be bound with black enameled leather, and the inside of the visor all around to be lined with green morocco leather pasted to the body with rubber cement. The sweat band to be of belgian sheep-skin, about two (2") inches wide: inside the sweat a band about an inch wide of heavy enameled leather. All to be well stitched in place. A shell ventilator, according to pattern, to take the place of the top piece or spike when desired.

Ornaments and trimmings: The top piece to consist of a spike about three (3") inches high on a base of oak leaves, according to

An official photograph of the enlisted overlays and side buttons for the 1881-pattern helmet and a cavalry helmet plate. At top is the castle of engineers, followed by the flaming bomb or ordnance personnel, the caduceus for hospital stewards, the crescent for commissary sergeants, and crossed flags for signal corpsmen. The hooks on the side buttons never were adopted for enlisted men, however, these extensions being restricted to the helmets of infantry, cavalry, artillery, and signal officers instead. Also note the enlisted base used underneath the spike (top right) or the plume staff for mounted troops. *ARSW*

Paper labels inside two of the early contracts for the 1881-pattern helmet let to Raymold and Whitlock, the manufacturer who provided all the helmets of the model for over a half-dozen years. For instance, the first contract to this firm was let on May 5, 1881, for 16,000 helmet bodies followed by an additional order on May 22, 1882 for 15,000. The June 4, 1883 contract was for 18,000 helmets at $1.29 each. Note the stamped sheet brass washer which is imprinted with the Raymold and Whitlock name on the inside of the 1883 contract helmet. This item was used to support the plume staff assembly, but was to be inserted with the concave away from the top rather than toward the top as shown here. USCM and AHS

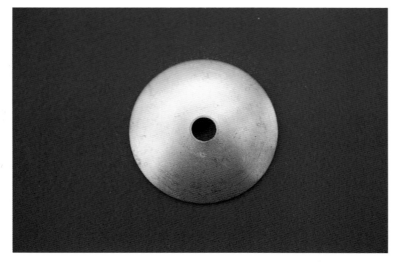 

A 1 inch diameter concave washer was placed underneath the plume of enlisted 1881-pattern dress helmet.

An "open-washer" held the rod that ran through the mounted plume staff as well as helped to support the weight of the staff, if properly inserted with the concave side up in the helmet. MC

1881-pattern enlisted infantry plate with German silver numbers indicating the soldier served with the Twenty-fourth U.S. Infantry, one of two regiments comprised of all African Americans in the ranks. JG

sample, and to be made to screw into the base of the ventilator as shown in sample.

Eagle with shield and motto, and side buttons, according to pattern, for each arm of service. All to be yellow metal.

The number of the regiment, or device of corps, to be in white metal and be borne on the lower half of shield on eagle's breast, according to sample.

The standard sample to be followed in all respects as to shape, quality of materials, workmanship & c.

To be of six (6) standard sizes, numbered one to six (1 to 6) inclusive, corresponding to the trade sizes, 6 3/4 to 7 3/8 inclusive.

Even with these descriptions, further details seemed necessary insofar as trimmings were concerned. In this light, General Orders No. 52, Headquarters of the Army, June 14, 1881, provided slightly more information on the overlays for helmet plates, along with mention of helmets for cavalry and light artillery enlisted personnel for the first time. This order stated in part:

Helmets for mounted troops. Body of black felt, or suitable material, as per pattern in the office of the Quartermaster General, with leather chin-strap. Brass eagle with motto, shield and crossed arms, according to arm of service. Number of regiment or device of corps in white metal (German silver) on shield. Brass side buttons

1881-pattern heavy artillery enlisted dress helmet worn by Forest Andrews, a member of the Sixth U.S. Artillery, one of two artillery regiments formed as a result of the increase of the U.S. Army during the Spanish-American War. The contract date on the helmet body is November 29, 1897, with the Philadelphia firm of Wm. H. Horstmann. JB

1881-pattern commissary sergeant's helmet plate with overlay. Plates for noncommissioned staff corps personnel, as well as Engineer Corps, Signal Corps, and Ordnance Corps enlisted men, had overlays but no crossed cannons, sabers, or rifles unlike the artillery, cavalry, and infantry rank and file. Photograph by Gordon Chappell.

1881-pattern ordnance helmet with German silver flaming bomb insignia. CF

1881-pattern light artillery enlisted dress helmet with silver numeral on the shield to indicate the wearer's regiment. RB

1881-pattern Engineer Corps dress helmet with German silver castle overlay. Photograph by Gordon Chappell.

bearing device of corps or arm of service. Top piece, plume socket, and rings, all brass. Horsehair plume, and cords and bands of color according to arm of service.

Helmets for foot troops. Of the same pattern and material as for mounted troops.

By 1882, a more detailed delineation of metallic ornaments for the new helmet, along with updated requirements for the helmets themselves once more were set forth. The following description remained basic for several years thereafter:[15]

Eagles.—Eagles according to pattern made of No. 24 sheet-brass (high); American eagle displayed proper with national shield on breast and bearing in beak a scroll with motto 'E pluribus unum;' olive branch in dexter talon and branch of arrows in sinister. For troops of the line the distinguishing arms are displayed under the shield, viz: Artillery, the crossed cannon; cavalry, crossed sabers; infantry, crossed rifles, and upon the lower part of the shield is borne the regimental number in German silver. For the staff and staff corps, the crossed arms are omitted and the distinguishing badge, in German silver, is borne upon the lower part of shield, viz: For hospital stewards, the caduceus; for commissary sergeants, the crescent; for engineers, the castle; for ordnance and ordnance sergeants, the shell and flame, and for Signal Service, the crossed flags.

Fort Laramie's Post Ordnance Sergeant Leodegar Schnyder wears an infantry plate on his 1881-pattern helmet rather than the correct staff plate. He does display the regulation German silver ordnance bomb overlay, however. GC

The crossed quill and key device was adopted for the helmets of post quartermaster sergeants in 1885, and the wear of these overlays and side buttons were extended to the enlisted service detachment at the United States Military Academy in 1900. WR

When flat the eagle is about the following dimensions: Greatest width between tips of wings four and one-quarter (4 1/4") inches; from upper edge of scroll to tip of tail three and seven-eighths (3 7/8") inches, It shall be molded to the form of helmet shell and be provided with three (3) wire loops by which to fasten it.

Spike and base (foot troops).—Spike to be of polished high brass, according to pattern, hexagonal, fluted surface, with screw of brass to fit socket in top of helmet. Height of spikes three (3") inches; widest diameter one (1") inch; length of screw (in the clear) three-fourths (3/4") of an inch; base of No. 24 sheet-brass (high); oak-leaf design according to pattern, eight (8) points, bed in center to received base of spike and hole cut for spike-screw.

Plume socket (for mounted men's helmets).—To be of high brass, according to pattern. An inverted fluted cone and mitered top (four points), front ornamented with the national eagle and shield and a single star surmounting eagle head. Spherical base, into the mouth of which the cone is securely brazed, and which is formed into a hexagonal pedestal at the bottom similar to that of spike so far as to rest firmly upon the oak-leaf base and be bored for the plume pin. Height of spherical base (including mouth and pedestal) about one and one-half (1 1/2") inches; of cone two (2") inches; diameter of cone at top one (1") inch, at bottom five-eighths (5/8") of an inch; diameter of spherical base one (1") inch. Plume pin, with ornamental head and plain washer (each about one and one-fourth (1 1/4") inches in diameter), about four and three-quarters (4 3/4") inches in length, the thread of which shall be cut so as to screw into the ventilator socket in top of helmet. For the lower end of pin a large open washer or disk with beveled edge to bear against the inside of helmet shell for better security of the top piece, and be kept in place by a small brass thumb nut. Diameter of disk, about two and one-half (2 1/2") inches.

The oak-base to be the same as described for foot helmets.

Side buttons.—Side buttons to be of high brass, according to pattern, with flat brass double stems. Devices on buttons in high relief: For engineers, the castle; for ordnance, the shell and flame; for hospital stewards, the caduceus; for commissary sergeants, the crescent; for Signal Corps, the crossed flags; for artillery, the crossed cannon; for cavalry, the crossed sabers; for infantry, the crossed rifles.

A light artillery corporal wearing the correct uniform for the 1885-1902 period, including the 1881-pattern helmet. NA

A post quartermaster sergeant wearing the correct uniform for the 1885-1902 period, including the 1881-pattern helmet. NA

CHEVRON FOR
POST QUARTERMASTER SERGEANT.

GILT BUCKLE

BUCKLE FOR WHITE TROUSERS.

HELMET SIDE BUTTONS.
POST Q. M. SERGEANTS.

DEVICE FOR HELMET, EAGLE, AND
FORAGE CAP, POST Q.M.SERGEANTS.

LYRE FOR MUSICIANS

Both the crossed quill and key overlay for post quartermaster sergeants and the lyre for regimental bandsmen were authorized in October 1885, as were side buttons with the quill and key. Conversely, no lyre side buttons ever were called for as regulation. *ARSW*

Numbers.—Numbers to be one-half (1/2") inch in height and made of No. 18 German silver, according to pattern, with two soft copper wire stems to hold them to shield.

Devices.—Devices for staff and staff corps to be German silver, according to pattern. Designs are mentioned in description of eagle, and stems as for numbers.

Scrolls and rings (mounted troops).—Scrolls and rings. One on each side, between the leaf-shaped points of top piece, its lower edge one-half (1/2") inch below these points. The scroll is three-fourths (3/4") inch diameter, ornamented to correspond with the fastening on the top piece. On the top of the scroll, in the center, is an eye of thin wire three-sixteenths (3/16") of an inch high, holding a thin brass ring one-half (1/2") inch in diameter, to keep the cords and bands in position. The stem of the scroll is formed in two pieces of thin brass wire to fasten to it at the inside of the helmet. All to be high brass.

NOTE—Or*naments and trimmings for foot troops.*—The top-piece to consist of a spike on a base of oak leaves, according to sample, and to be made to screw into the base of ventilator, as shown in sample. Eagle with shield and motto, and side buttons, according to pattern, for each arm of service. All to be of yellow metal.

Infantry band mounted helmet with white plume and white cords as authorized in 1885. Photograph by Gordon Chappell.

The number of the regiment or device of corps to be in white metal (German silver) and be borne on the lower half of shield on eagle's breast, according to pattern.

For mounted troops. The top ornament to consist of a horse-hair plume (color according to arm of service) and a yellow-metal plume-socket, as described in specifications, which rests upon the oak-leaf base. Eagle with shield and motto, and side buttons, according to arm of service. All to be yellow metal.

The number of the regiment or device of corps, in German silver, to be borne on the shield, as described for foot troops.

Because of this change from the original intent of General Orders No. 4, Meigs made it clear that the helmet eagle "with shield, with crossed cannons, or rifles, or sabers" would bear "the number of the regiment, or the insignia of the staff corps" upon the shield. This fact, and the adoption of side buttons indicating the arm of service resulted in another pronouncement from Meigs requiring the depot at Philadelphia to furnish the new helmet complete to the field. For this reason, he stated it was necessary for requisitions to indicate the arm of service and number of regiment so they could be placed "on the shield of the eagles to fill" incoming orders, once the new helmet was available.

The band at the U.S. Military Academy in the infantry helmet with white cords, band, and plume circa 1890. FAM

In another variation on the theme, this infantry bandsman has a fountain plume of feathers on his helmet, but wears no cords, and displays the regimental number on the plate, rather than a German silver lyre, probably indicating that the image was taken prior to 1885. FAM

As one example of the diversity that was found in regimental band uniforms this infantry musician wears the mounted helmet with white bands and cords, but his mounted 1881-pattern helmet is topped with red and white feathers. NA

Thus, distillation of the helmet and its components was nearing completion after an ongoing process which can be traced in part from some of Meigs' exchanges on the topic. One telling letter noted that the summer helmet, field officers' helmet, and infantry helmet "recommended by the Miles Board were made on the same block...."[16] These designs had been well received by several officers. Having reviewed this matter, Meigs reached the conclusion that only one style of officers' helmet should be adopted, so that all that an individual had to do upon transfer or promotion was "to change the ornaments and not the helmet itself."[17] Elsewhere, Meigs revealed that the Miles Board helmets had been paid for by his department, but were held by the manufacturer, Allien. This company had made some claims as to having proprietary rights to the helmet. While Meigs in fact preferred that firm's design over one from Horstmann, having tried on the sample along with the models from Horstmann that General Sherman had approved, he realized that "These two great military furnishing houses" (Allien and Horstmann) were "jealous rivals." Furthermore, he attached "little importance to Messrs. Allien's claim." Meigs considered that although the firm's helmet was advocated by the Miles Board, the helmet as adopted

Hospital steward in the 1887-pattern full dress uniform, including helmet with German silver Geneva cross overlay. NA

In 1887 the overlay for dress helmets of hospital stewards and all enlisted medical personnel was changed to a German silver Geneva cross. The side buttons also bore the same device. FAM

in 1881 was the result of "a new movement and that the helmet as adopted" was one that had been selected because of the wishes of many officers who signed a petition for the model authorized by the general orders.

It was this later helmet, which had been designed by Joseph Starkey, an employee of Horstmann, that was to be the official headdress of the U.S. Army.[18] Nor did Starkey's involvement end with his role in the basic helmet design. In February, he met with Meigs and presented "a very good eagle cased and dressed," which was "struck from a very good die of excellent detail." Meigs thought "the cast of the eagle to be a very satisfactory one," as he did sidebuttons, which Starkey presented in the same "portfolio." Meigs related the sidebuttons "would be satisfactory to me."[19] Having found acceptable trimmings, some $10,000 was to be set aside during the next fiscal year for the purchase of these helmet ornaments and ones for the forage cap.[20]

At the same time four helmets, which were adopted as standard by the general of the army, along with an Allien helmet, were sent to the Philadelphia depot.[21] To make certain that there were no deviations from these standards, Meigs also called for additional prototypes of the new

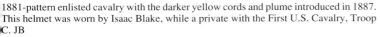

1881-pattern enlisted cavalry with the darker yellow cords and plume introduced in 1887. This helmet was worn by Isaac Blake, while a private with the First U.S. Cavalry, Troop C. JB

A cavalry private in the full dress uniform with darker yellow adopted in 1887, including for the cords, bands, and plume of the 1881-pattern helmet so that fading would be less a problem than with the 1872-pattern cords, which were lighter in color. FAM

enlisted helmet to be ordered so that samples could be sent to the various chief quartermasters around the country. Funding was limited for this purpose.[22] Consequently, only fifty preliminary examples were to be made.

Likewise, Meigs took other precautions to ensure that the helmet as produced would not vary from the pattern. To this end, he requested that Captain John Rodgers from Philadelphia be issued official orders authorizing him to travel to the various factories where the helmets and spikes were being fabricated under contract to insure the government specifications were met.[23] As a further precaution, he approved the expenditure of $90 for photographs of the new helmets, and required a set of the pictures, under the title *Standard Helmets and Trimmings*, be sent to each of the depots.[24]

Even as these quality control measures were underway, Meigs lauded the new helmet. He manifested this attitude in a letter to a lieutenant from the Nineteenth U.S. Infantry, which read in part: "Officers will be as likely to purchase the soldiers' uniform helmet which, in the opinion of the Quartermaster General will be quite good enough for anybody, to wear on frontier service, and generally in towns and cities,

except on service in public ceremonies and festivals where officers desire to be particularly well dressed."[25] In some instances officers did procure enlisted bodies, which became available after a contract for 16,000 new pattern helmets had been let to Raymold and Whitlock of New York, on May 5, 1881.[26]

This headgear followed the specifications officially established for foot troops only less than two months earlier.[27] Indeed, the enlisted dress helmet called out in 1881 remained almost unchanged until 1889, when the composition of the body was modified.[28]

The change in composition of the helmet body was the result of a certain degree of dissatisfaction, not only with this piece of headgear's makeup, but also for campaign hats and forage caps, as well. This state of affairs prompted Captain John Rodgers to report:

It having been observed that a gradual falling off in the quality of these articles of headgear had taken place, the Quartermaster General , at the last annual contract letting, directed that bids upon samples, to be submitted by bidders, should be invited. As a consequence, samples of superior quality than those prescribed by existing standards and specifications were received. Those most suitable for service, and whose cost was within the means of the Department, were selected, and contracts awarded accordingly. New standards and specifications will hereafter be adopted from these deliveries.

What Rodgers did not mention, was the new helmets produced beginning in 1889 had a profile that differed from earlier specimens, as indicated by comparing earlier contracts with ones that were let starting with a May 14, 1889, order to B.M. Whitlock.[29] What is more, several new overlays and side buttons, along with some new cords from time to time, would be introduced to add to the variety.

In the latter instance, after a general survey of line units, it was determined that mounted helmets were desired for infantry regimental bandsmen. While mounted helmets had been granted on rare occasions in the past, as of 1885, white cords and bands, along with white horsehair plumes, were sanctioned for all infantry bands, if desired. Further, a German silver lyre was to replace the regimental numeral on the helmet for all bandsmen, not only of infantry, but also of cavalry and artillery. This overlay was joined by a crossed key and quill of German silver for the new non-commissioned staff position of post quartermaster sergeant, as were crossed flags, now with a burning torch in the center, for Signal Corps enlisted men.[30]

Within two years, yet another overlay was replaced by a new version, the former caduceus being ousted by a Geneva cross in silver for medical enlisted personnel. Side buttons with smaller versions of the German silver Geneva cross separately applied by a pair of fine wires to a gilt, stippled-backed disk formed another part of the helmet's orna-

mentation.[31] This was the only instance in which enlisted side buttons were made in two pieces.[32]

The same year, 1887, was the first time that the cords and bands for 1881-pattern helmets were given a more than cursory mention. In fact, Quartermaster Specification No. 188, April 5, 1887, offered significant particulars as to how these decorative drapes were:

To be made of worsted No. 26, and 'machined cord,' dyed a fast color to shade of sample.

The bands are loop-plaited, fastened to the scroll-ring, and festooned on front and back of helmet, the festoons reaching in front to the upper edge of chin-strap, and approaching the lower edge of back within two (2) inches.

The loop-plaiting is about one (1) inch wide, and ends under the scrolls on the left side in a tassel of sixty (60) to seventy (70) fringes one and three-fourth (1 3/4) inches long. Through the braided head, about three-fourths (3/4) inch diameter, passes the continuation of the bands in the form of two cords, each five (5) feet eight (8) inches long, with two (2) slides netted over a fuller's board three-fourth (3/4) inch in diameter, five-eighths (5/8) of an inch high. Three inches from the lower end the cords are fastened together by a braided knot, holding a loop about two and three-fourths (2 3/4) inches long. At the end of each cord is also a small braided knot, and an aiguillette, plated flat in three strands of smaller cord, in oval shape, two and three-eighths (2 3/8) inches long, two and three-fourths (2 3/4) inches wide. From the lower end of each aiguillette is suspended another tassel of from sixty (60) to seventy

In 1891 a dress helmet with a black plume, cords, and bands was prescribed for enlisted men of the Signal Corps. WR

In 1890 a dress helmet with a longer plume made up of red and white horsehair, along with red and white cords, crossed German silver arrow overlays, and crossed arrow side buttons was produced for Indian scouts. It is unlikely that these helmets ever were issued on a large scale. Photograph by Glen Swanson. GS

(70) fringes, one and three-fourths (1 3/4) inches long, with braided head three-eighths of an inch high, three-fourths (3/4) inch diameter.

Another component of the helmet was described more clearly in 1887, too. This was the plume, which according to Specification No. 187, adopted April 5, 1887, was: "To droop from the top of socket over back and sides of helmet." The horse-hairs which made up the plume were to be "sewed together at one end, giving the latter the form of a flattened knob about one and five-eighths (1 5/8) inches diameter, with star-shaped brass eyelet in center to admit the pin of the top piece." The length from the eyelet to the end was to be fourteen inches. The entire plume was: "To be made of good horse-hair dyed a fast color to shade of standard sample."

This meant light artillery plumes were to be scarlet; signal corps were orange; those for infantry bands white; and, as of 1887, cavalry troopers were to have a darker shade of yellow than in the past, the earlier hue being subject to fading. Because of this problem, the lighter yellow plumes, as well as cords, were to be replaced by the deeper color. Consequently, at least the unissued cords were to be redyed, although it seems that the plumes in stock were not.[33]

Two years after the adoption of the darker cavalry hue, one of the dress helmet variations was deleted from the inventory. In 1889, the Signal Service underwent a radical change in its uniform. This transformation was rather minor for officers, who ultimately returned to the chapeau, but enlisted men had a more dramatic turn of affairs because they no longer were to receive a dress uniform. Among other things, they ceased to wear the mounted helmet with orange trim. Instead, the *Regulations of the United States Army* prescribed only one ensemble for all functions, among which was a new type of forage cap described as follows:

For all Enlisted Men—Dark-blue cloth, the diameters at the top and base to be the same, the quarters not less than 1 1/4 or more than 1 1/2 inches high, and of the same height in front and at back. The seam around the top shall be without welt, and neatly stitched on each side. The band shall be without a welt, and neatly stitched on each side. The band shall be 1 1/2 inches wide, with welt 1/2 inch in diameter at the top and bottom; the bottom welt shall be 1/2 inch from the base of the cap. A band of lustrous black mohair braid shall be worn between the upper and lower welts. The visor shall be of patent leather, molded to shape and sloping downward

Details of the cords for the Indian scout helmet, which were made of cord with intermixed scarlet and white threads, a unique two-tone feature not found on other dress helmets of the era. Note how the bands are connected to the scroll and ring below the plume socket base. MC

In the early 1890s the .45-70 Springfield "trapdoor" began to be replaced by the .30-40 Krag bolt action rifle. No doubt the infantry plate for infantry soldiers in the Regular Army continued to bear the old Springfields. This example exhibits Krags, raising a question as to whether this was a prototype for a unadopted change to the newer longarm, or more likely it was made for some national guard unit, or officer's use. Note that no regimental number appears on the shield, indicating that the item was probably never worn. JG

Side view of the enlisted helmet body with slightly modified profile found on helmets made under contract starting in the late 1880s through 1902. WR

In 1899 German silver forked lightning bolts were adopted for the newly created position of electrician sergeant. RB

at a angle of not less than 20° nor more than 30° from the horizontal. Inside band shall be of leather, to extend to within 1 inch of the top; sweat-lining shall be of morocco. Four black metal eyelets, two on each side, shall be placed in the quarters for ventilation. A small button shall be placed on each side, beyond the ends of the visor.

Cap Ornaments

For all Enlisted Men.—The Signal Service device of crossed flags and torch embroidered on dark blue cloth, in silk and bullion, in high relief, attached to the front of the cap, the center midway between buttons over the upper welt.[34]

It seems improbable that this type of headgear was produced, or if it were, it was not issued on a widespread basis, especially because a new dress uniform was introduced in 1891. This included a mounted helmet once more for enlisted men, this time with black cords, bands, and plume.[35] Regardless of the fact that the 1889 Signal Service enlisted cap was most probably a product of imagination rather than a reality, its crossed flag devices with torch represented a permutation of an actual insignia which had been adopted for signal officers' forage caps covered in General Orders No. 4, Headquarters of the Army, January 7, 1878. This order called for a white flag with red star in the center (dexter) crossing over a white flag with a blue square (sinister), and intersected by a gold torch and surrounded by a diminutive gold wreath.[36] Several years later, General Orders No. 30, Headquarters of the Army, April 14, 1884, directed that an officer's cap badge of: "A gold embroidered wreath of oak leaves, the size prescribed for officers of the other staff corps, on dark blue cloth ground, encircling two crossed signal flags and a burning torch...."

The early type bands and cords were composed of soft bundles of threads (left) while beginning sometime in the mid to late 1880s harder cased threads were woven together to form these cords and bands (right). Also note the two different colors of yellow, the lighter hue being that adopted in 1872 and the dark shade being the regulation starting in 1887. The difference in early and later cords and bands construction particularly is evident on those specimens for the 1890 Indian scout and 1891 Signal Corps helmets. JB

Cap insignia for enlisted men of the Signal Corps were not as clearly defined for this same period. Originally, no device was prescribed for the cap, but presumably enlisted signalmen eventually wore the same crossed German silver flags that were designated as overlays on the helmet by General Orders No. 9, Headquarters of the Army, January 27, 1882.[37] Some three years later a torch was added to the overlay, in accordance with General Orders No. 77, Headquarters of the Army, July, 13, 1885. Perhaps the same badge was to be added to the enlisted forage cap, but certainly General Orders No. 74, Headquarters of the Army, August 20, 1891, made it clear that yet another version of the crossed flags and torch (the flags being square-shaped rather than the wavy design illustrated in the 1888 published uniform regulations) was established as the proper cap insignia for enlisted men, this being placed in the center of a thin brass wreath.[38]

Throughout this time frame, the silver regimental number and crossed cannon, sabers, and rifles, remained status quo for officers of artillery, cavalry, and infantry, respectively. Further, the flaming bomb in gold embroidery was retained for ordnance officers, and the silver castle with gold wreath remained for engineer officers. Finally, all general staff corps and general officers retained the silver embroidered US in a gilt wreath on their forage caps, with one exception. Underscored by General Orders No. 79, Headquarters of the Army, November 4, 1883, the Adjutant General Department was a unique departure from other staff officers in that they had: "A gold embroidered wreath on dark blue cloth ground, same as for general officers, encircling a solid silver shield bearing thirteen stars...," rather than the script U.S.

In 1883, another more widespread change was permitted in that officers' forage cap straps were to be of gold cord in lieu of the old leather chin straps. This accessory had been employed in a number of individual instances prior to being sanctioned by General Orders No. 102, Headquarters of the Army, December 26, 1883. Officers were given until March 1, 1884, to obtain the gold on silver cap-strap and attach it to the forage cap.

Besides these evolutions relative to forage caps of officers and signal enlisted men, a few other additions to insignia appeared in the 1880s. One of these was the replacement of the silver U.S. for hospital stewards by a German silver caduceus in accordance with General Orders No. 9, War Department, January 27, 1882. The device was essentially the same as worn on the helmet plate, but affixed directly to the front of the cap by wires. The enclosing gilt wreath was retained and placed on the cap's front separately from the caduceus. The cap devices for hospi-

DEVICES FOR HELMET EAGLES FOR ENLISTED MEN OF STAFF CORPS AND BAND MUSICIANS (FULL SIZE).

HOSPITAL CORPS.

ENGINEERS.

German silver overlays for enlisted personnel (from top left to bottom right): Hospital Corps adopted in 1887; Engineer Corps prescribed in 1881; quartermaster sergeants (and after 1900 for the West Point Service Detachment) beginning in 1885; Ordnance Department adopted in 1881; Signal Corps as specified in 1885; commissary sergeants introduced in 1881; and lyres for regimental bandsmen as of 1885. The numerals were used to designate the regiments of artillery, cavalry, and infantry soldiers. A pair of small wires soldered to the rear of the devices served to attach them to the helmet place GS.

POST QUARTERMASTER SERGEANT.

ORDNANCE.

SIGNAL CORPS.

COMMISSARY SERGEANT.

BAND MUSICIANS.

HELMET NUMBERS FOR ENLISTED MEN OF THE LINE
(FULL SIZE).

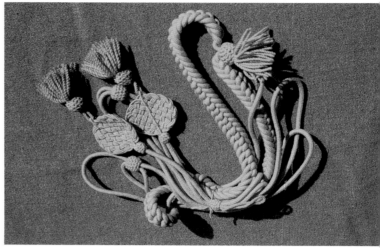

Side buttons for the 1881-pattern enlisted helmet, starting at the top left and proceeding in order: artillery and cavalry were adopted on July 27, 1872; infantry, signal, commissary, ordnance, and engineer models were adopted on June 14, 1881; crossed flags with torch buttons were prescribed for Signal Corps enlisted men on July 13, 1885 and a quill and pen for quartermaster sergeants came into existence on October 3, 1885; Hospital Corps personnel were to receive the Geneva cross on August 11, 1887, Indian scouts the crossed arrows on August 11, 1890, and electrician sergeants were to be set off by lighting bolts as of April 24, 1899. CF

An unissued set of 1887-pattern cavalry cords as shipped from the depot separate from the helmet. Photograph by Gordon Chappell. JG

Front view of an 1881-pattern infantry company grade officers' helmet, which belonged to John Leefe while he served as a captain in the Nineteenth U.S. Infantry Regiment. This helmet was produced by the firm of Henry V. Allien as indicated by the slightly pointed visor and distinctive trim made by that supplier. MC

The 1881-pattern heavy artillery company grade officer's helmet was similar to that worn by infantry lieutenants and captains, except that the plate displayed crossed cannons rather than crossed rifles, as did the side buttons. RB

Rear view of a company grade foot officers' helmet.

tal stewards represented the only major change for many years, the other enlisted insignia of the early 1880s continuing, for the most part, as those settled upon in the middle of the previous decade. This point can be ascertained by a review of specifications adopted May 6, 1882.[39]

Bugles for musicians.—Bugles for field and band musicians: Of sheet-brass (high) No, 28, representing an old-style bugle with circular crook, and a cord sling three (3) fold around lower part, terminating in two (2) tassels on one and, one (1) tassel on the other side. Height across crook, one and one-fourth (1 1/4") inches; width from mouth-piece to outer edge of bowl two and one-fourth (2 1/4") inches. Brass-wire loops same as on letters.

Castles (engineers).—Castles; of sheet-brass (high) No. 28, representing an ancient castle with three (3) towers. Height of center tower, seven-eighths (7/8") of an inch; of side towers one and one-fourth (1 1/4") inches each; of battlements between towers, five-eighths (5/8") of an inch; width at base one and seven-eighths (1 7/8") inches; at top of side towers one and three-quarters (1 3/4") inches. Two brass loops strongly soldered on back to fasten to cap.

Shells and flames (ordnance).—Shells and flames. Of sheet-brass (high) No. 28, representing a shell and flame. Diameter of shell three-quarters (3/4") of an inch; height of flame from upper edge of shell seven-eighths (7/8") of an inch; greatest width of flame one and one-eighth (1 1/8") inches. Brass-wire on back same as on letters.

Crescents (commissary sergeants).—Crescents: Of sheet white metal (German-silver), crescent-shaped. Width from point one and five-eighths (1 5/8") inches; height of arc one (1") inch; greatest width in center one-half (1/2") inch. Brass-wire loops on back same as letters.

Wreaths and caduceus (hospital stewards).—Wreaths. Wreath made of dead or unburnished gilt-metal, representing two olive branches, held at the bottom by a loop and knot, turning upward and bending in an oval shape, approaching each other at the top. Height one and one-half (1 1/2") inches; greatest distance between outer edges two and five-eighths (2 5/8") inches; greatest width of single branch five-eighths (5/8") of an inch. Brass-wire loops as on back of letters.

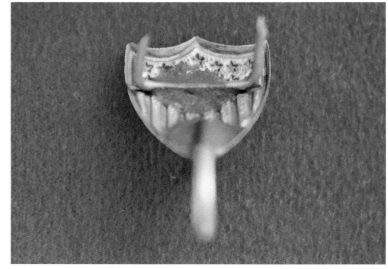

Front and rear view of the small gilt shield device with hook commonly used to secure the chinchain to the rear of the 1881-pattern officers' dress helmet and summer helmet. KC

The detachable spike and base for an 1881-pattern foot officers' helmet, in this case one made by Henry V. Allien as indicated by the distinctive simulated rope design on the acorn base. A number of variations from individual suppliers of officers' helmets existed. MC

A caduceus of German silver, similar to that on helmet eagle, to be worn within the wreath.

Crossed cannon (artillery).—Crossed cannon: Of sheet-brass (high) No. 20, representing two cannon crossing each other at the trunnions, muzzle upward; length two and one-eighth (2 1/8") inches; breath at breeches two (2") inches; at muzzle one and seven-eighths (1 7/8") inches. Four brass-wire loops as on back of letters.

Crossed sabers (cavalry).—Crossed sabers: Of sheet-brass (high) No. 20, representing two cavalry sabers in scabbards, crossed in the middle, with hilts and edges upward. To be shaped or curved so as to fit the front of cap. Length of sabers three (3") inches; height from hilt of one to point of other one and one-fourth (1 1/4") inches; from point to point two and three-fourths (2 3/4") inches. Four brass-wire loops as on crossed cannon.

Crossed rifles (infantry).—Crossed rifles: Of sheet-brass (high) No. 20; two rifles crossing each other at a point equidistant from the butt to muzzle; muzzles pointing upward and outward; hammers upward, their position crossed, making the upper space form an angle of 137°; length of rifle two and five-eighths (2 5/8") inches; diameter at point of crossing about one-eighth (1/8") of an inch; to be shaped or curved so as to fit the front of cap; the whole ornament occupying a rectangular space of about two and seven-eighths (2 7/8") inches wide, by one and three-eighths (1 3/8") inches high. Fastenings: Four brass-wire loops, firmly soldered, opening horizontally with the rifles, and placed about one-half (1/2") from the muzzles and butts.

Letters 'A' to 'M'.—Brass letters 'A' to 'M': Roman capitals, one-half (1/2") inch long, to be made of sheet-brass (high) No. 28; edges beveled. Two small brass-wire loops strongly soldered on the back of letter to fasten it to the cap.

Numbers '1' to '0'.—Brass numbers: Nos. 1' to '0,' inclusive, one-half (1/2") inch long, to be made of sheet-brass (high) No. 28; edges beveled. Small brass-wire loop same as letters.

Although enlisted cap insignia had been well defined as to the proper wear and manufacture, the fragile nature of these devices was a cause of some consternation. Because branch devices, letters, and numbers had been provided separately prior to the mid-1890s, and also due to the rather weak attachments on the back of the various cap insignia, the items sometimes fell off the headgear. This prompted a number of soldiers to strengthen their cap insignia by inventive means. A few enterprising individuals brazed the components together, or reinforced them

Right side view of an 1881-pattern foot officers' dress helmet. MC

Left side view of an 1881-pattern mounted officers' dress helmet, in this case for an infantry field grade officer as indicated by the white plume. MC

In addition to field grade infantry officers, adjutants of infantry regiments were to wear the mounted helmet with white plume as well, as seen here. The helmet was made by Henry V. Allien. NA

1881-pattern mounted infantry officers' helmet with the large silver regimental number correctly applied to the front on the plate. CF

John Leefe was promoted to lieutenant colonel of the Thirtieth U.S. Infantry, one of several new regiments raised as a result of the Spanish American War. His commission dated from October 1901, thereby indicating that this piece of headgear was purchased near the end of the life cycle of the dress helmet. MC

in various ways, such as filling the backs of insignia with lead.[40] Such an arrangement could be used for not only the forage cap, but also the old 1872-pattern dress cap insignia for foot troops.

Captain John Mendenhall went so far as to send a suggestion through the quartermaster in San Francisco with remarks that the cap ornaments furnished his Fourth Artillery gunners at Pt. San Jose, California, had fastenings that were "very poor...." The captain thought "if small staples were put on firmly they would last much longer."[41]

An infantry officer, Captain Augustus Corliss, went so far as to propose crossed rifles with the "number, and letter" attached "in solid form, so that they might be fastened to the cap by means of one loop."[42] The captain was told that this design would be frail and would increase the likelihood of breakage. Moreover, the cost was deemed prohibitive.[43] In this Corliss was a decade and a half ahead of his times.

Although the problem of enlisted cap insignia design was not resolved until the mid-1890s, new types of devices occasionally emerged because of increased recognition of specialists in the ranks. One such example arose from the granting of permission for regimental bands-

man to sport a white metal lyre on their caps per General Orders No. 104, Headquarters of the Army, October 3, 1885. This same directive indicated that the newly established post quartermaster sergeants were to attach a German silver crossed key and quill to their forage caps of the same type as worn on their helmet plates. It is probable that this badge was to be worn inside a wreath, but not until three years later did General Orders No. 6, Headquarters of the Army, February 8, 1888, spell out this point. This order called for, "a wreath dead and burnished gilt metal" to encircle the crossed pen and key, in keeping with the practice for hospital stewards over the previous years.

Even before the quartermaster sergeants gained clarification as to their cap devices, in 1887, the creation of the Hospital Corps under General Orders No. 56, War Department, August 11, 1887, ushered in yet another insignia for hospital stewards, along with acting hospital stewards, and privates of the newly established organization. This was to be a white metal cross for the forage cap of all enlisted men. Additionally, hospital stewards carried on the tradition of a wreath around their device, but the color was changed to white metal, although it is uncertain whether this special wreath was issued.

Captain Edward B. Williston, Second U.S. Artillery, cradles his 1881-pattern officers' helmet. Once again this example bears the distinctive Henry V. Allien helmet plate. NA

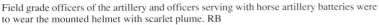

Field grade officers of the artillery and officers serving with horse artillery batteries were to wear the mounted helmet with scarlet plume. RB

Following this same line, General Orders No. 3, Headquarters of the Army, January 15, 1889, added the wreath to commissary sergeant's forage caps, although the wreath was dead or unburnished (yellow metal versus white metal). Additionally, the large crescent adopted in 1873 was replaced with a smaller German silver version which coincided with the helmet plate overlay, and which for the first time was described as being worn horizontally rather than vertically. For some unknown reason, post ordnance sergeants were not to be granted the same distinctive combination of wreath with insignia, but instead retained the flaming shell alone, as did all Ordnance Department enlisted men.

Besides these periodic adjustments to specific enlisted specializations, the introduction of a new design for buttons in 1884 constituted a change which eventually impacted upon all enlisted forage caps. The pair of small vest-size buttons that held the enlisted chin strap in place ultimately were to be of the 1884-pattern, rather than the old 1854-pattern. Evidently, though, the changeover was not immediate. For example, during 1885, 15,000 caps ordered under contract from B.Y. Pippey of New York had the old buttons, while the 15,000 procured in the same year from the firm of Hirschberg bore the new buttons.[44]

Another minute change to the cap came in 1885, when black silesia was added as a covering to the tarred board interior crown support.[45] During the next year, the side buttons on the cap having been adopted, it was noted that these would be fire-gilt, as was the slide on the chin-strap.[46] Both of these requirements had not been spelled out previously.

On January 5, 1889, however, new quartermaster specifications introduced slightly more visible alterations.[47] The band now was to be 1 3/8, not 1 1/2 inches wide, while the front was "to rise above the band straight and vertical one and one-eight (1 1/8) inches" instead of the previous 1 1/2 to 1 5/8 inches. Further, the back was reduced a half inch to 4 1/2 inches from the 5 inches of earlier models, while the crown was to be a quarter of an inch larger at 5 inches in diameter versus the old 4 3/4 inches. Additionally, the visor was to have a green underside and be bound "with fine black enameled leather" rather than being a raw edge. Inside, black satin replaced glazed muslin as lining, which was gathered over an elastic cord by strong thread. The elastic represented an addition, as did a black mohair or worsted 1/8 inch braid secured in a loop "under the sweat-leather at the back seam" so that the hat presumably could be hung up when not in use. Except for allowances to have

The US Artillery attaché at Aldershot in Great Britain wears the last of the 1881-pattern officers' dress helmets to be used in this 1905 photograph. KC

Another example of the patented method for easy removal of the plume staff, in this case for a mounted artillery officers' helmet. RB

A patented method for easy removal of the plume staff, which featured a spring activated attachment, was just one of many options officers had when purchasing their helmets. Note the shields that attached the gold officers' helmet bands have rings soldered to them, while the shield in the rear has a hook to secure the chinchain. SWHS

The quality of officers's helmets varied considerably, including this inexpensive pressed fur felt body that resembled an enlisted model produced by J.H. McKenney for purchase by company grade officers who did not want to spend a large sum for their headgear. Photograph by Gordon Chappell

either a line or staff button, "as may be required" on either side of the visor, later specifications barely differed from those set forth in 1889, but that was to change.[48]

For one thing, while the proposed signal corps enlisted forage cap of 1889 probably never was provided, its design foreshadowed an actual piece of headgear that did come into being in 1895. The cap adopted in that year reflected British antecedents. As early as the 1850s England's military had popularized a circular cap with sloping visor. By the Civil War, a similar style had made its way into the U.S. Navy for officers, and continued in vogue for decades thereafter. In the civilian world, firemen, police officers, railway conductors, streetcar operators, and even sportsmen (including players of the rapidly growing American pastime—baseball) favored such a cap, too. With this trend in motion, and considerable discussion of what constituted the proper cap during the 1870s through 1890s ongoing in many circles, the time seemed perfect for a new model.

To this end, on March 13, 1895, several officers met to discuss a design that would replace the chasseur style so long in use.[49] They submitted their proposal, which was adopted as Quartermaster Specification No. 367, on September 5, 1895. Officers were to purchase the new cap by July 1 of that year, while the rank and file were to be issued the headgear no later than January 1, 1896, at a cost against their clothing allowance of $.67, without insignia.[50]

The full description as first conceived and stated in Specification No. 637 was a cap:

Cloth.—To made of dark blue cloth, wool-dyed indigo, unless otherwise authorized by purchasing officer; to be fifty-four (54) inches wide; to weigh not less than fourteen (14) ounces to the linear yard; to contain sixty-two (62) thread to the inch in the warp,

Officer's 1881-pattern dress helmet of William H. Paine, First U.S. Cavalry. JB

In 1887 a darker shade of yellow was adopted for cavalry officers' helmets, as seen here for this specimen worn by Major Frederic Benteen late in his career. WC

A second example of the darker helmet plume for cavalry officers, in this instance one worn by Second Lieutenant Ben Dorcy, who received his commission to the Fourth U.S. Cavalry on May 10, 1899. AHS

Between 1881 and 1889 the chapeau was discontinued for Signal Corps officers, and a helmet with orange plume prescribed instead. Not until 1884 was a flaming torch added to the plate of these helmets that originally bore only the crossed flags. This example was worn by Second Lieutenant Leroy Emmons Sebree, who held his commission from 1878 through 1888. SI

John Upham became colonel of the Eighth U.S. Cavalry in 1892, and remained in command of the regiment until his death nearly six years later. His helmet exhibits some deviations from the norm in that he did not have the prescribed regimental numeral affixed to the helmet's eagle shield, and his cords are of a double strands of gold rather than triple strands that were regulation—both factors being emblematic of the considerable diversity found among officers' 1881-pattern helmets. SWHS

and fifty-eight (58) threads to the inch in the filling; to be capable of sustaining a strain of not less than thirty-two (32) pounds to the inch in the warp, and twenty-eight (28) pounds to the inch in the filling; the cloth to be well sponged without refinishing, before being made into caps.

Band.—The band to be one and one-half (1 1/2) inches wide, formed by the material of the body of the cap, between two welts, each welt at top and bottom projecting one-eighth (1/8) inch, the bottom welt being one-eighth (1/8) inch above the base of the cap; the band to be strengthened by a strap of strong split leather, about one-sixteenth (1/16) inch thickness all around, and two and one-quarter (2 1/4) inches wide, sewed in between the sweat band and the body of the cap with the lining of the cap between the two.

The height of the cap to be three and one-quarter (3 1/4) inches all around; the seam around the top without a welt and neatly stitched on each side; the diameter of the top from right to left to be six and one-half (6 1/2) inches, and from front to back seven and five-eighths (7 5/8) inches.

Visor.—To have a slanting visor of patent enameled leather, black above and green underneath, about one-eighth (1/8) inch thick, and bound with black patent leather to the depth of about three-sixteenths (3/16) inch, neatly stitched; the width of the visor from the lower edge of the cap to the inner edge of the binding at its widest part to be one and three-quarters (1 3/4) inches, and the entire visor to be molded to shape.

end finished to a point will project about one-half (1/2) inch, to permit strap to be adjusted at will; the sweat leather to be of Belgian leather, about one and seven-eights (1 7/8) inches wide, turned on the upper edge and properly cemented; the lining of strong black satin, cut and shaped to the inner body of the cap, the crown of the lining to be made with an interlining of black muslin of good quality, there being an interlining of hair cloth of good quality, cut and shaped to the entire inner portion of the crown of the cap, extending from the top to the lower edge of the body of the cap between the band and stiffening and the body. Each cap to have four (4) black metal eyelets for ventilation, two (2) on each side, placed above the band, the center of each eyelet to be about five-eighths (5/8) inch from the upper seam of the cap and one and one-half (1 1/2) inches apart from each other. Each cap to be finished with a loop of black Mohair or worsted braid not less than one-eighth (1/8) inch wide, and securely fastened under the sweat leather of the back of same.

The above specifications based on cap size 7 1/8. Materials, workmanship, and finish to conform to standard sample.

In spite of the fact that many elements of this headdress' specifications approximated the old forage cap, the quality was not considered adequate. This resulted in the promulgation of yet another standard published at Quartermaster Specification No. 417, on October 22, 1896. The cap as provided for in this description not only was improved as to the outer cloth, lining, and workmanship, but also was reduced in price to only $.57.[51]

Officers' 1895-pattern forage caps differed from those for enlisted men in several ways. The quality for officers' caps usually was superior, but officers were to have a black mohair band, as had been called for in the unadopted Signal Corps cap, or in the case of generals, a black velvet band. In either instance, the trim went around the crown. Further, the officer's cap cord of silver on gold was carried over from the previous regulations, as were the vest size buttons of the various branches, departments, and corps. Finally, the arms of the United States, most typically embroidered into the front of the cap, was to be worn by all officers. This did away with having to produce caps to order with the several branch devices that traditionally had been applied throughout much of the nineteenth century.

This was not so for enlisted men, who carried on with the distinctive devices that paralleled those issued through most of the post Civil

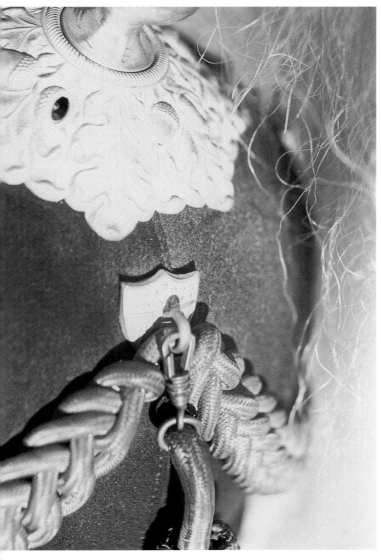

Detail of the attachment of the gold bands and the separate gold breast cords prescribed for officers' 1881-pattern mounted helmets. MC

Trimmings.—A small regulation button on each side immediately behind the ends of he visor for chin straps; the side buttons to be fire gilt; the chin strap to be made of good enameled leather in two parts, each part about ten (10) inches long and one-half (1/2) inch wide, fitted with a stout gilt slide on the end of the under part, and a leather keeper on the end of the upper part, through which the

Japanned tin case for Nelson A. Miles' chapeau de bras. WC

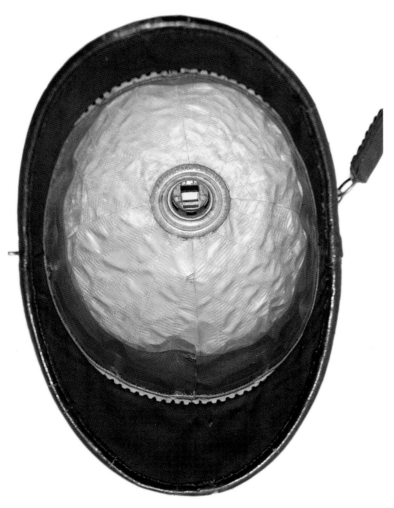

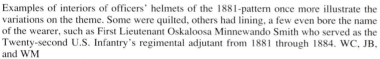

Examples of interiors of officers' helmets of the 1881-pattern once more illustrate the variations on the theme. Some were quilted, others had lining, a few even bore the name of the wearer, such as First Lieutenant Oskaloosa Minnewando Smith who served as the Twenty-second U.S. Infantry's regimental adjutant from 1881 through 1884. WC, JB, and WM

War era. There were very pronounced contrasts, however, in that the insignia provided for the 1895-pattern enlisted forage cap had company letters and regimental numbers or wreaths and devices integrally attached, as opposed to being issued separately. At long last, the new insignia were stouter in construction, and the means of attachment superior. A strong screw post with round nut replaced the rather weak wire loops of past patterns. Such upgrades had been under consideration for some time, and supposedly were well received once they actually were made and began to be issued for the first time during 1896 and 1897.[52]

These solid brass insignia were enumerated in Quartermaster Specification No. 419, adopted January 13, 1897. They were to be:

Material.—The devices to be made of solid bronze, struck by sharp keen dies, free from all imperfections. The numbers and letters are also to be struck from solid bronze and attached to the device by means of hard solder, the number above and the letter below, except where otherwise designated, supported on the back by an extra piece of bronze, also hard soldered to the device. At the back of each device there shall be an attachment, to connect the device with the body of the cap, consisting of a brass-threaded post about one-half (1/2) inch long, over which is passed a brass washer

Various japanned helmet canisters used to protect dress helmets when they were not in use. MC and GS

Japanned tin case with a staff chapeau of the type worn in the post Civil War era. FAM

Handsomely lined interior of a staff officers' chapeau de bras. WC

about five-sixteenths (5/16) inch in diameter, and the whole attachment made secure to the cap by a thumbscrew about one-half (1/2) inch in diameter, concave, and a hollow threaded post about one-quarter (1/4) inch deep, in the center to fit over the threaded post above described.

All ornaments to be shaped so as to fit the oval surface of the cap, and to have soldered to the backs thereof two (2) sharp needle points about three-sixteenth (3/16) inch long, for the purpose of holding the ornaments securely in position on the cap.

Infantry Device.—To consist of two (2) rifles crossing each other at a point equidistant from the butts and muzzles, the muzzles pointing upward and the hammers upward. Length of rifle two and five-eighths (2 5/8) inches; distance between the extreme points of the muzzles about two and one-quarter (2 1/4) inches, and between the butts about two (2) inches. All to be thoroughly gold plated and burnished, and to admit an assay of not less than 4.84 grains of gold to each dozen ornaments.

Artillery.—To consist of two (2) cannons crossing each other at the trunnions, muzzles upward; length of cannons about two and one-eighth (2 1/8) inches; distance between the muzzles about one and seven-sixteenth (1 7/16) inches, and between the cascabels about

one and seven-eighths (1 7/8) inches. All to be thoroughly gold plated and burnished, and to admit an assay of not less than 5.06 grains of gold to each dozen ornaments.

Cavalry.—To consist of two (2) sabers crossing each other at the center, representing two cavalry sabers in scabbards, with hilts and edges upward. The extreme distance between the guards to be about two and three-eighths (2 3/8) inches, and between the points of the scabbards about two and three-eighths (2 3/8) inches. Each ornament to be thoroughly gold plated and burnished, and to admit an assay of not less than 3.52 grains of gold to each dozen ornaments.

Engineers.—To consist of a castle, representing an ancient castle with three towers. The height of the center tower to be about seven-eighths (7/8) inch; side towers about one and one-eighth (1 1/8) inches; battlements between towers about five-eighths (5/8) inch; width at base about one and six-eighths (1 6/8) inches: at top of side towers about one and three-quarters (1 3/4) inches. The letter to be attached to the top of the center tower. The whole to be thoroughly gold plated, satin finished, and burnished, as shown in standard sample, and to admit an assay of not less than 10.03 grains of gold to each dozen ornaments.

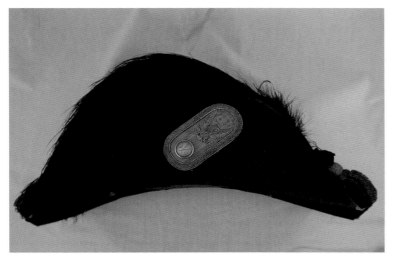

General and staff officers' chapeaus bore a general staff button. Signal officers and engineer officers wore special buttons on their chapeaus that bore crossed flags with a torch for the former and a fortification with eagle overhead bearing a banner on which the word "esseyons" was inscribed for the latter group. JG

Variant of the chapeau de bras of the early 1870s through the twentieth century, in this case with gold lace trim rather than black silk. JB

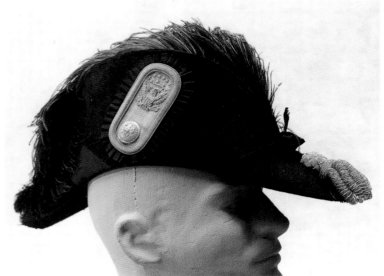

Typical examples of 1872 through 1910 era chapeau de bras, both attributed to Nelson A. Miles. Photograph by Glen Swanson. WC

Post Quartermaster Sergeant.—To consist of a wreath representing two (2) olive branches, held together at the base by a loop and knot, turning upward and bending in an oval shape approaching each other at the top. The distance between the two points of the wreath to be about one (1) inch; the extreme outside measurement across the wreath about two and five-eighths (2 5/8) inches; extreme height about one and one-half (1 1/2) inches. To have in the center of the wreath a silver-plated key and quill, crossing each other and supported by a silver-plated bar extending from side to side of the wreath: the key, quill pen, and bar to be to be silver-plated on white metal, and hard soldered to the wreath. The wreath to be thoroughly gold plated, satin finished, and burnished, as shown in the standard sample, and to admit an assay of not less than 9.24 grains of gold to each dozen ornaments.

Signal Corps.—To consist of a wreath representing two (2) olive branches, held together at the base by a loop and knot, turning upward and bending in an oval shape approaching each other at the top. The distance between the two points of the wreath to be about one (1) inch; the extreme outside measurement across the wreath about two and five-eighths (2 5/8) inches; extreme height about one and one-half (1 1/2) inches. To have in the center of the wreath two (2) crossed signal flags, with a torch in the center standing perpendicularly, all soldering and resting on a crossbar extending from side to side of the wreath and hard soldered to same. The signal flags, torch, and bar to be silver-plated on white metal. The wreath to be thoroughly gold plated, satin finished, and burnished, as shown in the standard sample, and to admit an assay of not less than 9.24 grains of gold to each dozen ornaments.

Commissary Sergeant.—To consist of a wreath representing two (2) olive branches, held together at the base by a loop and knot, turning upward and bending in an oval shape approaching each other at the top. The distance between the two points of the wreath to be about one (1) inch; the extreme outside measurement across the wreath about two and five-eighths (2 5/8) inches; extreme height about one and one-half (1 1/2) inches. To have in the center of the wreath a silver-plated crescent, cusps pointing upward, supported

by a silver-plated bar extending from side to side of the wreath, and firmly hard-soldered to same; the crescent and bar to be silver plated on white metal. The wreath to be thoroughly gold plated, satin fin

Staff officers (left) in their chapeau de bras cut a distinct figure from the company grade officers on the right in the 1881-pattern dress helmet. NA

Colonel Oliver Duff Greene, who received the Medal of Honor for distinguished gallantry at the Battle of Antietam, holds the chapeau de bras that was in vogue during the last quarter of the nineteenth century. USAPAM

Lithographs in a circa 1890 German publication illustrated the uniform of the U.S. Army, including the various items of headdress. LC

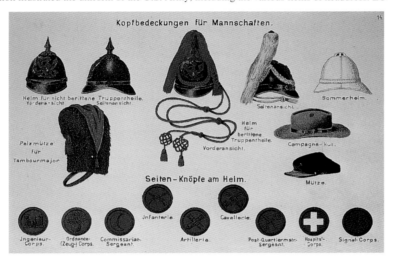

ished, and burnished, as shown in the standard sample, and to admit an assay of not less than 9.24 grains of gold to each dozen ornaments.

Hospital Steward.—To consist of a wreath representing two (2) olive branches, held together at the base by a loop and knot, turning upward and bending in an oval shape approaching each other at the top. The distance between the two points of the wreath to be about one (1) inch; the extreme outside measurement across the wreath about two and five-eighths (2 5/8) inches; extreme height about one and one-half (1 1/2) inches. To have in the center of the wreath a Geneva cross, the extreme measurements of which shall be about seven-eighths (7/8) inch, and each arm to measures about five-sixteenth (5/16)inch in width, supported by a silver-plated bar extending from side to side of the wreath and firmly soldered to same. The cross to be silver plated and highly burnished, and the wreath to be thoroughly silver plated, as in the standard sample, and to admit an assay of not less than 44 grains of silver to each dozen ornaments.

Hospital Corps.—To consist of a Geneva cross, the extreme measurements of which shall be about seven-eighths (7/8) inch, and each arm to measures about five-sixteenth (5/16)inch in width. To be heavily silver plated on white metal and highly burnished.

To admit an assay of not less than 10.84 grains of silver to each dozen ornaments.

Ordnance.—To consist of a shell and flame. The diameter of the shell to be about three-quarters (3/4) inch, and the height of the flame to be about one (1) inch. The whole to be thoroughly gold plated, and the shell burnished, and the flame stain burnished, as shown in the standard sample, and to admit of an assay of not less than 4.62 grains of gold to each dozen ornaments.

Field Musicians.—A device representing an old-style bugle with circular crook, and a cord sling three folds around the lower part, terminating in two tassels on one and one tassel on the other side. The height across crook to be about one and one-eighth (1 1/8) inches, and the width from mouthpiece to outer edge of bell about two (2) inches. The number to be placed in the center of the circle on a bar extending from side to side and hard soldered to the under side of the bugle, and the letter to be placed above the number and hard soldered to the upper turn of the center of the bugle. The whole to be thoroughly gold plated and highly burnished, and to admit an assay of not less than 3.3 grains of gold to each dozen ornaments.

Band Musicians.—To consist of a lyre the full height of which shall be about one and one-half (1 1/2) inches, and its greatest width about seven-eighths (7/8) inches, made in accordance with the pat

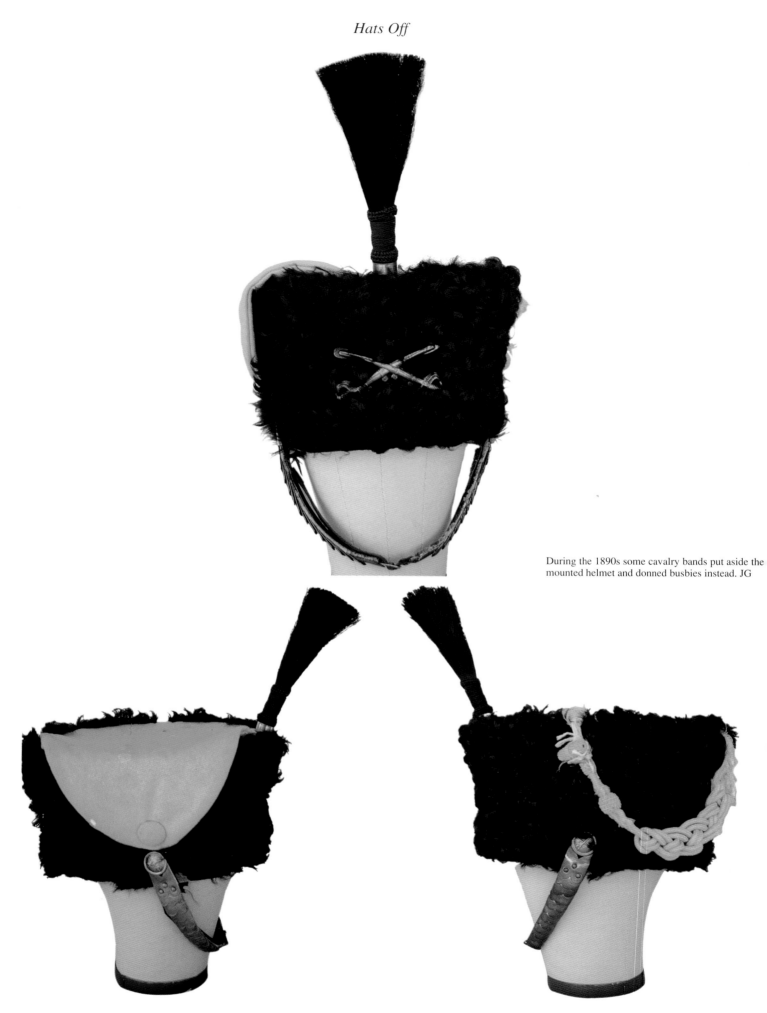

During the 1890s some cavalry bands put aside the
mounted helmet and donned busbies instead. JG

In this 1894 picture a bandsman of the Second U.S. Cavalry at Ft. Wingate, New Mexico Territory, wears the busby with his dress uniform. USAMHI

Musician John F. Boyer of the Fifteenth U.S. Infantry band sports a pillbox cap with his dress uniform in this circa 1895 portrait. FSHM

This specimen resembles Musician Boyer's cap but the band is of white facing material, the branch color adopted for infantry in 1884, rather than black mohair. It is not possible to determine whether this piece was made for an officer of the First U.S. Infantry, or possibly for the regimental band. Photograph by Gordon Chappell. AHS

tern of the standard sample. To admit an assay of not less than 25.33 grains of silver to each dozen ornaments.

Trumpeter of Cavalry.—Same as prescribed for cavalry devices.

The regimental sergeant majors of artillery, infantry, and cavalry; the battalion quartermaster sergeant, and the battalion sergeant major, engineers; the saddler sergeants, cavalry, and the chief trumpeters, cavalry; the principal musicians, infantry and artillery; and the chief musicians, artillery, cavalry, and infantry, are the same as the cap ornaments herein before described for artillery, infantry, cavalry, and engineers, except in each case the letter is omitted.

The U.S. Mint Assayer in all cases to determine the amount of gold or silver.

All numbers or figures to be one-half (1/2) inch long, and all letters Roman capitals one-half (1/2) inch long.

All ornaments to be like and equal to the standard samples in every particular.

Although these guidelines remained in place for many years to come, occasionally additional forage cap insignia would be added. For instance, in 1899, the creation of electrician sergeants brought about silver forked lightning bolts in a dead or unburnished wreath, while in 1900, the U.S. Army Service Detachment at West Point also were to display an unburnished or dead wreath on their caps with white metal Roman letters "Q.M.D." (Quartermaster Department) in the center.[53]

By 1901, military medical personnel experienced yet one more change of identity. To begin with, just five years earlier, their full dress uniform had been discontinued, meaning that the short-lived spiked helmet with Geneva cross overlay and side buttons ceased to be issued.[54] The forage cap insignia with silver Geneva cross, however, remained in use. Then, the publication of General Orders No.19, Headquarters of the Army, February 19, 1901, brought an end to that device as well.

In this circa 1875 portrait Major Louis H. Carpenter of the Tenth Cavalry posed in a pillbox cap. While not universally popular, this style saw unofficial wear by officers in a number of regiments during the 1870s and 1880s. Gordon Chappell Photograph. LF

Soon after that date, a 7/8 by 7/8 inch Maltese cross (Cross of St. John) was to be the standard insignia for all caps, the by now traditional wreath being added for hospital stewards.

While the medics were undergoing a readjustment of image, their comrades in the artillery were facing a change, too. In 1901, the old system of regiments was abolished. Instead, a Corps of Artillery was instituted whereby all field artillery batteries were given consecutive numbers from one through thirty, while their counterparts in coast artillery companies likewise converted their former affiliations to numerical designations, starting with one and running through 130.[55] As an outward manifestation of this structure, which lasted until 1907, appropriate numbers were to be attached to the campaign hat, except for field artillerymen, who from 1905 to 1907 had bronze crossed cannons with the battery number below, except in the case of staff NCOs.[56]

As far as enlisted 1895-pattern forage caps devices were concerned, the crossed cannons were retained, but without any numbers for noncommissioned staff. All other artillery enlisted personnel wore their battery or company number below the cannons.[57] Another initiative which

related to the 1895-pattern cap relative to artillerymen came in 1898 when uniform regulations allowed gunners and their officers at Fort Barrancas, Jackson Barracks, Key West, Sullivan's Island, Washington Barracks, and Fort Monroe to have "white linen caps." The last mentioned garrison had long been given some sort of summer headdress, as noted earlier. Besides straw hats and summer helmets, a special issue item, head-nets, were allowed for distribution for summer wear in the Department of Dakota, especially at Fort Assiniboine, to combat mosquitoes. Some 2,000 were purchased and distributed.[58]

Another limited item was in vogue for Fort Monroe's student officers at least, who obtained cap covers as early as 1884.[59] These removable accessories were reflective of the French Foreign Legion's "white kepi," or the British covers which had been in service in India since the Sepoy Rebellion.[60]

Foreign influence aside, these caps covers were to gain use beyond the posts for which they first were adopted, especially after the United States began to send troops to far off Pacific and Caribbean climes. Indeed, by 1900, "during the warm season if authorized by post com-

One of the Seventh Cavalry's officers, Captain Thomas McDougall (top row left) also elected to wear a pillbox cap. So did his spouse. Note that McDougall's fellow officer, Second Lieutenant Benjamin Hodgson (front row center), also has on a pillbox cap in this picture taken at Ft. Lincoln, Dakota Territory in the early 1870s. LBBNM

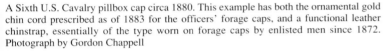

A Sixth U.S. Cavalry pillbox cap circa 1880. This example has both the ornamental gold chin cord prescribed as of 1883 for the officers' forage caps, and a functional leather chinstrap, essentially of the type worn on forage caps by enlisted men since 1872. Photograph by Gordon Chappell

Captain Mason M. Maxon of the Tenth U.S. Cavalry's pillbox cap. Photograph by Gordon Chappell. FDNHS

manders" officers could avail themselves of a white linen cap as opposed to just a cover. No insignia was spelled out for this substitute for the summer helmet, although general officers were to wear gold lace cap cords, measuring approximately 2/3 inch wide, presumably held in place by staff buttons. Gold bullion cap cords of the type worn with the blue forage cap were called for in the case of the staff corps and staff officers, while 1/8 inch diameter silk cords that were in yellow for cavalry, white for infantry, and red for artillery, were the only decorative elements, there being no mention of insignia.[61] Some individuals went beyond the regulations and added insignia, or even procured a khaki version of the cap, despite the fact that no official allowance existed for this shade of forage cap.

Such individual whim certainly was not unknown when it came to military headgear fashion. For example, the pillbox cap, yet another British-inspired item, had long been included in some military wardrobes in the United States.[62] For the most part, a few officers, chiefly in the post-Civil War era, donned the rakish cap for off duty wear.[63] On occasion, their wives even acquired this jaunty piece of headgear, which according to one source, "may have owed more to the popularity of the pert 'Eugenie,' also a diminutive style of hat."[64]

Besides officers and some of their ladies, certain regimental bandsmen seemed to have been provided with pillboxes as well. This was in keeping with the long-standing practice that allowed regimental commanders to "make such additions of ornaments" to the uniform of his musicians as he judged proper, providing that the cost for this customizing was not drawn from appropriated funds. This practice extended to other types of non-regulation headgear for bandsmen as well. Various bearskins, shakos, and even busbies were acquired on occasion, often reflecting fashion trends of the times. Indeed, the 1901 uniform regulations went one step further by prescribing black lynx skin shakos ("bearskins") for drum majors.

This fur headdress was strictly ornamental, but the army long continued to provide various other fur headdress as protection against the cold. None of these caps had met with total satisfaction. As a consequence, another track was followed, when in 1884, a canvas winter hood came unto the scene, these being perceived as having more warmth than fur headgear. According to Quartermaster Specification No. 109, adopted on April 17, 1884, these "canvas caps" were to be "made of 6 ounce cotton duck, dyed brown, lined with light blanket cloth next to the duck, and with light-colored cotton jean in the inside...." A pair of buttons were to close the cap's cape around the throat, and a "vest size, brown 'lasting' button" was attached to "the top for finish." A visor, which could be folded upward and held in position by a hook and eye, was bound in 3/4 inch brown tape, as were the edges of the cap.

Two years later, red wool lining replaced the cotton jean, this latter material being considered warmer. Additionally, the area of issue for the hoods was expanded from the original prescription for posts in the Departments of Dakota, Columbia, and the Platte, to "all troops stationed in extremely cold regions when the necessity for such issues is certified by Department commanders, to troops at West Point, N.Y., and those not attached to any military department upon the approval of the head of the staff department to which they belong."[65] Even these changes did not produce the desired response in that by 1887, the secretary of war permitted fur caps to be issued in lieu of the canvas cap, if commanders so desired to request them.[66] This option eventually spelled the end to the canvas hood. By August 25, 1902, a muskrat fur cap, delineated in Quartermaster Specification No. 580, brought an end to the hood.

This cap was described in great detail as opposed to the one called for on March 12, 1879, as the following information indicates when compared to the old fur cap that simply had been referred to as "according to standard sample, of muskrat skin, with ear flaps, cape, and visor, according to pattern." In contrast, the 1902-pattern cap was spelled out as:

Some officers choose to wear their 1872-pattern forage caps without leather chin straps, or in other instances added various types of ornamental gold cord straps instead, as this surgeon or staff officer has done. MM

General officers' forage caps had a black velvet band as a distinguishing feature as this headgear does which belonged to Major General Winfield Scott Hancock. Note the type of gold cord, which was adopted in lieu of the leather chinstrap in 1883. SI

Major Marcus Reno's Seventh U.S. Cavalry forage cap with the 1883 pattern officers' gold cord.

Material.—Fur portion to be of full furred and seasoned trapped muskrat skins (winter or spring skins only), thoroughly dressed with butter or oleomargarine, and cleaned with white or yellow sawdust (no alum or vitriol or other chemicals to be used), each skin to be sufficiently large to admit of the half crown being cut in one solid piece, except one small additional piece is allowed at each side to make required width. The lining to be good quality brown satin, counting about one hundred and twenty (120) threads to the inch of warp and about two hundred (200) threads to the inch of filling, sustaining a tensile strength of thirty-six (36) pounds both in the warp and the filling: the sateen weighing about two and one-fourth (2 1/4) ounces to the linear yard, thirty-six (36) inches wide. Interlining of good quality cotton wadding in the body of the cap, with an interlining in the cap and ear-laps of furniture hair cloth, medium weight, as shown in sealed standard sample, counting about sixty-two (62) threads to the warp and forty-two (42) threads to the filling.

Measurements.—Height of crown to be stout seven (7) inches on the pelt, full in circular slant, as shown in the sealed standard sample. The greatest depth of the ear-laps to be about five (5) inches, continuing around the cap, forming in the back a cape about three (3) inches, with a visor in the front, properly shaded, its greatest depth about two and three-fourths (2 3/4) inches; in the fur composing the section of the cap embodying no more piecing of the fur than is shown in the sealed standard sample. At the top of each ear-lap a black tape string about nine (9) inches long and one-half (1/2) inch wide for the purpose of extending over the crown of the cap and tying to hold the ear-laps and cape in position. The lining and interlining of the body of the cap to be quilted in block pattern, as shown in sealed standard sample, not less than twelve (12) stitches to the inch; the joining of the body of the cap to the lining thus prepared to be neatly and securely sewed with about six (6) stitches to the inch. The ear-lap and cape to have an interlining of furniture

A second lieutenant of artillery wearing the officers' forage cap with crossed cannons to designate his branch. USCM

Captain William Thompson, Fourth U.S. Cavalry in his forage cap circa 1885. The sabers were gold embroidery and the number silver embroidery. NA

The Sixth Infantry's Captain Stephen Baker exhibits both the 1883-pattern officers' cord and the profile of the officers' forage cap. His insignia was embroidered to a cloth background of dark blue material that matched the cap then was applied to the front above the visor. GS

A Second U.S. Artillery officers' forage cap of the 1883-1895 period. RB

Forage cap insignia of a Signal Corps officer c. 1885. Note that this example was sewn to a cloth background that could be applied to the front of the cap, rather than embroidered directly to the cap. JB

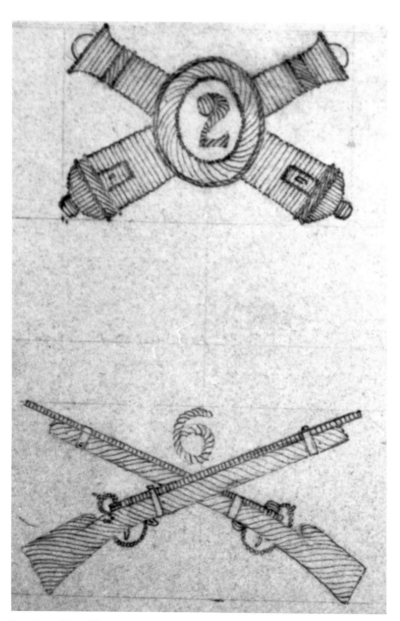

Drawings of the artillery and infantry officers' forage cap insignia of the 1875-1895 period. NA

hair cloth to give that portion of the cap stability, and applied as shown in the sealed standard sample.

The measurements and descriptions based on size seven and one-eighth (7 1/8), all other sizes to be in proportion.

To be like and equal to the standard sealed sample in every particular.

For years to come, this cap remained on the books for winter wear. However, as in the past, it was to be provided at cost to the men when post commanders deemed this headdress necessary.[67] As of 1902, for those men who did not wish to spend their own funds, or in instances where local commanders did not believe the fur headgear was required, brown cotton duck, blanket lined caps were available for troops "in extremely cold regions and to troops at West Point."[68] An olive drab wool hood lined with material of the same color was yet one more initiative in 1902. This item was to be secured under the collar of an olive drab overcoat by means of a half dozen buttons, when weather conditions made the extra protection necessary.[69]

While initiatives to protect troops from the winter remained an ongoing concern, the quest for an improved campaign hat likewise continued to be considered. As early as 1882, Major J.C. Breckenridge, a Civil War artillery officer who had become a member of the Inspector General's Department, returned from an official tour in the West. There he found considerable desire for a fur hat rather than one of wool. Moreover, he indicated that there was a sustained interest in a light colored campaign hat for troops serving in hot climates, much as correspondence of the mid-1870s had indicated and been noted in *Circular No. 8.*[70] To this end the new quartermaster general, Rufus Ingalls, turned to Captain Rodgers in Philadelphia for assistance. Rodgers was to obtain several colors and types of hats for review, to which the officer replied that he considered: "The only proper substance to use in the manufacture of hats of this character is *fur* felt." He went on to admit: "They will cost considerable [sic] more to begin with than wool hats, but a reasonable careful man can make two of them last through a term of enlistment, whereas he would want five of the wool ones." To partially offset

Engineer soldier's forage cap of the 1880s through mid-1890s. JG

In 1889, bound visors were adopted for enlisted forage caps as standard. This was among several subtle changes that were made to the cap's specifications during its last years of issue. The insignia is for the First U.S. Cavalry, Troop F. CF

this increased price, Rodgers suggested elimination of the Brasher ventilators, which could be replaced by a much less costly eyelet.[71]

Ingalls agreed with Rodgers and asked permission from the secretary of war to order 1,000 fur felt drab hats for experimental issue, although the cost would be approximately $2.00 each as opposed to the $.67 for the 1876-pattern black wool hat.[72]

The secretary gave his blessings. In 1883, among other units, Troop I, Sixth Cavalry stationed at Fort McDowell, Arizona Territory, were provided with the experimental drab hat. The company commander and many of his comrades from other organizations who tested the hat responded favorably.[73] With these positive endorsements, another 1,000 hats were ordered, but these were to have "larger ventilators in the side" than the trial models.[74] In fact, the improved hat was so successful, by

Sides and rear of the 1889-pattern enlisted forage cap. JB

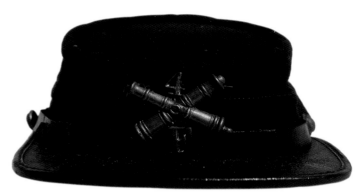

An 1889-pattern enlisted forage cap with the insignia of the Fourth U.S. Artillery, Battery F. RB

Interior of the 1889-pattern enlisted forage cap.

In 1882 a caduceus replaced the German silver US within a wreath as the insignia for hospital stewards, this device remaining regulation until 1887. The reinforcing bar is an example of how individual methods were employed to strengthen issue enlisted forage cap insignia that were made up of individual flimsy components. Photograph by Gordon Chappell

1885, the secretary of war was informed the Quartermaster Department thought it best "to purchase no more of the present standard pattern black, all wool, hats." Instead, the quartermaster general proposed future purchases should be "confined entirely hats of drab colors." Nevertheless, an option remained for those who still favored the 1876-pattern, because as quartermaster representatives pointed out: "If a demand for black, instead of drab colored hats should be made hereafter, there will be no difficulty to procure them."[75] Under the circumstances, then, the black and drab hats saw service side by side, although the latter type soon dominated, as indicated by photographs taken in the late 1880s and early 1890s, as well as by the contracts let for the 1883-pattern.[76]

This drab, fur felt version became standard on December 14, 1883:

Mixture,—To be composed of two-third best coney and one-third fine blown nutria.

Weight.—Hat bodies to be weighed—4 3/4 ounces heavy.

Shape.—Block to be 5 3/4 inches deep to center of tip.

Brim.—To be 2 3/4 inches wide in front and rear, and 3 inches wide at sides; to be of double thickness, and to have two rows of stitching, as shown in sample."

Color.—To be a drab or other suitable color, as per sample.

Trimmings.—To be trimmed with 8-ligne union band—same quality as on hat—to be sewed on by hand. Sweat to be imported lined leather, 2 3/4 inches wide, sewed to the reed by zigzag stitch. A wire gauze ventilator to be on each side of the hat, 3 1/2 inches from brim—to be of size as on sample hat.

The hats to be doe finished, as per sample.[77]

Because the sample hat apparently did not survive, it is difficult to ascertain some specifics about this piece of headgear, most notably the gauze ventilator. Such features had been found on 1872-pattern helmets provided by certain contractors, and occasionally were inserted in the top of 1872-pattern officers' caps in lieu of the specified Brasher device. From archaeological specimens, along with an extent black version of the hat, it seems that the adopted standard screen had a diameter of approximately a half inch.

The details of the wire gauze soon became a moot point in that the ventilators were discontinued altogether in 1889, when a new drab campaign hat specification was set forth. Another element which changed was the number of stitches on the brim, a third row being added.[78] The

A member of the Second U.S. Artillery, Battery F, appears to have attached the regimental number and battery letter to his 1872-pattern crossed cannon insignia. He wears the 1872-pattern enlisted forage cap. FAM

Regulations were mute as to what device was to be worn on the enlisted Signal Corps forage cap of the 1870s and 1880s. One bit of evidence is found in this portrait of Signal Corps Second Class Private R.L. Sutton in the 1872-pattern forage cap and with crossed German silver flags on his forage cap. This image was taken in the mid-1880s. JG

Left to right: side buttons worn on enlisted forage caps from the Civil War through 1884; 1884-pattern forage cap side button for all enlisted men, except staff non-commissioned officers; non-commissioned staff forage cap side button. KC

1889-pattern specifications also went into considerably more depth as to the composition of the fur, as follows:

Mixture.—To be composed of fur in the following proportions and kinds, for twenty-four (24) dozen hats; Fifteen (15) pounds Y.C. Ex. Ex. coney; thirty (30) pounds Y.C. No. 1 coney; sixteen (16) pounds W.C. No. 1 coney; twelve (12) pounds W.C. mottled coney; five (5) pounds W.C. hare's bellies; ten (10) pounds blown nutria; ten (10) pounds American rabbit.

A large German silver crescent measuring approximately two inches in length and one inch in height was regulation for the forage caps of commissary sergeant from 1873 through 1889. GS

Weight.—Hat bodies to be weighed, four and three-quarters (4 3/4) ounces heavy.

Shape.—Block to be five and three-fourths (5 3/4) inches deep to center of tip.

Brim.—To be two and three-fourths (2 3/4) inches wide in front and rare, and three (3) inches as sides; and to have three rows of stitching on edge.

Color.—To be drab, shade of standard sample.

Trimmings.—To be trimmed with eight-ligne union band, same quality and style as on hat, to be sewed on by hand. Sweat to be imported lined leather, two and one-fourth (2 1/4) inches wide. sewed to reed by zigzag stitch. Each side of hat to have an opening for ventilation consisting of small punched holes of size, arranged in design, as on standard sample hat; the center of design to be about three and one-quarter (3 1/4) inches from brim.

The hats to be doe-finished, as per sample.

In many respects, the 1889-pattern mirrored the earlier drab campaign hat. Once more, the two patterns were issued and worn side by side, until quantities of the 1883-pattern had been exhausted, presumably sometime early in the 1890s.[79] Indeed, issue must have been complete in that there are no known surviving examples of the 1883-pattern drab hat!

This is but one indication of the fact that the drab had proved popular. Another piece of evidence was the admission in 1886 of the Quartermaster Department "that at some posts the enlisted men declined to draw the black woolen campaign hats originally adopted [1876-pattern], and preferred to draw only those of drab color...." The response was "to issue the black hats until exhausted" as a matter of economy, but presumably to order no more.[80]

Contrary to this, a few examples of yet another campaign hat, this one adopted in 1890, still remain, although they were made in far smaller numbers that the drab campaign hat. This was the distinct headgear introduced as part of an entire special kit, in 1890, for Indian Scouts.[81] Among other items there was to be an Indian Scout fatigue hat which was described as: "Of black felt, brim 3 1/2 inches wide, crown 3 1/2 inches high; brim to be well stiffened." The crown, unlike the drab hat, was not creased in the center, but instead was domed or rounded.

The introduction of the Indian Scout hat also resulted in the creation of more than the headgear itself. Circular No. 10 likewise called for: "Two arrows crossed, to be made of nickel or some white metal,

In 1885 the forage cap device for post quartermaster sergeants was to be a gilt wreath surrounding a German silver key and quill. KSHS

three inches in length, the letters U.S.S. in the upper intersection.[82]" A special hat cord was to be worn with this headgear, being: "Of white worsted cord, one strand of scarlet, terminating in two tassels 1 1/2 inches in length, same color and material as the cord." The insignia was the first one ever specifically sanctioned for wear with a campaign hat, while the cords traced their lineage to the 1855-pattern cavalry hat. The Indian Scout cords, however, were based on the pattern adopted for the 1858 enlisted "Hardee" hat, and consisted of four strands of twisted worsted that terminated in fringed tassels and were held together by a netted slide in order to allow the adjustment of size. Such cords had been retained even after the 1872 uniform change, in part because large stocks remained on hand after the Civil War's conclusion.[83] While not necessarily popular, according to the various figures reported in the *Annual Report of the Secretary of War*, troops continued to draw "fair numbers" of the cords as an option well into the 1880s.[84]

Further, certain new additions to the ranks, namely post commissary sergeants and quartermaster sergeants, whose branch colors were cadet gray and buff, respectively, did not exist before the Civil War, or in the case of engineers, had changed their branch color from yellow to white and red. Evidence indicates that provisions were made to provide appropriate cords for at least commissary sergeants, but there is no indication that engineers, signalmen, or quartermaster sergeants ever had cords issued.[85] Regardless, by 1887, the secretary of war permitted a gratuitous cord for each hat issued, until such a time as the supply on hand was depleted. The fact that of the 32,855 on hand in that year, only

Contract label inside a white cover for the enlisted forage cap of the 1872 through 1895 era. It is unclear whether these were made for the Regular Army or for militia use, but it is certain that during part of the 1880s officers attending the Artillery School at Ft. Monroe, Virginia wore such covers. JG

3,049 had been issued, caused quartermaster officials to take action to deplete the stocks of these unpopular items.[86]

At that point, by the late 1880s or early 1890s, the hat cord essentially disappeared (except for officers who continued to purchase the black and gold intermixed cords for all but generals, who were to have gold cords). Whether generals or lesser grades, all officers' cords were to end in acorns, as they had since being ushered in during the 1850s.[87]

FORAGE CAP BADGES FOR ENLISTED MEN
(FULL SIZE).

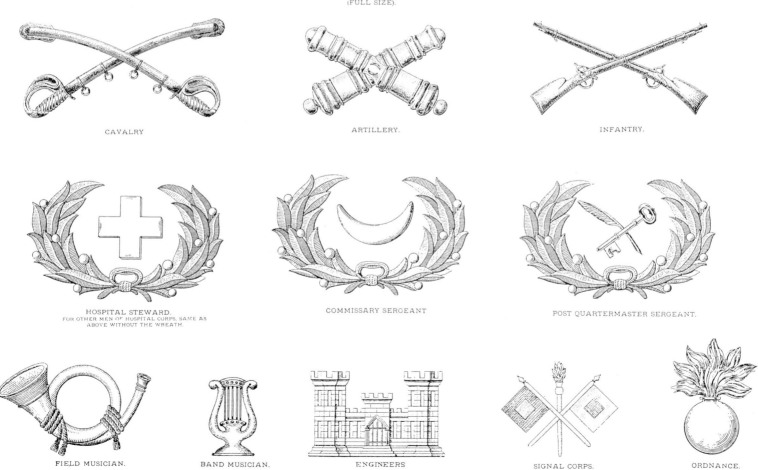

CAVALRY   ARTILLERY.   INFANTRY.

HOSPITAL STEWARD.
FOR OTHER MEN OF HOSPITAL CORPS, SAME AS ABOVE WITHOUT THE WREATH.

COMMISSARY SERGEANT   POST QUARTERMASTER SERGEANT.

FIELD MUSICIAN.   BAND MUSICIAN.   ENGINEERS   SIGNAL CORPS.   ORDNANCE.

Enlisted and non-commissioned officers' forage cap insignia as they existed by 1889. GS

Front and side views of the blue 1895-pattern officer's forage cap that belonged to Lieutenant Colonel W.L. Kiger, 160th Indiana Volunteer Infantry Regiment during the Spanish-American War. Officers' caps for regulars and volunteers were identical for the most part, except that the chin strap buttons usually bore the state seal for the latter, while regulation U.S. buttons were the norm for U.S. Army officers. JB

Hat cords would be revived in due course for the rank and file as well. This resurgence coincided with a dramatic change in the mission of the U.S. Army and the creation of yet another variation of the campaign hat.

These new dynamics occurred in the wake of the 1898 sinking of U.S.S. *Maine*, an event that plunged the United States into conflict with Spain. After the outbreak of the Spanish American War, yet another version of the drab campaign hat came into existence. In some respects, this headgear, adopted in 1899, harkened to earlier times in that screen vents were reintroduced for purposes of air circulation. It seems that the perforations in the 1889-pattern hat had not performed this function adequately, if the account of one officer can be taken as typical. While deployed to Cuba, a Tenth Cavalry troop commander, Captain John Bigelow, cut a hole in the crown of his hat to provide better air flow. His buffalo soldiers improved upon the idea and slit the hat's crown, but left these as flaps that could be closed during a "tropical rain."[88]

The band on 1895-officers' caps for generals was to be of black velvet, rather than black mohair. This cap belonging to Nelson A. Miles was furnished by Bent and Bush of Boston. Photograph by Glen Swanson. WS

Captain Charles William Foster of the Sixth U.S. Artillery Regiment wore an 1895-pattern forage cap with a silver chinstrap rather than the regulation gold pattern. Numerous variations of this nature were found among the caps bought by Regular Army officers, volunteers, and national guardsmen. There were even versions that could be telescoped like a top hat when not in use or others that were without stiffening so that they were rather formless. JG

Another example of the 1895-pattern officers' forage cap worn by C.O. Phillips of the 158th Indiana Volunteer Infantry. JB

Oilcloth covers, such as those one belonging to Lieutenant Colonel W.L. Kiger, 160th Indiana Volunteer Infantry Regiment, could be obtained for the 1895-pattern cap to offer some protection against the rain. JB

The officer who obtained this cap ignored the regulations and added an embroidered arms of the United States. In this case the insignia was integral to this particular piece of headgear, but removable versions existed to facilitate cleaning of the cap body.

Others who shipped overseas as part of the war effort desired one more means of making the hat more comfortable suggesting that headgear should be issued in larger sizes and made so that there would be "plenty of space between the sweat leather and the hat."[89]

Military authorities took the responses from the field to heart. In 1899, the Philadelphia Depot was instructed to obtain "1,000 hats with corrugated side ventilators similar to those abandoned in 1889, and corrugated insertions under the sweat bands, 500 of leather and 500 papier mâché, to be sent to Cuba for trial."[90] Additionally, the brims of some of the experimental hats were turned under and secured with three rows of stitching, while the other hat simply was to have the three stitched rows near the edge that was flat rather than overturned.

The overall idea seemed to gain support, and by the end of 1900 Horstmann & Co. made an improvement, which completed the process. The firm suggested a corrugated aluminum insert in the sweat band that would be more durable than the leather or papier mâché types. Once more, the Quartermaster Department decided to experiment, and bought 1,000 hats with the aluminum inserts and a like number with celluloid inserts, in both cases to be attached to the hat with a non-rustable wire. Once again, the large screen ventilators (approximately 1 inch in diameter as opposed to the smaller 1883-pattern) formed part of that hat. And once more, some had turned over brims, and others had brims with raw edges, but in both cases triple-stitched. Troops in Cuba and the Philippines received the hats for field trial. Later, during fiscal year 1900, some 350,000 hats with sweat band inserts were bought for general issue. Private purchase of campaign hats for officers continued throughout the period as well, and black models still were favored by some

officers, who elected to buy this shade that remained optional according to regulations until early in the twentieth century. Even when a drab hat was adopted universally in the early 1900s, black ones were retained officially for chaplains for years thereafter. Moreover, even toward the end of the Victorian era, straw hats saw some limited use in the Philippines as a replacement for the campaign hat and summer helmet.[91]

The reason for the continued private procurement of straw hats stemmed from the fact that the summer helmet never had a universal appeal. A medical officer serving at Fort Sill, Indian Territory, Assistant Surgeon C.N.B. Macauley, voiced some of the objections against this headdress. The doctor noted the men at that garrison quickly removed their forage caps after formation to don straw hats. Why did they resort to the non-regulation headgear? Perhaps it was because, as Dr. Macauley concluded, the summer helmet's brim was insufficient to protect the eyes and the ears in front and the nap of the neck in the rear. Further, he thought, "Nine tenths of the present white helmets have so small a ventilating space that hair of ordinary thickness checks all draught."[92] As a solution, the surgeon sought a helmet with pugagaree and other improvements, including an extended visor, as well as a gutta purcha or imitation jet series of insignia based on the forage cap design,

Khaki versions of the 1895-pattern cap, although not mentioned in regulations, were nonetheless bought by some officers and a few men alike. JB

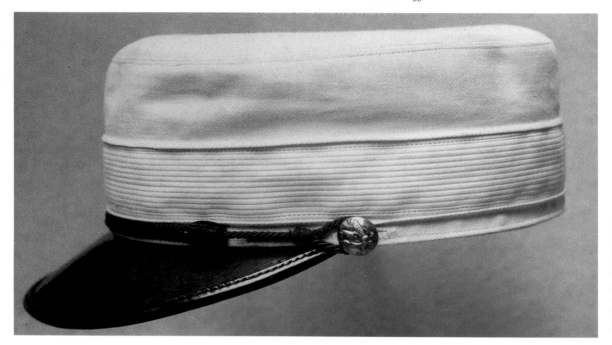

White cap or caps made with white bodies were permitted for officers, however, although these were to be without insignia, and be plain except for two side buttons and a 2/3 inch gold lace chin strap for generals, and an 1/8 inch chin strap for all other officers, those for staff officers being of gold, and those for cavalry, artillery, and infantry officers being of silk in the color of the arm. NA

which could be affixed to the helmet to designate corps or branch. Most of these suggestions were ignored, but a model with longer rear visor ultimately was adopted toward the end of the nineteenth century, and would be issued into the early 1900s. Another practice that lasted into the next century came about in tandem with activity related to an improved campaign hat. This was a renewed interest in hat cords. In 1899, with all earlier stocks evidently issued or sold, some nine different types of mohair cords with acorn ends were prescribed for enlisted men. Those for engineers were to be of alternating red and white stripes. In turn, scarlet was for artillery; yellow for cavalry; green for Hospital Corps; light blue for infantry; crimson for ordnance; gray for post commissary sergeants; buff for post quartermaster sergeants; and black for Signal Corps.[93] Within a few months, a minor adjustment was made when infantrymen were to have their blue cords replaced with white ones.[94]

Subsequent army regulations continued to prescribe the hat cord for years to come, which according to paragraph 83 of the 1902 regulations pertaining to enlisted men was to be "3/16 inch diameter, of material, conforming in color to that of the corps, department or arm of service; to be sewed fast to the hat." In that year another version of the service or campaign hat was adopted, one that did away with the corrugated insert in the sweat band and the screen vents, and which was to be adorned with cords of the same colors as settled upon in late 1899, except that those for the Hospital Corps would be white and maroon intermixed; for Ordnance Corps black and scarlet intermixed; and for Signal Corps orange and white intermixed.[95] These cords likewise were to be sewed fast to the hat. Several years later, in 1910, two more cords joined the list—a green one for Army Service School Detachment personnel and green intermixed with white for the U.S. Military Academy's Army Service Detachment.[96]

The officer on the right wears the white version of the forage cap without ornamentation in accordance with regulations. He has combined his headgear with the khaki uniform rather than the white 1895-pattern officers' summer blouse as one indication of the numerous combinations of headdress with uniforms that existed during the late nineteenth century. USAMHI

Second Lieutenant Samuel B. Arnold of the First U.S. Cavalry in the 1895-pattern officer's forage cap. UKL

An 1895-pattern enlisted forage cap with infantry insignia. JG

The 1895-pattern enlisted forage cap with the insignia of a Signal Corps non-commissioned officer.

Besides the revival of cords in 1899, authority to wear insignia on the campaign hat crown, including corps badges, came under consideration. One example of this trend appeared in a letter written by the Second Cavalry's colonel, whereby he cited "the very common practice" among his troopers to add "crossed sabers & c. on the hat."[97] This prompted the quartermaster general to suggest a further step by requesting permission to provide a "hat cord for each arm of the service," along with the addition of "the number of the regiment in brass."[98]

By July 1899 the matter had been pondered and approved, with regimental numbers, company letters, and hat cords being permitted. At first the insignia to indicate regimental and company affiliation was restricted to artillery, cavalry, and infantry soldiers, while engineers were to have company letters only, and Indian Scouts would continue to be issued their special crossed arrows.[99] The numbers and letters were priced at a mere penny apiece; the scout's more costly device was valued at a quarter each.[100]

In the beginning, the numbers and letters were of lightweight, hollow brass, similar but not identical to the numerals that once had adorned the collars of the 1872-pattern enlisted dress coat and the 1872-pattern forage cap.[101] By 1902, they were to be made in a "dull bronze finish."[102] In either case, the thin metal devices measured one-half inch high, and were attached by a pair of wires affixed to the back side.[103] In certain respects this insignia represented a reversion to the old, less satisfactory system of attachment, thereby prompting a revisiting of the subject. Later in 1903, heavier prongs were introduced, along with a thicker (approximately 1/16 inch) gauge dull bronze metal for the letters and numbers.[104] This alteration followed an earlier scheme that occurred in 1902, when the previous Indian Scout white metal insignia with crossed arrows was changed to the simple heavy bronze one-piece "USS." At the same time, "Native troops in the Philippines" were to bear a subdued "P" on their campaign hats, while men serving in the "Porto [sic] Rico Provisional

Side view of an 1895-pattern enlisted forage cap. JG

1895-pattern enlisted forage cap worn by William W. Gibb, Seventh U.S. Cavalry, Troop E, who enlisted on July 11, 1898. JB

The back of the insignia prescribed for use with the enlisted 1895-patten forage cap had a screw post and round nut to secure it to the front of the headgear, as well as small prongs to help retain it in place. This example is for an artilleryman. GL

The 1895-pattern enlisted forage cap with the insignia adopted in 1901 for hospital stewards. AHS

Regiment" were to bear the letter "P.R." on the crowns of their headgear.[105]

The matter was not closed with the strengthened insignia because some question remained as to why non-commissioned officers of the regimental staff and other specialists did not have insignia for their campaign hats.[106] Consideration of this matter resulted in the publication of General Orders No. 197, War Department, December 31, 1902, which among many other things required:

> The number of the regiment and letter or number of the company, troop, or battery, made of dull-bronze metal, to be placed on the front part of the crown, the regimental number to be above the company letter or number. Enlisted men of field artillery will wear crossed cannons, with the number of the battery below them, all of dull-finish bronze metal. Post non-commissioned staff officers will wear the device in dull-finish of their respective corps...."

By the next year, General Orders No. 163, War Department, October 4, 1905, again underscored that for infantry and cavalry enlisted men: "The number of the regiment, and for those assigned to a troop or company, its letter, the number to be placed above the letter." The order went on to prescribe the number only for coast artillerymen. As noted previously, this was in keeping with the fact that from 1901 to 1907, the artillery had been reorganized into coast and field artillery units and the

regiments abolished. Thus, all artillerymen were assigned to numbered batteries, without regimental affiliation during this period.

Nonetheless, field artillerymen enjoyed an additional distinction under General Orders No. 163, in that they wore not only the number, but also crossed cannons, the numeral being cast below the device. In turn, sergeants major of artillery wore the cannon without any numeric designation, a practice that started in 1901. All post non-commissioned staff officers continued with the same devices essentially as assigned for the 1895-forage cap, with a few exceptions, but without the wreath and in dull bronze. This included master electricians, electricians, and master signal electricians, with their lighting bolts. Finally, all enlisted men of the Ordnance Department, Hospital Corps, Signal Corps (except master electricians), and the army service detachment at West Point gained permission to wear their respective insignia, but without wreaths in the case of non-commissioned officers from these organizations. A year later, General Orders No. 183, War Department, October 31, 1906, repeated this prescription for the "dull-finish metal devices" verbatim, but added a "R.S." for the recruiting service, and a "P.G." for enlisted men posted as military prison guards.

The 1902-pattern campaign hat, on which these various insignia were to be worn, was adopted as standard on January 29, 1904, by Quartermaster Specification No. 651. The hat had several features of note.

The white enlisted summer helmet (left) adopted late in the nineteenth century with a steeper visor than the 1880-pattern, and its khaki counterpart that began to be produced during the Spanish American War (right). RB

The color guard of the Ninth U.S. Infantry have put aside their 1881-pattern enlisted dress helmet for the plain 1880-pattern summer helmet at Madison Barracks, New York, during hot weather in 1896. They have combined the helmet with the 1884-pattern infantry enlisted dress coat. Note that the helmet is devoid of all insignia, as was proper for enlisted men. T&L

For one thing, the corrugated sweat band inserts and screen vents both were discontinued, the latter items being replaced again by perforations on either side of the crown. This time, the design was a five-pointed star rather than the previous snowflake-like ventilators. Further, the edge of the brim was turned upon itself and fastened in place. In addition, there was an eyelet of the same heavy fur felt as the hat affixed on each side of the brim near the base of the crown "for fastening a strap or cord, the use of which is authorized."[107] The color and the fore and aft crease remained in place, however, thereby giving the new campaign hat a similar appearance to its drab predecessors.

This piece of headgear's appearance, according to the secretary of war's annual report in 1904, had come about "Owing to the gradual deterioration of the quality of campaign hats heretofore procured under contracts...." As a result, the quartermaster department launched into consultation with various manufacturers and procured experimental samples "from which a hat composed of a higher grade of materials" was selected, "and which while more expensive" was thought to be "more durable and give greater satisfaction." Once specifications were drawn up, some 100,000 hats were bought under contract. Once in hand, and after old supplies were exhausted, they were to be issued to the U.S. Army and militia, thereby supposedly ending "future complaints" over the subject of the campaign hat.[108] The following year the secretary contended: "This hat proved a vast improvement in all respects over the old style and has given satisfaction. It is in every way of better appearance, better quality, and better make than the old one...."[109]

BELOW: In this 1888 image, enlisted men of the Hospital Corps detachment at Ft. Gibson, Indian Territory (Oklahoma) stand in formation with their officer all wearing the 1880-pattern summer helmet. Note that the officer has added the optional spike to his helmet, a feature that was not seen on the headdress of enlisted personnel. National Library of Medicine, USAMHI

The campaign hat was but one of many types of headgear that would be redefined early in the twentieth century. Even before the 1902-pattern campaign hat was announced, an exclusive dress cap was delineated as a replacement for the chapeau of Corps of Engineer officers. As of March 1902, this item was:

> To be of dark-blue cloth with three cloth welts, 3 1/2 inches total depth; diameter across the top, 8 3/4 inches for a cap of size 7; the top to be 1/8 inch larger or smaller for every size above or below size 7. The sides to be made in four pieces, to be 1 1/2 inches between upper welts, and semi-stiff. Between the two lower welts a band 1 3/4 inches wide, to be arranged as follows: Scarlet, 1/8 inch; white, 3/32 inch; gold lace 1/2 inch; white 3/32 inch; scarlet 1/8 inch; white 3/32 inch; gold lace 1/2 inch; white 3/32, inch; scarlet, 1/8 inch.

> Visor to be of black patent leather, 1 3/4 inches deep at center; to droop at an angle of about 45 degrees. A gold cord as now prescribed to be held at the sides of the visor by two small gilt engineer buttons.

> Cap badge shall be the coat of arms of the United States in gold embroidery of the pattern now prescribed, edged with scarlet silk, excepting the scroll and stars, arrows, and laurel branch, and placed so that the tip of eagle wings shall be 3/4 inch below top welt of cap.[110]

The order permitting this new style was signed by Lieutenant General Nelson A. Miles, the same officer who had headed up the 1879 Board, and who nearly three decades later had become the commanding general of the U.S. Army. Miles himself had favored such a cap, which has come to be referred to at least by some sources as a "bellcrown," because its flared out like an upside-down bell. Miles in fact wore a cap of the style early in the twentieth century with his full dress uniform, taking such an initiative based on the long-standing tradition that the senior officer in the army would have latitude to design his uniform. Nearly a half century earlier, Winfield Scott had exercised this prerogative, and Miles did so after he came to command.

Previously, the chapeau de bras had been the required finery for engineer officers on dress occasions, as it had been for general officers, staff departments, and the Signal Corps (after 1887). The design of this long accepted headdress changed little since the 1870s, but its decades of duty were about to come to a close in nearly every case, when sweeping uniform changes that had introduced the 1902-pattern campaign hat, among other items, likewise brought about a whole new generation of headgear, many pieces of which formed the basis of articles worn through the twentieth century.

This headdress was but a component of a widespread new uniform regulation that came about in following the Spanish-American War, when yet another uniform board met to deliberate what the U.S. Army should

1898, these officers of the Tenth U.S. Cavalry posted to Cuba have acquired the white summer helmet, all of which seem to be standard enlisted versions covered with drill and with the longer rear visor that was adopted late in the Victorian era. USAMHI

adopt as its outward appearance. The Engineer Corps officer's ensemble presaged the board's vision that was made known to the rank and file as General Orders No. 81, Headquarters of the Army, July 17, 1902. Although the commanding general, Nelson Miles, approved the order, both he and President Theodore Roosevelt expressed objections to particular elements of the document. This resulted in revisions that superseded the July 17 directive, which was supplanted by General Orders No. 132, Headquarters of the Army, December 31, 1902.[111] This command, along with the subsequent specifications that resulted, gave rise to dozens of types of headgear, including the colorful full dress caps for officers and enlisted men alike.

In the former case, General Orders No. 132 enumerated two basic types, one for generals (who incidently were the only ones that still were to retain the chapeau after generations of that headdress' existence), and another for all other officers as follows:

For general officers, full-dress.—A full-dress cap, to be of the same size and make as the full-dress cap for other officers, except that it will have a blue-black velvet band between the lower welts 1 3/4 inches wide and mid-way thereon an embroidered design of oak leaves in gold 1 inch wide surrounding the cap; and on the visor an ornament of oak leaves embroidered in gold on the upper surface, as described below.

All General Officers (dismounted) shall wear the chapeau.

For officers of cavalry, artillery, infantry, and engineers, and other officers of the staff corps and departments when in full dress.—

be dark-blue cloth, with three cloth welts; total depth, 3 1/2 inches; diameter across the top, 8 3/4 inches for a cap of size 7, the top to be 1/8 larger or smaller for every size above or below the above head size. The sides to be made in four pieces; to be 1 1/2 inches between upper welts and stiffened with hair cloth and wire around crown. Between the two upper welts a band 1 3/4 inches in width to be arranged as follows: Gold lace 1/2 inch wide; background 3/4 inch wide; gold lace 1/2 inch wide. The background between the bands of gold lace will be as follows. Of silk, color being that of the facings of the corps, departments, or arm of service (see par. 51). Visor to be of black patent leather, 1 3/4 inches deep at the center and of green color underneath; to droop at an angle of 45 degree; to be ornamented with oak leaves embroidered in gold on the upper surface for all officers above the rank of captain. Cap to be provided with flat gold cap strap, 5/8 inches wide, to be held at the sides by two small regulation gilt buttons. The cap badge shall be the coat of arms of the United States embroidered in gold, as per pattern, and so placed that the tip of the eagle wings shall be 3/4 inch below the top welt of the cap. All the details to be in accordance with sealed pattern in the office of the Quartermaster General. No departure therefrom will be permitted.

The enlisted men were to have their own version of the cap which was to be:

Of dark-blue cloth, of same pattern and shape as that prescribed for officers; between the upper and lower welts a band 1 3/4 inches

Some members of the Third U.S. Volunteer Engineers at Cienfuego, Cuba, were issued the 1880-pattern summer helmet during their Spanish American War service. USAMHI

wide, to be arranged as follows: A stripe of cloth of the color of the corps, department, or arm of service, at top and bottom, the intervening space of 3/4 inch to be the color of the cap, the whole forming a detachable band; a black-enameled leather chin strap fitted with a stout fire-gilt slide and a leather keeper, secured at both ends by small gilt, regulation buttons, one on each side immediately back on the ends of the visor.

Some of the bands were in the traditional colors, such as scarlet for artillery, yellow for cavalry, red and white for engineers, cadet gray for commissary sergeants, buff for quartermaster sergeants and the West Point service detachment, but infantry returned to light blue from white, while signal corpsmen abandoned the black and white prescribed in 1889 for a reinstatement of orange and white. Further, ordnance personnel now had a black and scarlet as their color rather than crimson, while enlisted medical personnel abandoned green for maroon and white. Green, however, would make a resurgence, but not for medical men. Rather, as of 1910 the shade was introduced as facing for cap bands and chevrons, along with the piping on full dress coats for men in service school detachments.

For the most part, insignia adopted for the 1895-pattern forage cap was retained for the new enlisted 1902-pattern full-dress cap, with certain notable exceptions such as the Hospital Corps, where the caduceus made a comeback over the Maltese cross, and for quartermaster ser-

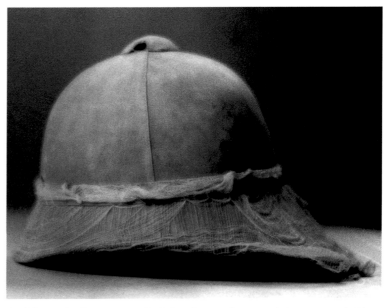

A soldier serving in some mosquito-infested outpost has appended a more practical item to his khaki summer helmet, a net attached puggree-style to help keep pesky insects away from the face. For a short period, nets had been an issue item, but for troops serving in the upper Great Plains near the Canadian Border, rather than for overseas duty. FSHM

Other units were provided with the later pattern summer helmet with longer rear visor. Khaki versions of these came into being soon after the United States began to send troops overseas. For instance, these men, who are members of the Philippine Scouts, wear the khaki helmet, and even have added a few non-regulation touches, such as the 1881-pattern dress helmet eagle. USAMHI

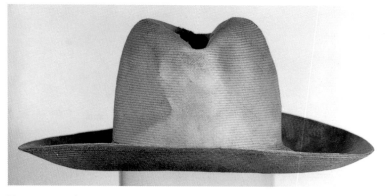 

Even overseas the summer helmet was not universally adopted. For instance, hats of this type were purchased by some troops in the Philippines. USAPAM

geants and members of the Army Service Detachment at West Point who now were to sport the new wheel surmounted by an eagle with crossed sword and key device adopted in March of 1902.[112] General Orders No. 132 thus mandated:

> Insignia of yellow metal, except where otherwise specified and made in accordance to sealed patterns in the office of the Quartermaster General, will be attached to the front of the cap so that the top of the insignia will be slightly below the top of the cap. Designs as follows:
>
> Cavalry.—Crossed sabers, number of regiment in the upper angle and letter of troop in lower angle.
>
> Artillery.—Crossed cannons, with number of battery in upper angle or company in lower angle.
>
> Infantry.—Crossed rifles, number of regiment in the upper angle and letter of company in lower angle.

Although the Quartermaster Department provided summer helmets, some officers and enlisted men, such as this infantry first sergeant, continued to favor a straw for warm weather wear as indicated by this banjo strumming enlisted man relaxing during his off duty hours. His comrade on the left wears the 1883-pattern drab campaign hat with small brass screen ventilator in the crown. AHS

In the late 1800s Captain Matthew Batson commanded Philippine Scouts. While serving in the islands he obtained a locally made civilian straw hat to which he added a blue band, a custom officers' hats cord, and an embroidered arms of the United States. USAMHI

Engineers.—The castle with letter of company above it.

Ordnance Sergeants.—Shell and flame in white metal, inclosed in a wreath of gilt metal.

All Enlisted Men of the Ordnance Department.—A shell and flame in gilt metal.

Post Commissary Sergeants.—Crescent of white metal, the points up, inclosed in a wreath of gilt metal.

Post Quartermaster Sergeants.—Insignia of the Quartermaster's Department, in white metal, inclosed in a wreath of gilt metal.

Electrician Sergeants.—A symbol resembling forked lightning, of white metal, inclosed in a wreath of gilt metal.

Hospital Stewards.—A caduceus of white metal, inclosed in a wreath of gilt metal. For acting hospital stewards, lance acting hospital stewards, and privates of the Hospital Corps, a caduceus of gilt metal, without wreath.

Non-commissioned officers of the Signal Corps.—Two crossed signal flags and a burning torch of white metal, inclosed in a wreath of gilt metal. For all other enlisted men of the Signal Corps, two crossed signal flags and a burning torch of gilt metal.

During the 1880s the Quartermaster Department sought replacements for muskrat caps and buffalo overcoats. In the former instance, a brown canvas hood with red lining was introduced in 1884, and a slightly altered version was specified two years later, although neither of these cold weather accessories entirely replaced the fur cap. JG

Black and gold intermixed hat cords ending in acorns were adopted in 1858 for all officers save generals. The basic pattern remained standard well into the twentieth century. This example was worn by John Leefe in the last quarter of the 1800s. MC

Enlisted men of the Army Service Detachment at the U.S. Military Academy, West Point, N.Y.—The insignia of the Quartermaster's Department in gilt metal.

Band Musicians.—A lyre of white metal. Engineers to have a castle of yellow metal in the center. Cavalry and infantry to have a number of the band, of yellow metal, above the lyre.

Field Musicians of Engineers.—A bugle of yellow metal, with a castle of white metal in the center of, and letter of the company, in yellow metal, above the bugle.

Field Musicians of Infantry and Trumpeters of Cavalry.—Bugle with letter of company or troop in center, and number of regiment above the bugle.

Field Musicians of Artillery.—A bugle with number of the company or battery in the center.

This insignia did double duty, as did the basic cap, in that by removing the detachable cap band this headdress could be converted from full dress to dress. This was not the case for officers, who had a special dress cap that for all intents and purposes was identical to the full dress cap save for the fact that the gold lace and colored background or embroidered oak leaves in the case of general officers were replaced by a plain "band of blue-black velvet" for generals, and "for all other officers, by a band of lustrous black mohair braid. The visor ornament of gold oak leaves is also excepted."

Officers further gained a new summer cap, which once more was much like the dress cap save being made: "Of white linen or cotton duck, with removable top,...the band between the two lower welts to be of white braid; the visor to be as prescribed for the dress cap." As an alternative, the 1880-pattern officers' summer helmet covered in white facing material was continued. Enlisted men likewise kept the summer helmet but covered in drill, both white and khaki versions remaining in stock. There were no white caps for the other ranks, though. But that situation changed in 1904.

Accordingly, General Orders No. 197, War Department, December 31, 1904, instituted a white service cap, which was to be the "Same

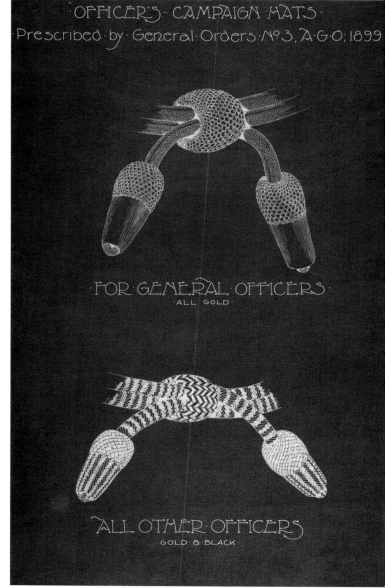

Pattern drawings of hat cords for generals (gold) and all other officers (black and gold intermixed) c. 1890. NA

In the decades after the Civil War civilian type slouch hats continued to be obtained by a number of officers, including Nelson Miles, who favored somber black hats reminiscent of the type worn by many in the Union Army. WC

Interior of one of Nelson Miles' campaign hats of the post-Civil War period. WC

This image was taken after Miles became a general officer in 1880. He holds his trademark black campaign hat. DJB

The Quartermaster Department began to experiment with drab campaign hats, which were adopted as official in 1883. The 1883-pattern campaign hat, as adopted, not only came in a lighter color, but also had small screen mesh side ventilators on each side of the crown following the design previously found on the 1872-pattern enlisted helmet. Regulations provided for black versions of the hat as well as drab ones, but the former rendition was most common. Officers—such as seen here as indicated by the hat cord and staff officer's insignia—tended to be the predominant users of the black hat, while the rank and file favored the drab model. No extant drab examples have been discovered to date. Additionally, this 1883-pattern black version, with the correct double stitching on the brim, is the only known surviving specimen. JG

as prescribed for officers, omitting the white braid." Unlike the officers' cap, which bore a detachable gilt metal arms of the United States, the enlisted rendition was to be without ornament, the small gilt side buttons and patent leather chin strap being the only addition to the basic headgear. Once again, this same general orders allowed the white summer helmet to be worn as an alternate to the new cap, as well as continued to provide for the khaki helmet, in both cases as long as supplies remained in stock.

Furthermore, General Orders No. 197 permitted an alternative to the khaki helmet by introducing a cotton service cap in that color. There also was an olive drab cap which for officers was to be of serge, as described in paragraph 33 which read in part:

> To be made with three welts: Total depth, 3 1/2 inches; diameter across the top. 8 3/4 inches for a cap of size 7; the top to be 1/8 inch larger or smaller for every size above or below the size above named. The sides or bell to be made in four pieces, seams equidistant; to be 1 1/2 inches between welt joining top pieces to bell and top welt of band.
>
> To have a band of lustrous mohair braid of olive-drab color 1 3/4 inches wide between the two lower welts.

In 1890, Indian scouts also were authorized scarlet and white intermixed hat cords. Two types of this accessory evidently were made as seen here. JG

While the drab campaign hat began to prevail, the 1890-pattern Indian scout campaign hat was black. This rare piece of headgear had a domed-shaped crown rather than the high crown standard campaign hat that was creased front to back. SI

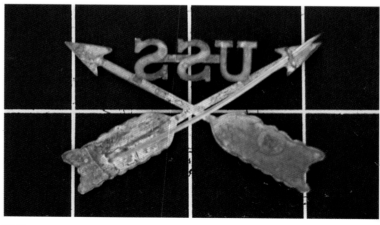

While most enlisted campaign hats of the 1880s through mid-1890s were worn devoid of insignia, a large German silver crossed arrows with the letters USS (U.S. Scouts) insignia held in place by a stout pinback was prescribed for the 1890-pattern Indian scout campaign hat. WR

Some Indian scouts elected to wear this insignia on non-regulation headgear, as did Robert White, an Oglala who served in Troop C. NSHS

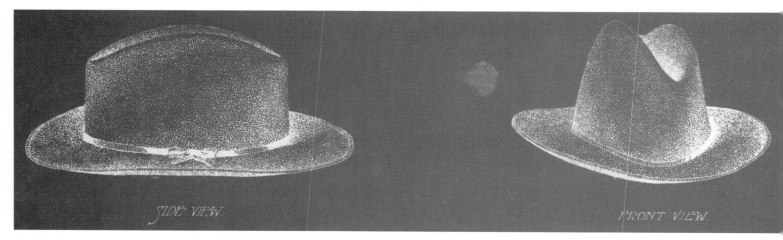

Specification drawing of the side and front view of the 1889-pattern campaign hat, as issued. While the illustration is for an officer's hat, the enlisted version essentially was identical. The brim was triple stitched. NA

Black 1889-pattern campaign hats were available, although not as popular as the standard issue drab type. Nonetheless, during the Spanish American War the darker hat was made by several firms, chiefly for sale to officers. JB

Most extant black campaign hats are marked in the sweatband "U.S. Army Regulation Hat", or with similar wording, as seen here. JB

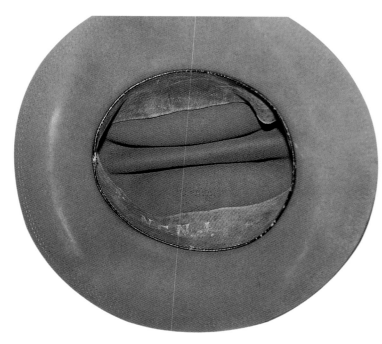

Some drab 1889-pattern campaign hats also were made for private purchase and often marked "U.S. Army Regulation Hat." JB

This veteran charted his tour of duty as well as indicated his unit affiliation on his 1889-pattern campaign hat. JB

Sometimes a dark ink stenciled insignia indicated the wearer's unit during the Spanish American War, as was the case with this 1889-campaign hat. JB

Company, troop, or battery letters where appropriate, and regimental numbers were prescribed for enlisted campaign hats in 1899, as seen in use here on an 1889-pattern drab campaign hat. RB

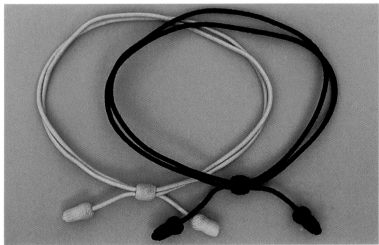

Worsted enlisted hat cords with acorn ends likewise were called for in 1899. Scarlet designated artillery troops, while light blue was prescribed for infantrymen in July, but was changed to white in September of that same year. JG

While the drab 1883-pattern campaign hat was relatively popular, the fact that it no longer had the screen ventilator featured in the 1883-pattern, but rather a perforated "snowflake" design prompted some individuals to modify their headgear to promote circulation. For instance, a simple brass grommet might be inserted into the crown for this purpose. JB

Another means to increase circulation in the 1889-pattern campaign hat was to cut holes in the crown to create flaps that could be opened to promote air flow, or closed when it rained. J.H. Westerhoff of Company C, Second New Jersey Volunteer Infantry, made this sort of modification to his campaign hat as well as made slits in the crown to allow him to carry his toothbrush on his hat. Three-quarters of a century later, troops in Vietnam continued a parallel practice by attaching insect repellent or other personal items to their helmets. JB

To have a visor of dark enameled leather, lined on underside with dark-green embossed leather, securely cemented to body of visor with the best rubber cement. The visor to be of black enameled leather to a depth of about 3/16 inch, upper edge of binding to be neatly turned in and stitched; the width of the visor at its widest part to be 1 5/8 inches, to be molded to shape at an angle of 45 degrees.

Trimmings: Chin strap to be made of best enameled black leather, with the necessary keepers of the same material; to be held in place by two small regulation buttons of dull-finish bronze. Lining to be best quality olive-drab cotton and worsted serge, cut and shaped to inner body of the cap, crown to be joined at the seam of the crownpiece of the cap, stitched therewith and to the band to hold lining securely in place. No stiffening of any kind to be used in crown or bell. The inside band to be of strong flexible material protected by a sweat leather of best quality, leather properly sewed in, turned on upper edge, and securely cemented.

Each cap to have four enameled-metal eyelets, as near color of serge as possible; to be placed above the band, two on each side of cap, the center of each eyelet halfway between upper welt of band and crown seam and 1 1/2 inches apart.

The cap badge shall be the arms of the United States, of dull-finish bronze metal, detachable.

The identical specifications were to be followed for the khaki cap, except that there was to be no mohair band, and the cover was to be removable from the cap's base. Nearly identical caps in khaki and olive drab were adopted under General Orders No. 197 for the common soldier as well. The chief differences from those procured by officers were neither of the enlisted models had mohair braid, and an additional eyelet 5/8 inch from the edge of the crown was pro-

Charles Earnest of Tenth Pennsylvania Volunteer Infantry wearing his mint condition 1889-pattern drab campaign hat before the ravages of field service and time took their toll. JB

Men of Troop D, Fourteenth U.S. Cavalry display the troop and regimental brass as called for in 1899, along with the hat cord with acorn tips also adopted in that year. All wear the 1889-pattern drab campaign hat, the prevalent field headdress of the late Victorian era U.S. Army. UKL

vided at the front of the cap to permit the attachment of the screwback insignia.[113] These devices were the same as required for the full dress/dress caps, except that they were to be of dull-finish bronze metal.

Also, according to War Department's 1905 annual report: "New standard samples of all metallic ornaments, gilt and bronze, prescribed for officers and enlisted men, strictly conforming to the provisions of War Department General Orders, No. 197, series of 1904, have been procured and adopted."[114] These devices were viewed as "greatly improved" in that the designs had been updated so that they were "strictly in conformity with the arms used by the respective organizations." This was most noticeable for infantrymen, who were thereafter to wear crossed Springfield .30 caliber bolt-action rifles rather than the .45-70 "trapdoors" that had been the norm since 1875. In addition, the new insignia were smaller in size than those worn previously. For instance, the wreaths worn by non-commissioned staff officers were reduced from their width of 2 5/8 inches to 1 7/8 inches. All other devices, except those for bands-

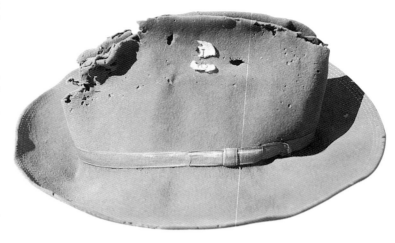

The remains of the X Corps, Second Division badge appears on this 1889-pattern campaign hat that was worn by Sergeant Charles Earnest, Tenth Pennsylvania Volunteer Infantry. JB

Regimental bandsmen sometimes went one step beyond regulations and added a lyre to their campaign hats rather than just the number of their regiment. JB

Variations in insignia were not the only deviation from regulations. Some late nineteenth century soldiers even continued to substitute privately purchased, civilian style slouch hats instead of wearing the issue campaign hat, as exhibited by this infantry first sergeant. JB

Throughout much of the history of the United States Army field headgear has been a matter of individual taste. A case in point, many of these New York Volunteers have customized the regulation drab campaign hat. They have reconfigured the crown into a point, rather than the regulation fore and aft crease. USAPAM

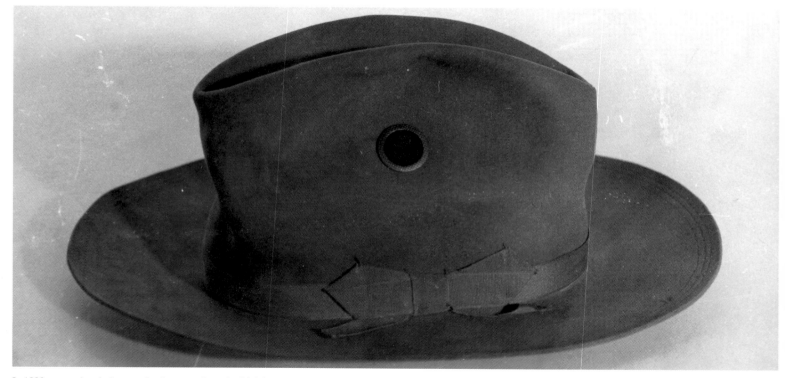

In 1899 yet another drab campaign hat was adopted, which in some respects harkened back to those issued in the early 1880s. The brims of the 1899-pattern hats, however, were triple stitched, while the 1883-pattern had only double stitching on the outer brims. Further, the earlier headgear had a smaller screen vent on each side of the crown. AHS

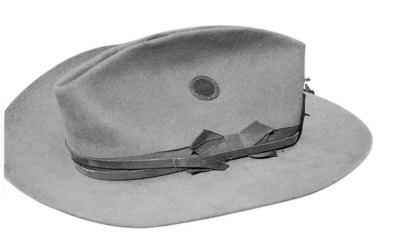

Left side and inside of an 1899-pattern campaign hat. JG

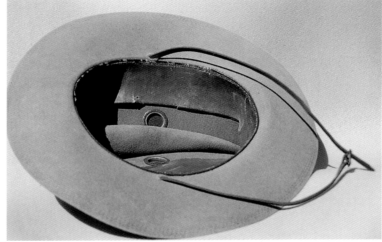

J.D. O'Keefe of Company I, Twenty-sixth U.S. Volunteer Infantry, added a leather thong strap to his 1899-pattern campaign hat. JB

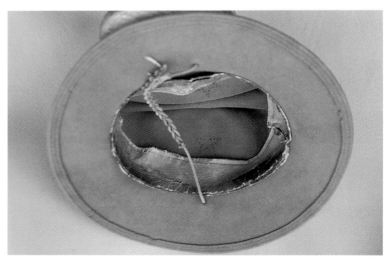

1899-pattern campaign hat with VIII Corps badge attached. JB

Another variation of a homemade chin strap was secured to this 1899-pattern drab campaign hat, the braiding representing a bit of individual intiative. JB men, medical personnel, signalmen, and West Point's Army Service Detachment, were decreased in size accordingly.[115] In the process, a slight adjustment occurred in the insignia of infantry musicians serving in companies and cavalry troop trumpeters in that the regimental number was to go above the bugle device and the company or troop letter in the center. This change represented a reversal of the placement previously prescribed.[116]

Similarly, artillerymen found some reworking of their insignia as well. Under General Orders No. 197, the number of the battery or company was to appear below the crossed cannon devices on the various caps. Then, General Orders No. 169, War Department, August 14, 1907, returned to the practice of the regimental number appearing above the cannons and the battery letter below, at least for field artillerymen. Conversely, coast artillerymen persisted in wearing the company letter below the cannons, and would continue to do so until 1916. This same order called for field artillery senior non-commissioned officers simply to exhibit the regimental number above the crossed cannons, while silver crossed cannons within a gilt wreath were introduced for the full dress/dress caps of regimental non-commissioned staff officers of the coast artillery and a subdued version for the service cap. Senior field artillery non-commissioned wore crossed cannons with the number only.

An 1899-pattern campaign hat with infantry hat cord and company letter with regimental numeral above, worn by Private Henry F. Goedecke, Fourth U.S. Infantry, Company D. The black crepe band, while non-regulation, was adopted to the hat as a sign of mourning, typical of Victorian custom. JB

Signalmen in the field, operating early in the twentieth century, wear the 1899-pattern campaign hat. NA

Corporal Goedecke's 1899-pattern hat with its black mourning band and other accessories can be seen on the table next to him in a portrait he had taken in the Philippines while on duty during the turn-of-the century. JB

On June 6, 1900 Nelson Miles became the commanding general of the army, a post he held until retirement on August 8, 1903. He wore a custom full uniform, including a cap with slight bellcrown and a small visor, as seen in this photograph taken early in the twentieth century. The basic design of this cap soon would inspire the headdress for all U.S. Army personnel. KC

Lieutenant General Nelson A. Miles in a custom white dress hat, probably of his own design. This image was taken just prior to his 1903 retirement. NA

Besides senior coast artillery NCOs being singled out with their new cap device, all enlisted men posted to coastal defenses, especially those serving on mortar crews, gained permission for another distinctive article. Because the traditional campaign hat was not entirely satisfactory for these gunners, on January 21, 1909, Quartermaster Specification 1009 allowed a work hat for these men as part of their fatigue uniform—a type of headgear that first had been prescribed for oilers and firemen in the army's harbor-boat service in 1904. This was to be a round "blue denim hat made of six sections with a matching brim stiffened with canvas and ten rows of stitching."[117] A white version of the hat was authorized for cooks, sailors, and crews of the same organization. The 1909 version of this cap consisted of six sections of blue denim, "containing not less than sixty threads to the inch in the warp and forty threads to the inch in the filling" which were to be secured together

This full dress cap with the three silver stars of a lieutenant general was made around 1902 by Horstmann. It resembles the headgear worn by Nelson A. Miles in his final years in uniform, and in fact is attributed to him. It may be a prototype for the 1902-pattern full dress generals' cap. Photograph by Glen Swanson. WS

This full dress cap, also from the Nelson A. Miles estate, follows the pattern adopted in the 1902 regulations for all general officers. This one was produced by M.C. Lilley & Co. and has the new 1902 type eagle buttons and Arms of the United in place. Photograph by Glen Swanson. WS

This general officers' dress cap was closer to the one actually adopted as regulation in 1902. It likewise was retained by Lieutenant General Miles either as a sample or for personal wear. This example was made by B. Pasquale of San Francisco. Photograph by Glen Swanson. WC

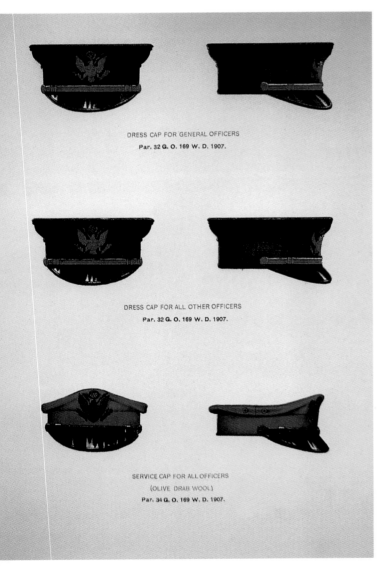

DRESS CAP FOR GENERAL OFFICERS
Par. 32 G. O. 169 W. D. 1907.

DRESS CAP FOR ALL OTHER OFFICERS
Par. 32 G. O. 169 W. D. 1907.

SERVICE CAP FOR ALL OFFICERS
(OLIVE DRAB WOOL)
Par. 34 G. O. 169 W. D. 1907.

Official Quartermaster Department illustrations of the dress cap for general officers and all other officers, as well as the olive drab wool service cap. KC

On March 17, 1902, Engineer Corps officers received an entirely new full dress uniform with visored cap. This outfit was the forerunner of a similar full dress prescribed for all company grade and field grade officers at the end of the year under General Orders No. 132, dated December 31, 1902. FAM

inside by 1/2 inch tape. The size was to be stamped on the inside with red indelible ink.

A slightly different model was adopted on December 23, 1910, as Quartermaster Specification 1102 which read in part: "*Materials.*—Blue denim, baling linen, cotton thread, six cord, No. 50, and one half (1/2) inch cotton tape, all to be Army standard." The material was to be cut into six sections, and held together by seams "securely stayed on the inside by black cotton tape one-half (1/2) inch in width. The band was "to be five-eighths (5/8) of an inch in width" while the sweat band was "to be one and one-quarter (1 1/4) inches in width, edge turned over and stitched." Finally, the brim was "to be two and one-half (2 1/2) inches

The 1902-pattern dress cap for officers below the rank of brigadier general had black mohair trim until 1912, when this headgear was discontinued and the full dress cap prescribed for use with both dress and full dress. JB

1902-pattern company grade artillery officer's full dress cap. RB

1902-pattern company grade full dress cap of a medical officer. EB

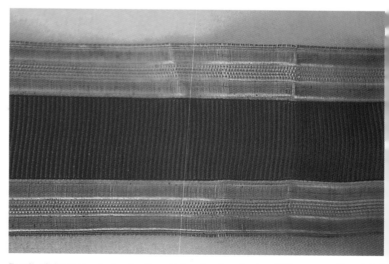

The 1902 uniform regulations allowed general officers to retain the chapeau de bras for certain formal occasions, but discontinued the use of this headdress for all other U.S. Army officers. Additionally, a full dress cap was adopted in 1902 for general officers with embroidered oak leaves on the visor and around the black velvet band that ran around the cap. KC

Detail of the grosgrain band with gold lace borders for the 1902-pattern officers' full dress cap, in this case for artillery because of the scarlet color. RB

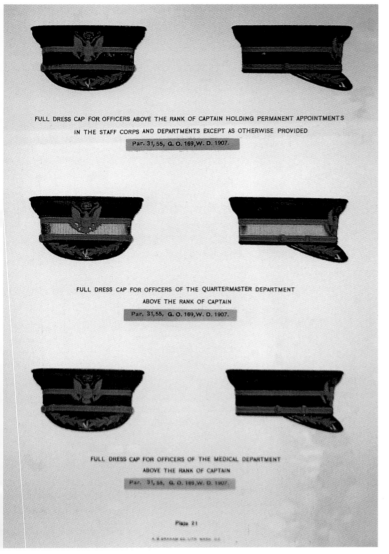

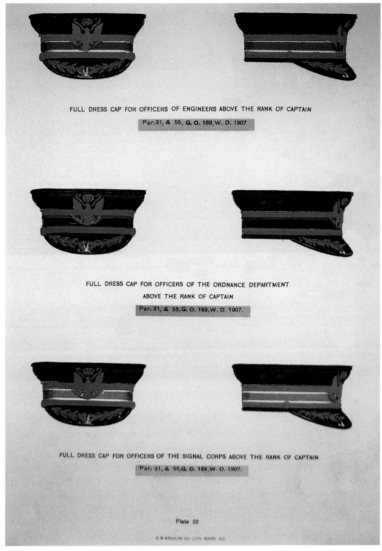

ABOVE AND FOLLOWING PAGES: Official Quartermaster Department illustrations of 1902-pattern full dress caps for both field grade (with embroidered oak leaves on the visor) and company grade officers (plain black visors). KC

wide, bound with the same material, and to be interlined with blue denim or baling linen, strengthened with about ten rows of stitching." Once introduced, the "Daisy Mae" as it came to be nicknamed after the character in the *Little Abner* comic strip, remained in use with few changes, not only for artillerymen, but also over time, for many other branches with only slight change until finally being abandoned early in World War II.[118]

Another piece of headgear that would boast a long service usage was the campaign hat adopted on September 8, 1911.[119] The new hats differed in several ways from the earlier forms, particularly in how they were blocked. All previous styles were to have crowns that were creased fore and aft. The new version was to be a "Montana Peak," a term that stemmed from the configuration of the crown, which was pointed somewhat like the top of a mountain. Such a style had been favored by a number of cowhands in the nineteenth century, and some military personnel sometimes unofficially shaped there campaign hats in this manner, especially during the Spanish American War.[120]

Now Uncle Sam sanctioned the practice, thereby leading to Specification 1145, adopted on January 2, 1912. The hat was:

To be composed of 62 1/2 per cent double ring Saxony hare's fur and 37 1/2 per cent best Coney center backs, cut from prime full winter English or Scottish skins.

Mixture.—The double ring Saxony hare's fur to be thoroughly mixed and blown through a six-section blower by itself. The best Coney center backs to be thoroughly mixed and blown through a six-section blower by itself. The two furs thus mixed to be then thoroughly mixed together and blown through not less than twelve sections.

Weight.—From this mixture to be weighed four and one-half ounces for a seven and one-eighth (7 1/8) inch hat; other sizes proportionally lighter or heavier.

Color.—To be olive drab, of the shade of the standard sample. Dye to be fast and to be applied during the process of shrinking and sizing. The finished hat to stand an exposure to ordinary weather conditions for a period of thirty days without material change in color.

Stiffening.—The brim to be stiffened with what is know as Wine stiffening, it being understood to be a shellac cut with alco-

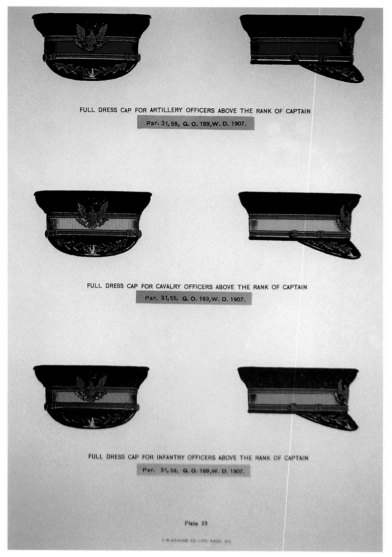

FULL DRESS CAP FOR ARTILLERY OFFICERS ABOVE THE RANK OF CAPTAIN
Par. 31, 55, G. O. 169, W. D. 1907.

FULL DRESS CAP FOR CAVALRY OFFICERS ABOVE THE RANK OF CAPTAIN
Par. 31, 55, G. O. 169, W. D. 1907.

FULL DRESS CAP FOR INFANTRY OFFICERS ABOVE THE RANK OF CAPTAIN
Par. 31, 55, G. O. 169, W. D. 1907.

Plate 23

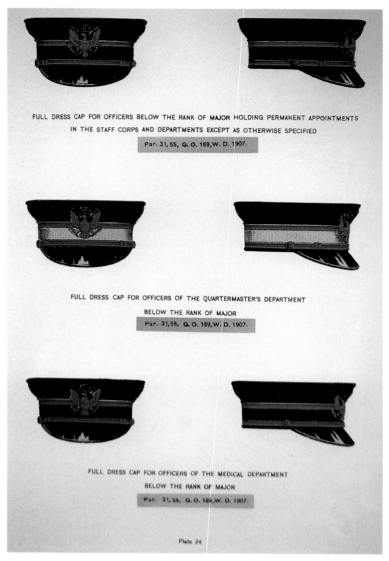

FULL DRESS CAP FOR OFFICERS BELOW THE RANK OF MAJOR HOLDING PERMANENT APPOINTMENTS
IN THE STAFF CORPS AND DEPARTMENTS EXCEPT AS OTHERWISE SPECIFIED
Par. 31, 55, G. O. 169, W. D. 1907.

FULL DRESS CAP FOR OFFICERS OF THE QUARTERMASTER'S DEPARTMENT
BELOW THE RANK OF MAJOR
Par. 31,55, G. O. 169, W. D. 1907.

FULL DRESS CAP FOR OFFICERS OF THE MEDICAL DEPARTMENT
BELOW THE RANK OF MAJOR
Par. 31, 55, G. O. 169, W. D. 1907.

Plate 24

hol (denatured). The crown to have no stiffening. The brim to withstand soaking in water for a period of forty-eight hours without becoming soft or flabby.

Trimming.—To be trimmed with a one (1) inch union band and bow, the color of the band and bow to stand the same exposure test as prescribed for the hat. To have a turned and cemented edge roan leather sweat band about one and three-fourths (1 3/4) inches wide, securely fastened to hat and which will be attached by a zigzag stitch a nonrustable reed, covered with an oiled muslin backing of not less that one-half (1/2) inch in width and of double thickness throughout.

Shape.—To be what is known as 'Montana Peak' crown, to be about five and one-half (5 1/2) inches deep with four indentations, pressed or blocked to conform to shape of standard sample, and the brim three (3) inches wide.

Ventilation.—The front, rear, and sides of the hat to have a drab color eyelet, with opening three-sixteenths (3/16) of an inch after being securely fastened. The center of the eyelets to be approximately two and three-fourths (2 3/4) inches from base of crown.

Eyelets.—For receiving the tying cords, to be inserted through the brim at about one and one-fourth (1 1/4) inches forward of the center of each side, and about one-fourth (1/4) of an inch from the band. One to be inserted from the upper side through a round piece of felt of same material as the hat (about one-half (1/2) inch in diameter in order to leave the upper edge of the eyelet one thickness of felt above the level of the upper brim, and the other inserted from the under side for the purpose of leaving an upper and under finished edge to the eyelet. Eyelets to conform to those in the standard hat.

Tying cords.—To have a good quality braided cord with metal tips, conforming closely in color to the hat.

Finishing.—The entire hat to be made in a workmanlike manner, and all operations in the forming, sizing, blocking, and finishing, to be thoroughly and carefully done.

There were seven sizes of the hats, ranging from 6 3/4 to 7 1/2. Further, hat cords of the type adopted in 1899 for enlisted men commonly were with this headgear, while officers persisted in wearing their appropriate gold and black intermixed cords, or gold cords (general officers). With the passage of time, the front ventilator eyelet offered an ideal means for the application of screwback devices, such as the post-World War I distinctive unit insignia, to be applied. Prior to the First World War, however, the campaign hat usually was devoid of ornamentation, save for the hat cord. Further, in its earliest form, the crown's four equidistant "dimples" was a matter of blocking, but examples made

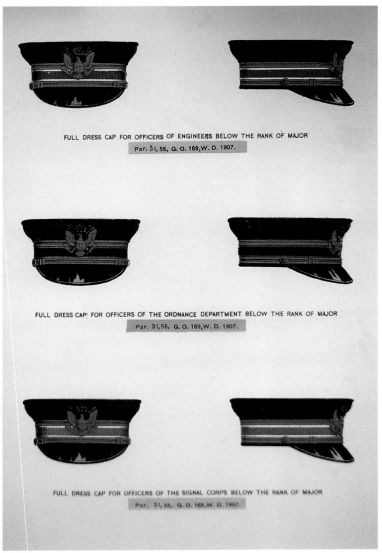

FULL DRESS CAP FOR OFFICERS OF ENGINEERS BELOW THE RANK OF MAJOR
Par. 31, 55, G. O. 169, W. D. 1907.

FULL DRESS CAP FOR OFFICERS OF THE ORDNANCE DEPARTMENT BELOW THE RANK OF MAJOR
Par. 31, 55, G. O. 169, W. D. 1907.

FULL DRESS CAP FOR OFFICERS OF THE SIGNAL CORPS BELOW THE RANK OF MAJOR
Par. 31, 55, G. O. 169, W. D. 1907.

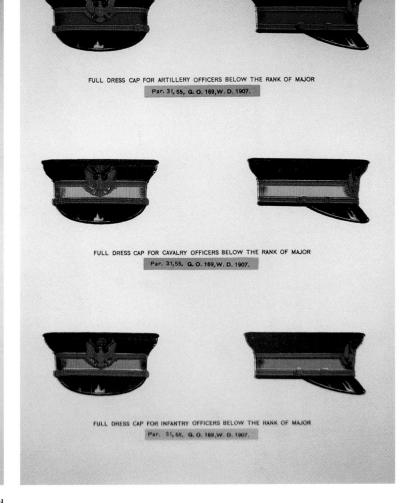

FULL DRESS CAP FOR ARTILLERY OFFICERS BELOW THE RANK OF MAJOR
Par. 31, 55, G. O. 169, W. D. 1907.

FULL DRESS CAP FOR CAVALRY OFFICERS BELOW THE RANK OF MAJOR
Par. 31, 55, G. O. 169, W. D. 1907.

FULL DRESS CAP FOR INFANTRY OFFICERS BELOW THE RANK OF MAJOR
Par. 31, 55, G. O. 169, W. D. 1907.

many years later had to be treated with stiffening so that they would retain this shape.

The Montana Peak was not the only item of headdress for which new specifications were written in 1912. Following the convening of yet another uniform board in 1911, a number of important decisions were reached that essentially brought about a series of headgear that still have readily identifiable descendants in use to this day.[121] First of all, the officer's full dress cap was adopted for dress wear as well, the previous dress cap with mohair band being eliminated from the uniform tables of wear with the exception of chaplains, veterinarians, dental surgeons, and acting dental surgeons. According to paragraph 9 of *Regulations and Specifications for the Uniform of the United States Army*, published in 1912, the full dress cap and dress cap became one. The design from the 1902 version changed slightly though, in that only the front of the cap was stiffened rather than the entire crown. Specifications from 1912 made this clear:

(a) General officers except the Quartermaster General and Chief of Coast Artillery.—To be made of dark blue cloth of adopted standard.

Badge.—Coat of arms of the United States embroidered in gold or gilt bullion in the front of the cap, taking in half of the upper part of velvet band and lower half of the two front quarters.

An officers' 1902-pattern olive drab service cap with correct metal subdued insignia, which was removable from the cap. RB

Band.—To be blue-black velvet, about 1 3/4 inches wide, upon which is embroidered oak leaves of gold or gilt metal bullion. The leaves to be about 1 inch in length and each group of two leaves about 3/4 inch in width. The velvet band with the gold leaf to encircle the cap.

Chin strap.—To be 3/8 inch in width and 9 inches long, of gold lace stitched on red Russia leather, edged to edge, fastened at each end of visor with a regulation small gilt button.

Crown.—Of dark-blue cloth of adopted standard, measuring about 10 1/2 inches from front to rear and 9 1/2 inches from side to side; to be stiffened in front by means of hair-cloth springs sewed between the quarters and lining, falling without stiffening to the rear. To have two black japanned eyelets 1 1/2 inches from the welt seam and about 3/4 inch on each side of side seam quarters.

Visor.—To be black patent leather, cut to slope to an angle of about 45° when attached to cap. To be lined with embossed green hatter's leather, and on outside two semi-circles of oak leaves em-

broidered in gold or gilt bullion. The leaves to be about 1 inch in length and each group of two leaves about 3/4 inch in width.

(d) Field officers [majors through colonels].—Same "General officers," par. 9 *(a)*, p.7.

Badge.—Same as "General officers."

Band.—A band consisting of two bands of gold lace about 1/2 inch in width on the top and bottom and in the center a silk band 3/4 inch wide, of the color of the corps of arm of the service. [see above from the 1902 regulations for colors]

Chin-strap.—Same as 'General officers.'

Crown. Same as 'General officers.'

Visor.—Same as 'General officers.'

(e) Officers below the rank of field officers.—Same as 'General officers.'

Badge.—Same as 'General officers.'

Band.—A band consisting of two bands of gold lace about 1/2 inch in width on the top and bottom and in the center a silk band 3/4

Engineer officers, including Captain Douglas MacArthur (front row, second from right) pose in their 1902-pattern Engineer Corps full dress officers' cap. The tall officer in the front row (third from left) is a major, and as such wears the gold embroidered leaves on the cap visor as was fitting for a field grade officer. FAM

A colonel of the Paymaster Department wears the field grade officers full dress cap of the 1902-pattern as indicated by the visor that bore embroidered oak leaves and a black grosgrain on the band, the color indicating the staff corps. JB

A veterinarian in the 1902-pattern officers' dress cap. FAM

Dapper First Lieutenant Henry Gibbins of Ninth U.S. Cavalry with his 1902-pattern olive drab service cap with shiny patent leather visor and chin strap. FAM

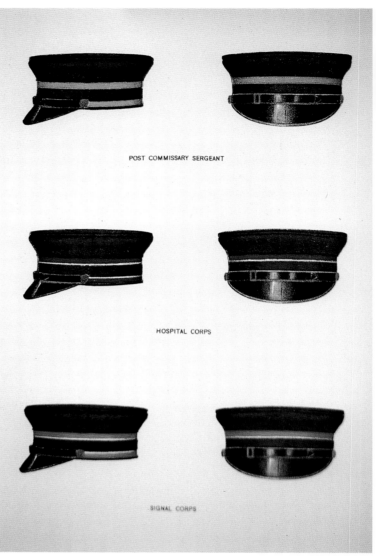

Official Quartermaster Department illustrations of the 1902-pattern officers' khaki cotton service cap, white service cap, and campaign hats, including the black version designated for chaplains. KC

ABOVE AND FOLLOWING: Official Quartermaster Department illustrations of the 1902-pattern enlisted full dress caps. KC

The 1902-pattern campaign hat cord for general officers continued to be gold while all other officers were to use the black and gold intermixed cord as in the past. KC

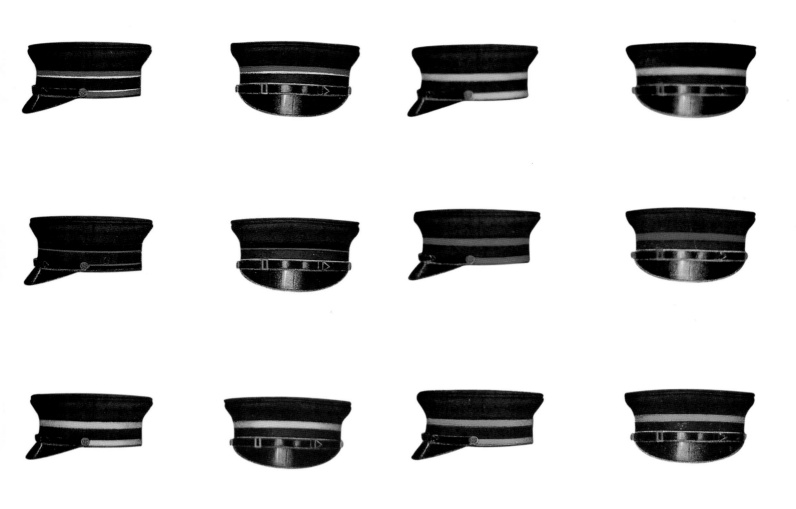

1902-pattern enlisted full dress cap with infantry insignia adopted in 1895, and that remained regulation for the first issue of the new 1902 uniform. CF

By removing the band from the 1902-pattern enlisted full dress cap, this headgear was converted to a dress cap, as is exhibited here for an infantry soldier. JB

The bugle device was retained for company musicians when the 1902-pattern dress cap was first adopted. This individual is a trumpeter with an artillery battery or company. RB

Private William H. Green was a member of the Ninth U.S. Cavalry Band at Ft. Riley, Kansas, when he appeared for this c. 1905 photograph. He wears the lyre prescribed for the caps of regimental bandsmen on the 1902-pattern dress cap. UKL

The original 1902-pattern full dress caps for enlisted men in the Artillery Corps displayed scarlet bands. Non-commissioned staff officers wore caps with crossed cannons that had no numbers, while those of field artillery batteries or coast artillery companies had numbers below their insignia. RB

The smaller enlisted artillery full dress and dress cap insignia adopted in 1905 is eviden[t] here. RB

inch wide, of the color of the corps of arm of the service. [see above from the 1902 regulations for colors]

Chin-strap.—Same as 'General officers.'

Crown.—Same as 'General officers.'

Visor.—Same as 'General officers,' except that a plain visor will be substituted for the embroidered visor.

(f) Chaplain, veterinarian, dental surgeon, and acting dental surgeon.—Same as 'General officers.'

Badge.—Same as 'General officers.'

Band.—To be plain band of black mohair braid about 1 3/4 inches wide.

Crown.—Same as 'General officers.'

Visor.—Same as 'Officers below the rank of field officer.'

While the full dress/dress cap with mohair band ultimately would be dispensed with, the other versions with gold oak leaves for generals and color coded bands for the various branches would be retained for formal wear throughout the remainder of the twentieth century, with some elemental changes. One of these would be the replacement of the embroidered badge with a detachable metal coat of arms in later years.

1902-pattern full dress cap prescribed for electrician sergeants and master electricia[n] sergeants with the insignia specified in 1905. RB

It should be noted that detachable badges, in subdued metal, fo[r] officers had been in limited use during the nineteenth century, and be[-] came the norm for the olive drab and khaki officer's service caps i[n] 1902. This continued to be the case in 1912, when a new service ca[p]

The 1905-pattern infantry insignia on the 1902-pattern enlisted full dress cap. CF

The 1905-pattern Hospital Corps insignia for sergeants first class of the Hospital Corps[.] EB

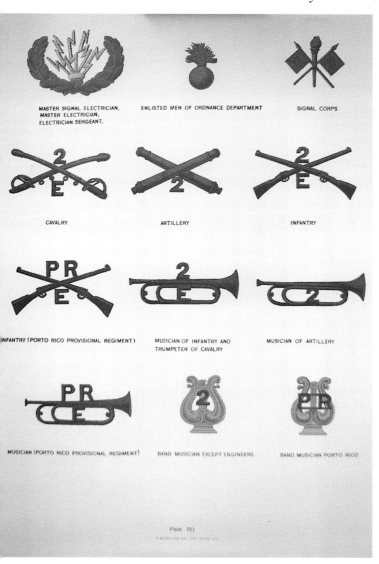

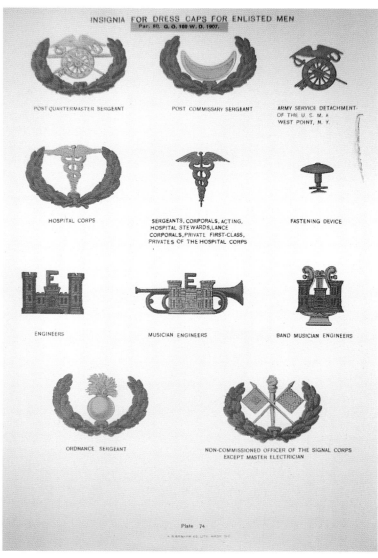

1902-pattern enlisted and non-commissioned staff full dress and dress cap insignia as specified in 1905. KC

lesign was adopted that would replace not only the previous OD model, but also brought an end to the use of the khaki model. The olive drab service cap of 1912, like its dress counterpart, was to be stiffened in the front only, thereby giving it the outline that would continue for generations to come, including the famed "sixty mission crush" of World War I. The 1912 model also introduced features that remained standard through the early 1950s, a brown visor and brown chin strap rather than the black leather of the 1902-pattern.

The officer's olive drab service cap as it came to be in 1912, then was:

To be made of 13-ounce olive drab woolen material, of adopted standard, of same general design and pattern as the dress cap, par. 9, p. 7.

Badge.—Coat of arms of the United States in dull finish bronze metal, taking in half the upper part of mohair band and the lower

Front and side views of the enlisted olive drab 1902-pattern service cap. CF

A khaki 1902-pattern summer enlisted service cap. CF

1902-pattern khaki enlisted man's cap with subdued insignia of the pattern specified in 1905 for master electrician sergeants, electrician sergeants, and signal electricians. RB

part of front two quarters; to be attached to the front of cap by means of a means of a threaded post inserted in an eyelet.

Band.—To be olive drab mohair braid about 1 3/4 inches in width around entire cap.

Chin strap.—Russet leather, about 1/4 inch in width and 9 inches long, fastened at each end of visor with a regulation small bronze button.

Crown.—Front to be *stiffened* by means of haircloth stiffening inserted between the lining and front quarter; crown to slope to rear with stiffening.

Visor.—Top piece of russet leather, lined with embossed green hatter's leather; to be waterproof.

Two observations relative to this description of the cap prompt further comment. First of all, the buttons mentioned as holding the chin strap differed from early models in that the 1912-pattern had a raised

rim for both gilt and dull versions, whereas those first adopted in 1902 had no outer rim. As was true in 1902, all branches and ranks had the same buttons except for Engineer Corps officers, who continued with the special "essayons" button.

Another change instituted in 1912 was the new enlisted olive drab service cap, which essentially mirrored the officer's cap with the exception that it did not have a mohair band, and the insignia, rather than being the arms of the United States, continued to be the subdued cap devices adopted in 1904-5. This remained standard until 1917, when a bronze disk bearing the coat of arms of the United States was adopted for all enlisted personnel, regardless of branch, in keeping with the device long associated with officers.

A further note relative to enlisted personnel had to do with the full dress cap. This item likewise underwent a slight modification, in 1912, that followed the other caps in that only the front was to be stiffened

Another version of the 1902-pattern khaki enlisted man's cap, with higher crown and subdued insignia for master electrician sergeants, electrician sergeants, and signal electricians. RB

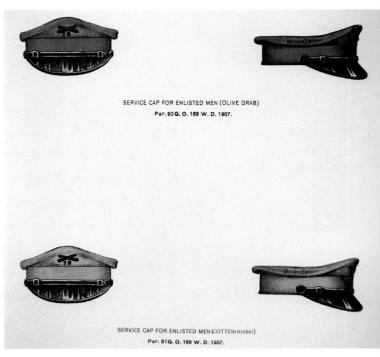

SERVICE CAP FOR ENLISTED MEN (OLIVE DRAB)
Par. 80 G. O. 169 W. D. 1907.

SERVICE CAP FOR ENLISTED MEN (COTTON KHAKI)
Par. 81 G. O. 169 W. D. 1907.

Official Quartermaster Department illustrations of the enlisted olive drab and cotton khaki 1902-pattern service caps with 1905 insignia for artillery. KC

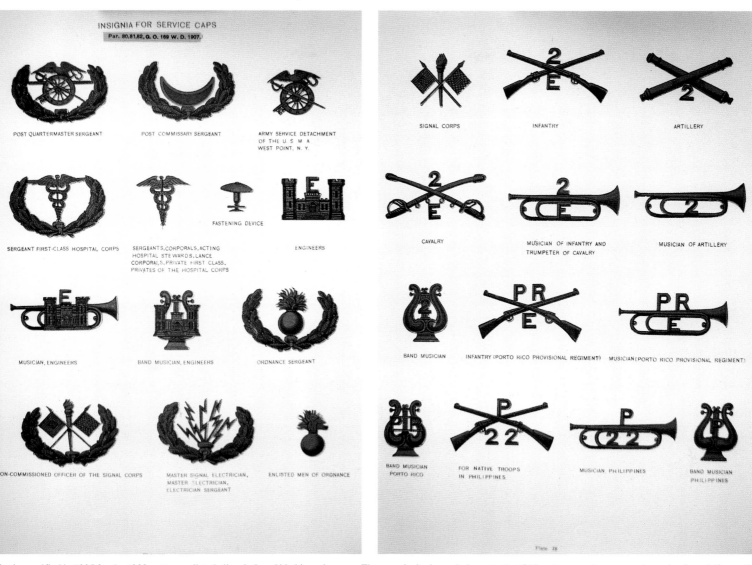

Insignia specified in 1905 for the 1902-pattern enlisted olive drab and khaki service caps. The same insignia carried over to the 1912-pattern service caps, and remained regulation until 1917. KC

rather than the entire crown. The measurement of the crown for all the 1912-pattern caps was different from their 1902-pattern counterparts, being fully one inch larger in diameter than the prior models.

This proved the same situation for the white service cap, which for all intents and purposes was identical in shape to the olive drab service cap. The cover continued to be of either white linen or cotton duck, and was removable to facilitate cleaning, rather than being permanently affixed to the cap, features which dated back to the 1902 regulations.[122]

Moreover, the visor remained black patent leather, not brown, although according to paragraph 11 of the *Regulations and Specifications...*, it too was to be lined with embossed green hatter's leather on the underside.

A removable gilt badge, once more the coat of arms, was retained too for officers as was the gold lace chin strap stitched to a 3/8 inch wide patent leather backing. Side buttons were gilt, and a white braid 1 3/4 inch band completed the officer's model.

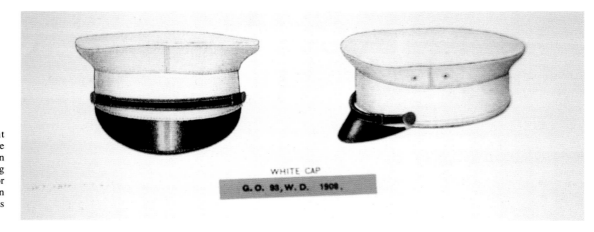

Official Quartermaster Department illustration of the 1902-pattern enlisted white summer cap. These were designed to be worn by medical personnel and recruiting personnel, but no provision was made for insignia, the cap being designed to be worn with the black chin strap and side buttons only. KC

In this group portrait of heavy artillery enlisted men at Ft. Totten, New York, non-commissioned officers, and officers appear in a range of 1902-pattern headgear. This includes the white summer service cap on the two officers in the center of the men, as well as campaign hats and full dress and dress enlisted caps. USA

Left side of the 1902-pattern service (campaign) hat with its star-pattern perforated ventilation and circular fur-felt reinforced eyelet, one appearing "on each side for fastening a strap or cord" to help retain the headgear in place. Note the brim was turned over, much like the 1876-pattern black campaign hat, rather than just stitched, as were the drab 1883, 1889, and 1899-pattern hats. SHSW

Captain H. Reeve, of the Third U.S. Infantry wears the 1902-pattern campaign hat with the black and gold intermixed hat cord that could trace it lineage to the pre-Civil War era. His campaign hat deviates from the standard pattern in that there are a pair of small grommets on the side of the crown rather than the perforated five-pointed star. NA

The enlisted pattern had no braid, and had a black leather chin strap of the type which was found on the full dress cap. This enlisted headgear saw limited use, however, in that after 1907 only Hospital Corps personnel and members of the General Recruiting Service were permitted to wear the white uniform. For enlisted men the hat supposedly was to be devoid of insignia, but the small rimmed side buttons adopted in 1912 were to be in place for both enlisted and officers' models to hold the chin strap.

Even as the white cap began to wane for enlisted men, so did the summer helmet. For instance, according to GO No. 197, Adjutant General's Office, January 1, 1904, the khaki helmet was to be worn in lieu of the service cap from May 1 to September 30 in the Department of the Gulf and the Department of Texas, and from June 1 to September 30 in all other posts within the Continental United States. The order went on to state that this would continue "until the supply is exhausted." Thereafter, both the khaki and white helmets soon began to be phased out as supplies dwindled, and no new contracts were let to replenish them. Even then, the final days of the khaki helmet were played out overseas, especially in the Philippines.[123]

Nineteenth century cork helmets were about to give way to a more durable type of headgear, one with a very different function. Indeed, by

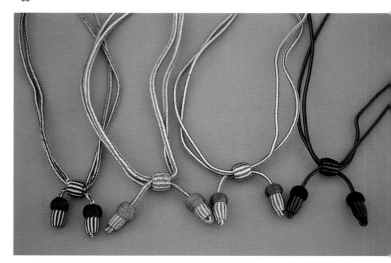

Examples of some of the enlisted hat cords for the 1902-pattern campaign hat from left to right: Hospital Corps; Signal Corps; Corps of Engineers; Ordnance Department. Scarlet remained regulation for artillerymen, yellow for cavalry troopers, blue for infantry soldiers, cadet gray for commissary sergeants, and buff for post quartermaster sergeants as well as the Army Service Detachment of the U.S. Military Academy. GL

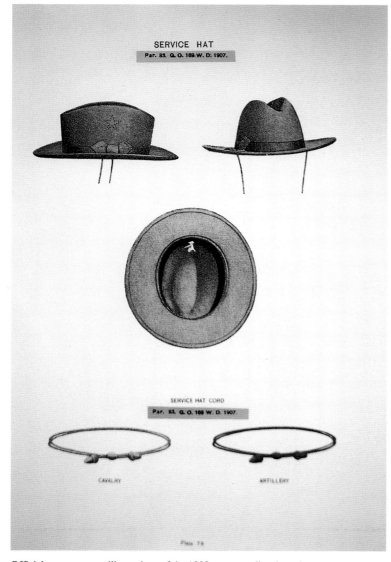

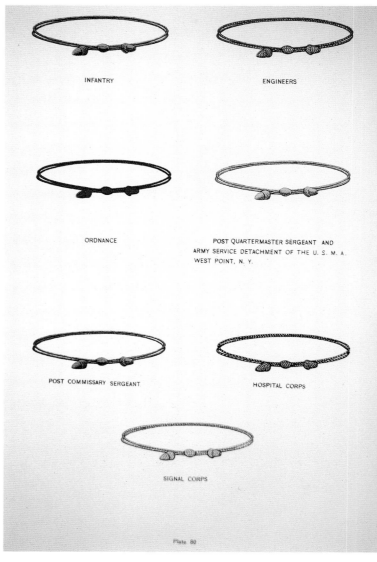

Official quartermaster illustrations of the 1902-pattern enlisted service hat with the cords for cavalry and artillery depicted. Note the tie string that was attached directly to the hat, a feature that was new to this piece of headgear. KC

1917, new concerns prompted U.S. Army officials to seek a helmet that rather than provide comfort against a tropical sun, instead was to protect the soldier from the enemy's lethal ordnance. As the American Expeditionary Force threw its hat into the ring to join in the fierce fighting of World War I, a new era dawned in the history of U.S. military. Headgear types soon changed after the arrival of the Yanks on the Western Front, but that story is better left to another telling.

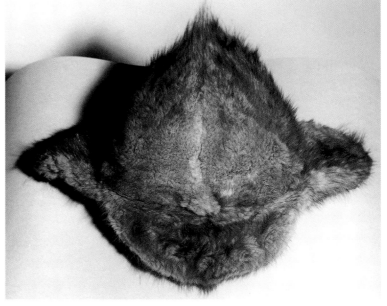

The Engineer Corps 1902-pattern hat cord consisted of red and white striping including on the slide and end of the acorn tassels, while the Indian scout cord had a white background intermixed with scarlet and a slide of scarlet. The tassels were flecked red and white. It is possible that this type of cord was adopted as early as 1899 for scouts, although this is speculation. The only specific mention of insignia for campaign hats worn by scouts was the dull bronze letters "U.S.S." for United States Scouts, although elsewhere regulations called for hat cords "conforming in color to that of the corps, department, or arm of the service; to be sewed fast to the hat." KC

A non-regulation company and regimental insignia for the enlisted 1902-pattern campaign hat. Such devices sometimes were made up for units, presumably as an initiative at the company, or troop level, and then purchased by the men in lieu of their issue insignia. JB

Front with flaps down and olive drab wool lining of an early twentieth century fur cap with contract label indicating the cap was procured from E.H. Taggart of Philadelphia on August 16, 1906. USCM

The enlisted 1902-pattern fur cap, full dress and dress cap, and campaign hat all are evident in this image taken by soldier-photographer Christian Barthelmess. All the men depicted here are with the Sixth U.S. Cavalry as they model the uniform that was ushered in by GO No. 132 in December 1902. CBF

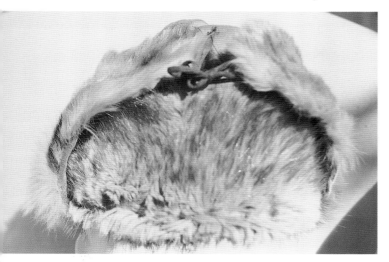

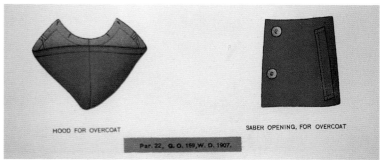

The olive drab overcoats adopted for officers and enlisted men at the end of 1902 had detachable cloth hoods to provide the wearer with extra protection against the cold and precipitation. GL

The fur cap issued early in the twentieth century was similar in many respects to the one first specified in 1879, as can be seen in this front view of one such cap. KC

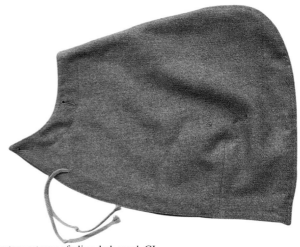

The interior of the 1902-pattern winter hood was lined in a light weight olive drab cloth while the outer part was of olive drab wool. GL

1   The hat would be replaced by a helmet that followed a pattern submitted by Captain Jonathan Rodgers. The Quartermaster Department had to be prepared to have these produced and distributed by July 1, 1881. M.C. Meigs to D.H. Rucker, January 9, 1881, LS, Clothing Br., 1881, Book A, OQMG, RG92, NA.

2   M.C. Meigs to J.F. Rodgers, January 17, 1881, ibid.

3   Ibid.

4   Ibid.

5   The forgoing text omits many details about the 1881-pattern helmet, particularly in regards to the numerous variations for officers. While additional information is treated in the captions accompanying illustrations, for a more satisfying discourse on this type of headgear the reader should delve into Gordon Chappell's excellent monograph, *Brass Spikes and Horsetail Plumes.*

6   *ARSW, 1882,* Vol. I, 303, noted that this action took place as of February 7, 1882. Prior to that time, the older pattern dress headgear continued in use. For instance, an order for thirty infantry pompons was filled for troops at Columbus Barracks, as just one indication that the helmet would take time to reach the troops as a replacement for the dismounted dress cap. Colonel S. Holabird to Captain A. Barrett, April 8, 1881, LS, Clothing Br., OQMG, RG92, NA. In a similar instance the Department of Texas' annual estimate for uniform items and clothing included among other things 114 eagles for the 1872-pattern enlisted caps as well as 10 crescents, 4 wreaths, 7 each white letters US, 2 shell and flames, 3138 crossed rifles, and all brass numbers and letters. These trimmings indicated there was at least limited issue of the old caps. As important, however, the projections likewise called for 8 hospital steward helmets, 7 commissary sergeants, 5 ordnance, 28 light artillery, 1,955 infantry and 590 cavalry helmets complete, which were to be supplied for the department through the Philadelphia Depot. M.C. Meigs to Chief Military Quartermaster of the Missouri June 6, 1881, ibid. Not all the old caps and pompons were to be sold, though. A small quantity were to be retained and supplied to the National Home for Disabled Volunteers. M.C. Meigs to Captain John Livers, August 15, 1881, ibid. The same letter indicated that cords and tassels would not be disposed of because these were intended for issue with campaign hats.

7   S.B. Holabird to Acting Assistant Quartermaster, Frankfort Arsenal, PA, May 28, 1881, ibid.

8   M.C. Meigs to J.F. Rodgers, January 17, 1881, ibid.

9   S.B. Holabird to Acting Assistant Quartermaster, Frankfort Arsenal, PA, May 28, 1881, ibid.

10   Chappell, *Brass Spikes and Horsetail Plumes,* 34.

11   M.C. Meigs to Secretary of War, April 5, 1881, LS, Clothing Br., OQMG, RG92, NA. Earlier all the serviceable helmets from the depots and posts in the Military Divisions of the Pacific and of the Missouri were recalled "in order that they may be altered and conform to the new pattern." M.C. Meigs to the Chief Quartermasters of the Military Division of the Missouri and the Chief Quartermaster of the Military Division of the Pacific, March 4, 1881, ibid.

12   Underestimation of the cost of converting the old pattern helmet "to conform to the new style" resulted in the need for approval of a higher budget, which was granted at a price not to exceed $.54 cents each or $6.50 per dozen. M.C. Meigs to D.H. Rucker, May 12, 1881, ibid.

13   One such indication of the continued issue of the old pattern is found in a directive to the military storekeeper at Philadelphia to: "Send to San Francisco depot 1,800 cavalry helmets complete, 100 light artillery helmets complete...." S.B. Holabird to J.F. Rodgers, April 19, 1881, ibid.

14   S.B. Holabird to Pettibone Mfr., January 19, 1881, ibid.

15   Constantine Chase to Commanding General of the Army, February 2, 1881, as reprinted in ibid. Captain Chase's letter contained a sketch of the cruciform base, which Meigs indicated was in fact different from the ornament for field grade and mounted helmets. He additionally stated: "The model adopted by the General of the Army for foot officers has the top piece sketched by Captain Chase." M.C. Meigs to Jonathan Tidball, Headquarters of the Army, February 4, 1881, ibid.

16   M.C. Meigs to Headquarters of the Army, February 4,1881, ibid.

17   These specifications were adopted on March 25, 1881, according to, *ARSW, 1881,* Vol. I, 304. In early January Meigs had directed that the specifications for trimmings and helmets be drawn up. He likewise underscored that he wanted the dies to be cut

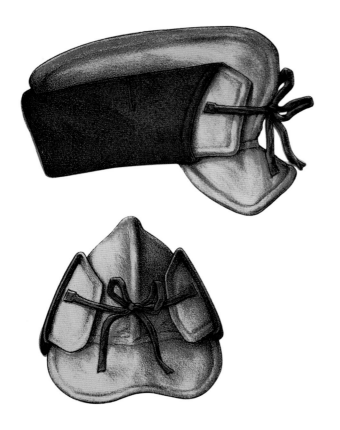

The 1902-pattern winter field cap was just one cold weather piece of headgear. It was lined with olive drab wool while the body was canvas. The basic pattern remained in use with few changes into early World War II. KC

The 1902 regulation sanctioned "black lynx-skin shakos with plume and tassel of color of the corps or arm of service, and leather chin straps with brass scales and side buttons" for full dress wear by drum majors. Those for cavalry were "to be of smaller dimensions than those of other arms." KC

well for the insignia. M.C. Meigs to D.H Rucker, January 9, 1881, LS, Clothing Br., OQMG, RG92, NA.

[18] *ARSW, 1882*, Vol.I, 320-23.
[19] Adopted on September 23, 1882, ibid., 323.
[20] C. Meigs to Major R. Batchholder April 14, 1881, LS, Clothing Br., OQMG, RG92, NA. This same letter went to all the other depots as well. Nearly a month later Meigs wanted to know how much the devices cost for the staff corps. M.C. Meigs to J.F. Rodgers, May 13, 1881, ibid.

[21] M.C. Meigs to D.H. Rucker, February 12, 1881, ibid.
[22] Ibid. In the same letter, Meigs once more called for a wider brim on the summer helmet, as he did in a prior communication.
[23] M.C. Meigs to D.H. Rucker, February 19, 1881, Book A, 1881, ibid.
[24] M.C. Meigs to Inspector General of the Army, January 31, 1881, ibid. Starkey came to Horstmann from London, and also was credited with designing the white helmet that officers and enlisted men of the U.S. Marine Corps were to begin using on July 1, 1881. "These helmets, for officers, are to be covered with white cloth, and for the

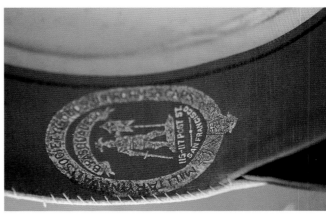

Side and interior views of the 1912-pattern officer's summer white service cap with removable cover belonging to Captain William H. Paine. Specifications for service caps of the 1912 pattern changed, with the profile sloping to the rear, a basic outline that continues on U.S. Army headgear to present times. JB

912-pattern officer's white summer service cap. Khaki and olive drab versions were in use as well, all with mohair bands which matched the color of the top of the cap. SWHS

912-pattern general officer's full dress and dress cap. SWHS

Front and side views of a 1912-pattern infantry company grade officers' full dress/dress cap. The buttons prescribed in that year were to have an outer rim, whereas those adopted in 1902 did not have the raised rim. DB

men, with white drill-ornaments and trimmings being made so as to be transferable." *A&NJ*, March 5, 1881, 635. Essentially, these helmets were the same as worn by the U.S. Army at the time.

[25] M.C. Meigs to D.H. Rucker, February 19, 1881, LS, Clothing Br., Book A, 1881, OQMG, RG92, NA. Just the day before Meigs had been less than enthusiastic about drawings for the eagle plate, which he described as "pretty good" but "the scroll has the defect complained about of being attached to wings so it can't be bent to fit the convex surface of the helmet." He wanted this corrected, along with pointing out that the lock of the rifles for the infantry plate looked more like a Winchester than the Springfield, and even at that, the lock was on the wrong side of the stock for one of the rifles depicted. Similarly, one of the sabers on the cavalry model had an incorrect left hand guard. M.C. Meigs to J.F. Rodgers, February 18, 1881, ibid.

[26] S.B. Holabird to D.H. Rucker, March 9, 1881, ibid.

[27] S.B. Holabird to J.F. Rodgers, March 9, 1881, ibid. This is a separate letter than the one sent on the same day by Holabird to Rodgers, thereby indicating the priority that the helmet had assumed.

[28] M.C. Meigs to J.F. Rodgers, April 6, 1881, ibid.

[29] S.B. Holabird to D.H. Rucker, April 19, 1881, ibid., asked when would the fifty "prototypes of the standard helmets" be available for distribution to the chief quarter masters of the military divisions as samples.

ABOVE: 1912-pattern Engineer Corps company grade officers' full dress/dress cap worn by Second Lieutenant Samuel Reigh Photograph by Gordon Chappell.

Front and side views of a 1902-pattern cavalry company grade officer's full dress cap (left), and a field grade cavalry officer's 1912-pattern full dress cap. Photograph by Gordon Chappell

A quartermaster captain in the 1912 officers' full dress/dress cap. The band was buff. KC.

Blue denin caps with white stitching had been adopted as early as 1904 for harbor boat service personnel, and some five years later for coast artillery troops. The basic design remained in service until early World War II. JP

30   This request also included visits to establishments where campaign hats, arctic over shoes, woolen flannel, and kersey, were being made. M.C. Meigs to Adjutant General, June 4, 1881, ibid.

31   M.C. Meigs to Capt J. Rodgers, March 29, 1881, ibid. Apparently these were reproduced as collotypes, bound with handwritten captions in red ink, and the "publication" given the title of *Standard Helmets and Trimmings.*

32   M.C. Meigs to Lieutenant George W. Spencer, April 22, 1881, ibid.

33   In addition to the "16,000 helmets untrimmed" priced at $1.69 each, Raymold & Whitlock of New York was given the contract for the original 16,000 helmet top pieces and spikes at $.09 each, while 16,000 helmet eagles at $.05 5/8, along with the award for 34,000 helmet side buttons at 5/8 cents each, and 16,000 white metal numbers at $.90 cents per hundred for singles and $1.80 for double numbers, all went to Horstmann Bros. & Co. of Philadelphia as did a contract for 25,000 1872-pattern forage caps at $.57 7/8 cents each. At the same time a purchase of 13,000 campaign hats was made with C.H. Tenney Co. New York furnishing these at $.69 each. M.C Meigs to D.H. Rucker April 28, 1881, ibid. Indicative of effort to supply the helmet to the field sometime during the summer, orders were being shipped to places such as Watertown Arsenal by mid-August. S.B. Holabird to J.F. Rodgers, August 17, 1881 ibid.

34   Chappell, *Brass Spikes and Horsetail Plumes*, 31 and 34. Further, according to ibid. 34, between July 1, 1881 and June 30, 1882 (fiscal year 1881) the Quartermaster Department had bought 36,680 helmet plates, 71,900 side buttons, 22.074 spike and oak leaf bases, 58,663 German silver numbers, and 2,500 staff corps overlays, but no new plume sockets or scrolls and rings, as further indication of the continued issuance of the 1872-pattern stocks of these trimmings.

35   See for example line drawings published as plates 1 through 3, in *ARSW, 1884*, Vol I, versus specifications found in, *U.S. Army Uniforms and Equipment, 1889* (Lincoln University of Nebraska Press, 1986), 292, and 345-6.

36   *ARSW, 1888*, Vol. I, 529.

37   Chappell, *Brass Spikes and Horsetail Plumes*, 92, provides an excellent illustration depicting the subtle change of the helmet's profile from 1872 through 1902. Moreover, ibid., 96-7, publishes a list of the many contracts that the Quartermaster Department had administered for the 1881-pattern enlisted helmet.

38   On October 3, 1884, the quartermaster general sent a circular letter to artillery, cavalry, and infantry regiments relative to opinions about band uniforms. Replies to this document are found in CCF, Box 1171, OQMG, RG92, NA. Many of the respondents desired the mounted helmets, even for foot bandsmen.

39   GO No. 104, HQA, October 3, 1885. It is interesting to note that GO No. 113, HQA October 31, 1885, required a helmet plate with "two crossed signal flags and a burning torch" for Signal Corps officers, in keeping with the new overlay for enlisted men of that organization that had been adopted by GO No. 77, HQA, July 13, 1885. The design for officers' plates can be traced to a memorandum dated May 9, 1884, in the office of the chief of the Signal Corps, which carried a drawing of the plate with torch for officers that was allowed by GO No. 113. Prior to that time it is unknown as to

Front and side views of the 1902 enlisted full dress cap (left) and the 1912 enlisted full dress cap (right) made under a May 24, 191. contract with A. Susskind Co.), both for cavalry troopers. Caps for enlisted men in other branches were identical except that the detachable bands were made of facing material in the color of the respective branch department, or corps, including in green for the Army Service School Detachment as of 1909, when a special large gilt disk with a cogged wheel surrounding a hammer and quill was adopted under GO No. 116, War Department, June 15, 1909, as the full dress and dress cap insignia. The other branches and arms continued to wear the insignia authorized in 1905. JB

1912-pattern enlisted olive drab service cap, with 1905-pattern enlisted field artillery insignia. RB

whether officers' plates had only crossed flags, or whether the few second lieutenants commissioned in the Signal Service had retained the chapeau in lieu of the helmet, despite regulations to the contrary as of 1881.

[40] GO No. 56, HQA, August 11, 1887, which likewise created the Hospital Corps, adding enlisted ranks beyond hospital stewards.

[41] It also should be noted that a pair of fine wires soldered to the back of the side buttons had been used to attach these trimmings to the helmet shell, but as of 1885 more stout strips of sheet brass were adopted that would be less likely to break. Chappell, B*rass Spikes and Horsetail Plumes*, 54.

[42] *ARSW, 1887*, Vol. I, 512. According to ibid., 1889, 649, "all the [cavalry] cords on hand in the general depots of the Quartermaster Department have been sent to the Philadelphia depot and redyed at a small expense."

[43] *Regulations of the United States Army, 1889* (Washington, DC: Government Printing Office, 1889), 209-10. The new Signal Service uniform as set forth in the 1889 regulations had been established by GO No. 18, HQA, February 16, 1889.

[44] GO No. 74, HQA, August 20, 1891. Side buttons for the 1891 helmet were to have the torch as well as crossed flags. The overlay was the same, but it seems the flags were more square in shape rather than the flowing design of 1881 and 1885. For more on this helmet consult, Chappell, *Brass Spikes and Horsetail Plumes*, 55-6.

[45] GO No. 86, WD, December 3, 1878 had authorized a forage cap badge for Signal Service officers, which may have been crossed flags within a wreath, according to, Leon W. Laframboise, *History of the Combat Support Branches Branch of Service Insignia* (Steeleville, MO: Watson Publishing Com., 1977), 200-1.

[46] *ARSW, 1882*, Vol. I, 298, noted that the chief signal officer had not apporved the use of crossed flags on the forage cap or the collar of the 1872-pattern dress coat, "hence the Signal Service is the only arm of the service without any badge on the garments referred to." Conversely, this same source indicated hospital stewards were to wear the caduceus within a wreath as their forage cap badge, and the caduceus on either side of the dress coat collar.

[47] There is some question whether the wavy flags were issued, although Lafromboise, *History of Combat Support Services*, 204, illustrates an example. Because many items in this source are replicas, it is unclear whether this is an actual specimen or one made for the author's collection.

[48] *ARSW, 1881*, Vol. I, 323.

[49] T.J. Sperry, "1872 Insignia Expedient Attachment Devices," XLI *Military Collector and Historian* No. 1 (Spring 1989): 43-5, offers example of this practice.

[50] Captain John Mendenhall to Chief Quartermaster Department of California, January 21, 1876, LR, OQMG, RG92, NA.

1902-pattern officers' winter olive drab service cap (left) and 1912-pattern officers' winter olive drab service cap (right), front and side views. In both cases, the mohair band was one of the chief distinctions between caps for officers and those for enlisted personnel whose caps did not have trim. Photograph by Gordon Chappell.

51 J.D. Bingham to Captain A.W. Corliss, April 9, 1877, ibid.

52 Ibid., and J.D. Bingham to D.H. Rucker, March 9, 1877, ibid. In another exchange, a like-minded officer was told his scheme to improve the fastening of cap insignia was also too costly. M.C. Meigs to Lieutenant R.D. Potts, March 8, 1877, ibid. Nearly a decade after these exchanges, quartermaster officials acknowledged "the well known fact that the cap ornaments now furnished are of necessity quite frail in their construction, especially in the back, where the loops are soldered to the body." Consequently, the insignia broke easily causing "some enlisted men" to resort "to various methods to fasten the letters and numbers to their devices, so as to avoid breakage in cleaning and fastening them to the cap." In reaction, the Quartermaster Department studied "this subject," and conducted experiments "to improve the ornaments without being compelled to provide a special die for each company of the service—quite a heavy expenditure."

53 *U.S. Army Uniforms and Equipment, 1889,* 345-58, published the descriptions and line drawings of helmet and forage cap ornaments and insignia as they had come to be by that date. Also see Quartermaster Specification No. 318, March 10, 1892, for a slightly later version of the enlisted cap insignia.

54 S.B. Holabird to M.I. Ludington, October 28, 1885, LS, Clothing Br., OQMG, RG92, NA.

55 Quartermaster Specification No. 143, April 3, 1885.

56 Quartermaster Specification No. 171, April 15, 1886.

57 *U.S. Army Uniforms and Equipment, 1889,* 227.

58 See for instance, Quartermaster Specification No. 324, April 12, 1892.

59 Howell, *United States Army Headgear, 1855-1902,* 83-4.

60 LR, March 12, 1895, File No. 2138, Secretary of War, RG 107; and LR, April 22, File No. C.L./62931, OQMG, RG92, NA.

61 GO No. 22, HQA, April 12, 1895.

62 Howell, *United States Army Headgear, 1855-1902,* 84; and GO No. 37, WD, June 12, 1897.

63 *ARSW, 1897,* Vol. I, 5.

64 GO No. 80, HQA, April 24, 1899, not only introduced the master electrician sergeant forage cap badge, but also many other uniform items for these specialists, including a German silver forked lighting overlay for the spiked helmet plate and brass side buttons with this same motif for the dress helmet. In turn, GO No. 14, HQA, February 12, 1900, created the enlisted service detachment at the U.S. Military Academy who previously wore the enlisted uniform of engineers. In 1900, however, they were to don a uniform that was similar in most respect to those issued to post quartermaster sergeants, including a spiked helmet quill and key overlay and side buttons. The cap badge, however, differed in that the letters "QMD" replaced the quill and key.

65 General Orders No. 37, HQA, August 13, 1896.

66 William Emerson, "U.S. Enlisted Cap Insignia 1905-1918," XXIX *Military Collector and Historian* No. 1 (Spring 1977): 23. Larry H. Addington, "The U.S. Coast Artillery and the Problem of Artillery Organization, 1907-1954," LX *Military Affairs* No. 1 (February 1976): 1-16, provides background for the various reorganizations of the artillery.

67 William K. Emerson, "US Army Enlisted Campaign Hat Insignia 1809-1907" XXIX *Military Collector and Historian* No. 4 (Winter 1977): 158-9.

68 William K. Emerson, U.S. Army Enlisted Cap Insignia, 1896-1905," XXIV *Military Collector and Historian* No. 1 (Spring 1972): 11 and 13. See also, Quartermaster Specification No. 594, January 22, 1903, for the status of all enlisted cap ornaments of the period.

69 *ARSW, 1882,* Vol. I, 299.

70 John P. Langellier, *Redlegs: The U.S. Artillery from the Civil War to the Spanish-American War, 1861-1898* (London: Greenhill Books, 1998), 57, reproduces a photograph of the officers attending the artillery school in 1884, most of whom have added white cloth covers over their standard chasseur forage caps. U.S Navy Ensign James H. Oliver is the only non-U.S. Army man among the group, but he too has donned the white cap cover. Further, Howell, *U.S. Army Headgear, 1855-1902,* 87, points out permission being given for white cap covers at both Fort Monroe and Key West in 1896. There are extant examples of white cap covers from the Manhattan Supply Company with a September 14, 1894 contract date as well. These are made for the 1872 through 1895 chasseur type caps, however, and it is unknown whether these were ordered for use by the U.S. Army or militiamen instead.

71 Christopher Wilkinson-Latham, *The Indian Mutiny* (London: Osprey Publishing, 1977), 33-5, 37, 39, and plates B, C, E, F, and H, all address the use of cap covers, often with a "neck curtain," which was in vogue for some British force on the Sub continent during the 1850s.

72 GO No. 39, HQA, April 2, 1900.

73 René Chartrand, "Canadian Volunteer Infantry, c. 1863-1870," XXXVII *Military Collector and Historian* No. 1 (Spring 1985): 25-36, also provides ample evidence of another North American military force who found the English pillbox cap worth emulating, including the Northwest Mounted Police. Not surprisingly, the Canadians added this style to their regulation kit, while their neighbors in the United States only unofficially did so on an individual, limited basis.

74 Howard Michael Madaus, "Dating the Earliest Use of the 'Pillbox Cap' in the United States Army" XXXII *Military Collector and Historian* No. 4 (Winter 1980): 177-9, indicates that the cap was being worn toward the end of the Civil War by a few soldiers serving in volunteer units, and cites three c. 1865 photographs that point to this conclusion. In fact, the cap seems to have been introduced even earlier, at least on a limited basis. See for instance, Anon. "Michael Bremer's Ante-bellum Daguerreotypes," I *Military Images* No. 3 (November-December 1979): 23, for an image of a medical officer taken between 1859 and 1861. Also, it is noteworthy that this style

The "Montana Peak" was adopted as official field wear in 1911. By the following year specifications were written and the hat began to be worn by officers and men alike, gradually replacing the earlier pattern. While insignia no longer was prescribed for the campaign hat, cords remained regulation. These designated the wearer's branch, as in this case where scarlet worsted cords indicated an artilleryman. The other colors were those established in 1902, to wit: yellow for cavalry; light blue for infantry; maroon and white for Hospital Corps; orange and white for Signal Corps; scarlet and white for Engineer Corps; gray for commissary sergeants; buff for quartermaster sergeants; scarlet intertwined with black for Ordnance Corps; and as of 1910, green for Army Service School Detachment personnel and green and white for the Army School Detachment, U.S. Military Academy Officers' cords continued to be gold and black intermixed for all save general officers who in turn sported gold cords. GL

was adopted as the undress cap for U.S. Marine Corps officers, as part of the 1875 uniform regulations, but no such official status was granted to U.S. Army personnel

75 Gordon Chappell, "The 'Pillbox' Cap in the United States Army c. 1866-1902," XXXII *Military Collector and Historian No. 1* (Spring 1980): 5. For a useful summary of this non-regulation style of headgear see, ibid., 4-15.

76 Quartermaster Specification No. 175, June 22, 1886, and *ARSW, 1886,* Vol. I, 505-6.

77 Ibid, 1887, 213, and GO No. 48, HQA, July 6, 1887.

78 Per GO No. 81, HQA, July 17, 1902, and GO 132, HQA, December 31, 1902.

79 GO No. 132, HQA, December 31, 1902.

80 Ibid. This order only mentions the hood for officers, but it in fact formed part of the enlisted outfit as well, once the new olive drab overcoats replaced the old light blue kersey patterns, early in the twentieth century.

81 Inspection Report, March 15, 1882, LS, Clothing, OQMG, RG92, NA.

82 J.C. Rodgers to Depot Quartermaster, April 29, 1882, CCF (Hats), ibid. It is interesting that eyelet concept was resurrected with the adoption of 1911-pattern "Montana Peak", a campaign hat discussed later in this chapter.

83 R. Ingalls to Secretary of War, July 18, 1882; and R. Ingalls to S.B. Holabird, July 17, 1882, LS, Clothing Br., Book B, 1882, ibid.

84 See for instance, CCF (hats), ibid.; S.B. Holabird to Secretary of War, October 18, 1883; and S.B. Holabird to M.I. Ludington, October 18, 1883, both in LS, Clothing Br., Book B, 1883, ibid.; *ARSW, 1883,* Vol. I, 56; and ibid., 1884, 311.

85 M.I. Ludington to S.B. Holabird, October 24, 1883; and November 17, 1883, LS, Clothing Br., Book B, 1883, OQMG, RG92, NA. The second letter required two hundred of the hats with larger ventilators to be shipped to the depot at San Francisco presumably for issue to troops in Arizona.

86 S.B. Holabird, Endorsement 8 to Adjutant General, USA, October 28, 1885, "Endorsements on report of trial of Drab Colored hats made by Lieut. Frank West, Troop 'I' 6th Cavalry, Fort McDowell, A.T., Aug. 31, 1883," Book B, 1885, ibid. The 9th endorsement was the secretary of war's approval to adopt the drab hat. The same series of correspondence noted: "Samples of those [drab hats] sent out for trial, and also of the present standard all wool black hat are submitted herewith."

87 For contracts to procure the 1883-pattern drab hat consult, Howell, *United States Army Headgear, 1855-1902,* 90. In spite of drab hats being in the majority, it should be noted that as late as the third edition (dated May 1, 1899) of *Regulations and Decisions Pertaining to the Uniform of the Army of the United States* (Washington, DC: Government Printing Office, 1899), paragraph 12, officers were permitted either a drab or a black campaign hat, except chaplains, who continued to be restricted to black ones only, through the early twentieth century. Paragraph 46 of this same document allowed straw hats during the warm season (if prescribed by the departmental commander), and required that "the color" of campaign hats was "to be uniform for both officers and enlisted men in each troop, battery, or company." Previously, according to GO No. 72, WD, AGO, December 2, 1887, officers were to wear only the "black felt" campaign hat, but in practice usually donned the drab model. In turn, the same general order set forth enlisted hats as either: "Of black or drab-colored felt, according to pattern in the office of the Quartermaster General; to be worn in garrison only on target practice, fatigue duty, and on marches and campaigns; the color to be uniform in each troop, battery, or company."

Troopers Goodniss and Simons of Company M. Tenth U.S. Cavalry donned the 1911-pattern campaign hat for this photograph taken soon after the issue of this type of headgear replaced the previous model. UKL

88 -7; 371; and ibid., 1885, 282. Some hats were obtained in 1883, and a limited number in a second lot during 1884, from William H. Hurlbut of New York, at cost ranging from $1.75 to $1.89 each. A larger quantity brought the price down to $1.67, when Raymold & Whitlock, a firm that had supplied dress helmets, delivered 8007 hats in 1884. Howell, *United States Army Headgear, 1855-1902*, 60.

89 As indicated previously according to *ARSW, 1888*, Vol. I, 529, new specifications had been drawn up in 1888 for campaign hats, helmets, and forage caps, all of which differed in a number of respects from previous ones.

90 A few minor changes in the specifications for the 1889-pattern hat point to the exhausting of the previous style early in the 1890s. One of the changes, prescribed in 1895, had to do with decreasing the weight of the 1889-pattern to 3 3/4 ounces, as called for by Quartermaster Specification No. 366, August 13, 1895. The other alteration came two years later, when the sweat band was to be turned over inch and attached to a thin strip of oiled silk (about inch) that was welted between the sweat band and the hat itself. Quartermaster Specification No. 426, March 11, 1897.

91 *ARSW, 1886*, Vol. I, 505.

92 Circular No. 10, War Department, August 15, 1890, introduced the Indian Scout uniform, including the hat, cords, and insignia as described above. Jacques Noel Jacobsen, Jr., "The Uniform of the Indian Scouts," XXVI *Military Collector and Historian* No. 3 (Fall 1974): 136-43, provides additional information on the subject. Also note that the Indian Scouts were to have a helmet with red and white cords and bands, a horse hair plume that was longer than the one for all other mounted troops, and a crossed German silver arrows overlay for the plate along with crossed arrow motif side buttons. It appears that few of these helmets ever were issued, however, although considerable quantities of all the components were produced.

93 Specification 318, March 10, 1892, set forth details on the construction of this insignia.

94 For example, M.C. Meigs to J.W. Sully, March 13, 1874, LS, C&E Br., Book A, 1874, OQMG, RG92, NA, instructed Ft. Rice's commanding officer to sell all the post's war stock at auction, except for the hat cords which could be worn with the folding campaign hat.

95 Howell, *U.S. Army Headgear, 1855-1902*, 62. As an example, as of June 30, 1882, there were 177,361 hat cords and tassels on hand, of which only 262 had been issued during the prior twelve months. Because of the relatively limited interest in the articles, 147,763 of them had been sold at auction during fiscal year 1882. *ARSW, 1882*, Vol. I, 306. As further evidence of the continuing numbers of these cords, by the end of June 1887 some 32,855 remained on the rolls. Ibid., 1888, Vol. I, 722.

96 In the mid-1870s pattern sample cords for ordnance enlisted men, hospital stewards, cavalrymen, artillerymen, infantrymen, and commissary sergeants were on hand, but no mention of cords for signal corpsmen or engineers were included in the inventory, making it appear that cords were not supplied to men in these organizations. M.C. Meigs to L.C. Easton, April 15, 1875, Book A, 1875, Clothing Br., OQMG, RG92, NA. No cords for Signal Corps enlisted men were mentioned. It would seem that the orange cords that formally had been issued to dragoons through the 1860s would be a logical choice, but perhaps all these had been disposed of at surplus sales or dispersed to troops during the early part of the Civil War.

97 rcular No. 2, HQA, February 25, 1887.

98 Leroy E. Ross, Jr. and William K. Emerson, "Hat Cords of the U.S. Army," XXVII *Military Collector and Historian* No. 4 (Winter 1976): 148. This article points out that it was not made clear until 1912 whether the slide and the acorns for officers below the grade of brigadier general would be intermixed or solid.

99 John Bigelow, Jr., *Reminiscences of the Santiago Campaign* (New York: Harper and Brothers, 1899), 42.

100 *Annual Report of the War Department, 1899*, Vol. I, (Washington, DC: Government Printing Office, 1899), 478.

101 Howell, *United States Army Headgear, 1855-1902*, 61.

102 Ibid., 61.

103 Philip M. Cavanaugh, "Non-Regulation U.S. Officer's Straw Hat, 1898," XXV *Military Collector and Historian* No. 2 (Summer 1973): 86, illustrates a hat of tightly woven straw with a cloth blue pugree style band and a gold bullion arms of the U.S. similar to the one embroidered on the front of the 1895-pattern officer's forage cap. An officer's hat cord was also worn with this headpiece that belonged to Captain Matthew Batson, a Fourth U.S. Cavalry officer who organized the "Macebebe Scouts" in the Philippines in 1898. According to this source: "Such straw hats were well known to troops serving in the Philippines...." In fact, a nearly identical example, but without the band, cords, and eagle, was found in the former Presidio Army Museum, which during the period served as a medical facility at the Presidio of San Francisco.

104 *ARSW, 1888*, Vol. I, 721.

105 Ibid., 721-2.

106 Quartermaster General Specification 470, July 19, 1899.

107 Quartermaster General Specification 476, September 12, 1899, and GO No. 168, HQA, AGO, September 14, 1899.

108 Quartermaster General Specification 689, November 17, 1902; GO No. 81, HQA, AGO, July 17, 1902; and GO No. 132, HQA, AGO, December 31, 1902.

109 Quartermaster General Specification 924, January 20, 1908, and GO No. 39, WD, March 10, 1910.

110 These were to be distinct symbols such as a figure eight for the Eighth Corps, in red for the first division of the corps; white for the second; and blue for the third. Moreover, "Officers and enlisted men belonging to a corps and not attached to a division will wear the corps symbol in red, bordered in white one-sixteenth of an inch and edged in blue one-thirty-second of an inch." GO No. 99, WD, July 15, 1898. According to Circular No. 60, HQA, November 19, 1898, only one badge could be worn at a

time. This restriction came as a result of some soldiers retaining the badges of one unit when they transferred to another, thereby defeating "the object of their use."

111 Letter from Commander, Second Cavalry to Adjutant General's Office, January 29, 1899, File Copy, U.S. Army Institute of Heraldry.

112 Fourth Endorsement from Quartermaster General, April 5, 1899, ibid.

113 *Annual Report of the War Department, 1899*, Vol. I, 97.

114 GO No. 111, HQA, August 16, 1900.

115 Emerson, "US Army Enlisted Campaign Hat Insignia 1890-1907", 159-60.

116 GO No. 80, HQA, December 31, 1902.

117 Emerson, "US Army Campaign Hat Insignia 1890-1907", 159, and Quartermaster Specification 607, April 2, 1903.

118 Quartermaster Specification No. 635, July 11, 1903.

119 GO No. 132, HQA, December 31, 1902.

120 Emerson, "US Army Campaign Hat Insignia 1890-1907", 159-60.

121 GO No. 81, HQA, July 17, 1902, and GO No. 132, HQA, December 31, 1902, both call for this strap and eyelet.

122 *Annual Report of the War Department, 1904*, Vol. II (Washington, DC: Government Printing Office, 1904), 5.

123 Ibid., 1905, 18.

124 GO No. 27, HQA, March 17, 1902. This hat was to be worn for full dress by engineer officers when serving with troops or when so directed by their commanding officer. The chapeau still could be worn, however, "on occasions of formal ceremony" in those instances where "engineer officers were not serving with troops." Ibid. J. Phillip Langellier and Jean Lenahan, "U.S. Army Engineer Officers Dress Uniforms, 1902-1903," XXXV *Military Collector and Historian* No. 4 (Winter 1983): 151-9, summarizes this transitional uniform that was prescribed for wear with this cap, as well as its subsequent replacement.

125 William K. Emerson, comp., *Uniform Regulations of the U.S. Army 1902* (Steelville, MO: J. Watson, 1976), 3.

126 GO No. 52, HQA, March 3, 1902.

127 GO No. 132, HQA, December 31, 1902.

128 Ibid.

129 *Annual Report of the War Department, 1905*, Vol. II, 18, underscored the olive drab cap's adoption which was "made upon the same lines as the present dress cap; that for enlisted men being plain, and for officers having a band of lustrous braid of darker shade than the crown." For some reason this report made no mention of the khaki cap.

130 Ibid., 18.

131 See Quartermaster Specification No. 744, February 20, 1905. Later, Quartermaster Specification No. 838, October 20, 1906, clarified the point that regimental, battalion, and squadron non-commission officers, along with chief musicians and trumpeters, would not have letters on their devices, nor would artillery personnel in these same positions have the number of the battery or company. It should be noted that cap devices for Recruiting Service personnel and enlisted men of the United States Military prison guard consisting of the white metal letters "R.S." and "P.G.", respectively inclosed in gilt wreaths, were included for the full dress/dress caps, and dull-finish ones for the service cap. There were also versions with numbers included for the recruiting district or company, respectively. Emerson, "U.S. Army Enlisted Cap Insignia, 1905-1918": 28 and 38. GO No. 154, WD, September 12, 1906, further indicated these designs were carried over to collar insignia.

132 GO No. 137, WD, August 10, 1905. As of 1906, it also should be noted that the field musicians serving as prison guards were to have the letter "PG" above their trumpets and the company number in the coil, while Recruiting Service field musicians had "RS" above and the number of the district in the coil. In addition, in 1905, the bands for the coast artillery were given their own numbers, as opposed to cavalry, field artillery, and infantry bandsmen who wore the regimental number on their lyre devices. Emerson, "U.S. Army Enlisted Cap Insignia, 1905-1918", 38.

133 It should be noted that one other addition to cap badges came into being with GO No. 169, WD, October 22, 1908. This order created special devices for cavalry and artillery enlisted personnel serving at West Point. The basic crossed sabers and crossed cannons were to be surmounted by the letter "USMA" above and the letters "DET" below. Further, the Army Service Detachment at West Point kept the quartermaster insignia, but added the letters "USMA" above and "DET" below, while similarly the academy's band was to sport a silver lyre with "USMA" above and "BAND" below. West Point's field musicians were to have the trumpet with "USMA" above and "F" for field musician below. There were gilt and subdued versions as required for the various caps.

This order was not carried out as first published, however, in that for some two years correspondence went back and forth between West Point and quartermaster personnel until settling upon the following scheme: the letters "MA and "DET" above and below respectively for the crossed cannons of artillery and the crossed saber of cavalry; the castle of engineers was to be surmounted by "MA" with "DET" on the face of the device; "MA" above the trumpet of field musicians with "DET" affixed to the trumpet coil; and a lyre within a wreath with "MA" on the face for the band. Quartermaster Specification No. 1075, August 12, 1910.

Even as discussions were ongoing relative to the proper insignia for the various en listed components at West Point, a decision was made to adopt another new insignia for the various service school personnel at West Point, Ft. Riley, and the other schools throughout the army. In 1909 a large disk of about 1 in diameter with a cogged wheel encircling a crossed quill and hammer, was specified. Emerson, "U.S Army Enlisted Cap Devices, 1905-1918": 24. During most of this evolution, insignia as adopted came in gilt and subdued versions, except for the Philippine Scouts, who for years had only dull bronze devices. Ibid: 38.

[34] Quartermaster Specification 691, adopted September 10, 1904.

[35] According to William K. Emerson, "Mounted Service School, 1913" XLIII *Military Collector and Historian* No. 3 (Fall 1991): 116, it seems other work caps were in use during the early part of the twentieth century as well, including what may have been a denim version of the 1895-pattern forage cap, as indicated by a photograph of a class of horseshoers at Fort Riley, Kansas' Mounted Service School. Some of the men also appear to wear old 1895-pattern forage caps, and the instructor apparently has on an officer's version of the cap with mohair band but without the eagle and gold cord chinstrap. Still a few more of the group have donned civilian billed caps, which probably were private purchases.

[36] *Annual Report of the War Department, 1912*, Vol. I, (Washington, DC: U.S. Government Printing Office, 1912), 20.

[37] Tom Lindmier and Steve Mount, *I See By Your Outfit: Historic Cowboy Gear of the Northern Plains* (Glendo, WY: High Plains Press, 1996), 32-42. provides a useful overview relative to cowboy headgear in the region where the "Montana Peak" seems to have originated.

[38] Randy Steffen, *The Horse Soldier, 1776-1943*, Vol. III (Norman: University of Oklahoma Press, 1978), 148.

[139] GO No. 193, WD, November 15, 1905, reiterated that the cover was to be removable, and further stated that the cap badge was to be "of gold or gilt metal, detachable", a detail not mentioned in GO No. 132, HQA, December 31, 1902.

[140] Previously GO No. 122, WD, July 13, 1904, stated khaki helmets were to be worn with the khaki uniform in the United States, until exhausted, instead of the campaign hat. The exception was "on occasions where the requirements of the service will necessitate wearing of the campaign hat. The helmet seemed to have a slightly prolonged career in the Pacific, however. See for instance, Robert L. Miller, "Military Funeral in the Philippines" XV *Military Collector and Historian* No. 4 (Winter 1963): 125, which clearly indicates the late use of khaki summer helmet in the Philippines Islands. The helmet was not necessarily popular, however, in that its cork body was rather fragile and could be damaged easily. In this light, the campaign hat was viewed as more desirable by some veterans. Interview with Edward Whitehead (Spanish American War volunteer and later regular army coast artillery master electrician) with John Langellier, c. 1975. Chappell, *Summer Helmets*, 30, notes the precise date by which the white and khaki helmets ceased to be issued "is a matter of conjecture." Chappell further proposed these helmets "seemed to fit in the American Edwardian Age as well as they had in the Victorian."

[141] Mark A. Reynosa, *U.S. Combat Helmets of the 20th Century—Mass Production* (Atglen, PA: Schiffer Military, 1997), 8-11, offers a cursory look at the M1917 helmet, one of several innovations in U.S. Army headgear that was spawned by WWI and its aftermath.

BIBLIOGRAPHY

Primary Sources

Unpublished

Record Group 92. Records of the Office of Quartermaster General. National Archives. Washington, DC.

Record Group 94. Records of the Office of the Adjutant General. National Archives. Washington, DC.

Record Group 107. Records of the Secretary of War. National Archives, Washington, DC.

Record Group 108. Records of Headquarters of the Army. National Archives. Washington, DC.

Record Group 112. Records of the Office of the Surgeon General. National Archives. Washington, DC.

Record Group 391. Records of U.S.Army Mobile Commands. National Archives. Washington, DC.

Record Group 393. Records of U.S. Army Continental Commands. National Archives. Washington, DC.

Published

Annual Report of the Secretary of War. Volume I. Washington, DC: U.S. Government Printing Office, 1872-1898.

Annual Report of the War Department. Volume I. Washington, D.C.: U.S. Government Printing Office, 1899-1912.

Army and Navy Journal. 1872-1890.

Bigelow, John, Jr. *Reminiscences of the Santiago Campaign*. New York: Harper and Brothers, 1899.

Bingham, Theo A. "Army Uniform." XX *Journal of the Military Service Institute*. 1897: 285-295.

Circular No. 8. Report on Hygiene of the United States Army and Circular No. 9, Report to the Surgeon General on the Transport of Wounded by Pack Animals. New York: Sol Lewis, 1974.

Emerson, William K. Comp. *Uniform Regulations of the U.S. Army 1902*. Steeleville, MO: J. Watson, 1976.

Everett, John P. "Bullets, Boots, and Saddles. Being Personnel recollections of Men Who Took Part in the Battle of the Big Horn in Montana Territory June 25, 1876, as Told to John P. Everett." IX *Sunshine Magazine*. September 1930. 4-10.

Fuller, Ezra. "Recollections of an Old Cavalryman." XXVI *Journal of the United State Cavalry Association* No. 1 (January 1916): 413-433.

General Orders and Circulars. Adjutant Generals Department. 1872-1912.

Graham, W.A. Ed. *Official Record of a Court of Inquiry convened...upon request of Major Marcus A. Reno...to investigate his conduct at...the Little Bighorn, June 25-26, 1876*. Pacific Palisades, CA: 1951.

Jacobsen, Jacques Noel, Jr. *Regulations and Notes for the Uniform of the United States Army 1857*. Staten Island: Manor Publishing, 1973.

Kimball, Maria Brace. *A Soldier-Doctor of Our Army James P. Kimball*. New York: Houghton Mifflin, 1917.

A Medical Report upon the Uniform and Clothing of the Soldiers of the U.S. Army, 15 April 1868. Washington, DC: Surgeon General's Office, 1868.

Nelson, Henry Loomis. *The Army of the United States*. New York: B.M. Whitlock, 1890.

_____."Army Uniforms in the United States." *Harper's Weekly*. March 1, 1890.

_____. "Reform in Army Uniforms." *Harper's Weekly*. August 30, 1890.

Quartermaster General of the Army. *U.S. Army Uniforms and Equipment, 1889*. Lincoln: University of Nebraska Press, 1986.

Regulations and Decisions Pertaining to the Uniform of Army of the United States. Washington, DC: Government Printing Office, 1899.

Regulations of the United States Army, 1889. Washington, DC: Government Printing office, 1889.

Rodenbaugh, Theo. F. *From Everglade to CaÈon With the Second Dragoons*. New York D. Van Nostrand, 1875.

Taylor, William O. *With Custer on the Little Bighorn*. New York: Viking, 1996.

Viele, Teresa G. *Following the Drum: A Glimpse of Frontier Life* Lincoln: University of Nebraska Press, 1984.

Bibliography

Secondary Sources

Book and Monographs

Boatner, Mark M. III. *The Civil War Dictionary*. New York: David McKay Company, Inc., 1959.

Brinckerhoff, Sidney B. *Military Headgear in the Southwest, 1846-1890*. Tucson: Arizona Pioneers' Historical Society, 1963.

Campbell, J. Duncan and Howell, Edgar M. *American Military Insignia 1800-1851*. Washington, DC: Smithsonian Institution, 1963.

Carmen, W.Y. *British Military Uniforms from Contemporary Pictures, Henry VII to Present Day*. London: Leonard Hill Ltd., 1959.

_____. *A Dictionary of Military Uniforms*. New York: Charles Scribner's Sons, 1977.

Chappell, Gordon. *Brass Spikes and Horsetail Plumes: A Study of* the U.S. Army Dress Helmet, 1872-1904. Gettysburg: Thomas Publications, 1997.

_____. *Search For The Well-Dressed Soldier, 1865-1890*. Tucson: Arizona Historical Society, 1972.

_____. *Summer Helmets of the U.S. Army, 1875-1910*. Cheyenne, WY: Wyoming State Museum, 1967.

Coffman, Edward M. *The Old Army: A Portrait of the American Army in Peacetime, 1784-1898*. Oxford: Oxford University Press, 1986.

Emerson, William K. *Encyclopedia of United States Army Insignia and Uniforms*. Norman: University of Oklahoma Press, 1996.

Howell, Edgar M. *United States Army Headgear 1855-1902: Catalog of United States Army Uniforms in the Collections of the Smithsonian Institution*. Volume II. Washington, DC: Smithsonian Institution, 1975.

Kube, Jan K. *Militaria: A Study of German Helmets & Uniforms, 1729-1918*. West Chester, PA: Schiffer Military, 1990.

Lafromboise, Leon W. *History of the Combat Support Branches Branch Insignia*. Steeleville, MO: Watson Publishing Co., 1977.

Langellier, John P. *Redlegs: The U.S. Artillery from the Civil War to the Spanish-American War, 1861-1898*. London: Greenhill Books, 1998.

Lindmier, Tom, and Mount, Steve. *I See By Your Outfit: Historic Cowboy Gear of the Northern Plains*. Glendo, WY: High Plains Press, 1996.

Long, Oscar F. *Changes in the Uniform of the Army 1775-1895*. Washington, DC: Army & Navy Register, 1898.

Lewis, Waverly P. *U.S Military Headgear 1770-1880*. Devon, CT: Printed by the Author, 1960.

McChristian, Douglas C. *The U.S. Army in the West, 1870-1880: Uniforms, Weapons and Equipment*. Norman: University of Oklahoma, 1995.

Matloff, Maurice, Ed. *American Military History*. Washington, DC: Office of the Chief of Military History United States Army, 1969.

Mollo, John. *Military Fashion*. New York: G.P. Putnam's Sons, 1972.

Müller, Heinrich and Kunter, Frizt. *Europäische Helme*. Berlin: Militarvelag der Deutchen Demokratischen Republik, 1971.

T*he Oxford Universal Dictionary of Historical Principles*. Oxford: The Claraden Press, 1955. 3rd Ed.

Rankin, Robert H. *Helmets and Headdress of the Imperial German Army, 1870-1918*. New Milford, CT: N. Flayderman & Co., 1965.

_____. *Military Headdress: A Pictorial History of Military Headgear from 1660 to 1914*. London: Arms and Armour, 1976.

Reynosa, Mark A. *U.S. Combat Helmets of the 20th Century—Mass Production*. Atglen, PA: Schiffer Military, 1977.

Risch Erna. *Quartermaster Support of the Army*. Washington, DC: Office of the Quartermaster General, 1962.

Schultz, Gerd M. *Helme und Mutzen der Armee, 1871-1945*. Munich: Jorg Minnergut, 1978.

Sefton, James E. *The United States Army and Reconstruction*. Baton Rouge: Louisiana State University Press, 1967.

Steffen, Randy. *The Horse Soldier, 1776-1943*. Volume III. Norman: University of Oklahoma Press, 1978.

Wilkinson-Latham, R.J. *Collecting Militaria*. New York: Arco Publishing, Inc., 1976.

_____. *The Indian Mutiny*. London: Osprey Publishing, 1977.

Periodicals

Addington, Larry H. "The U.S. Coast Artillery and the Problem of Artillery Organization, 1907-1954." LX *Military Affairs* No. 1. February 1976: 1-16

Anon. "Michael Bremer's Ante-bellum Daguerreotypes." I *Military Images*. No. 3. November-December 1979: 18-25.

Baird, L.C. "The Philadelphia Quartermaster Intermediate Depot." VI *Quartermaster Review* No. 6. May-June 1927, 18-19.

Cavanaugh, Philip M. "Non Regulation U.S. Officer's Straw Hat, 1898." XXV *Military Collector and Historian* No. 2. Summer 1973: 86

Chappell, Gordon. "The şPillbox' Cap in the United States Army c. 1866-1902." XXXII *Military Collector and Historian* No. 1. Spring 1980: 4-15.

Chartrand, René. "Canadian Volunteer Infantry c. 1863-1870." XXXVII *Military Collector and Historian* No. 1. Spring 1985: 25-36.

Darida, R., and Donnelly, Ralph. "United States Marine Corps Dress Cap Model of 1859." XXVI *Military Collector and* Historian No. 2. Summer 1974: 110.

Emerson, William K. "U.S. Army Enlisted Campaign Hat Insignia 1890-1907." XXIX *Military Collector and Historian* No. 4. Winter 1977: 158-162.

_____. "U.S. Army Enlisted Cap Insignia, 1896-1905." XXIV *Military Collector and Historian* No. 1. Spring 1972: 11-15.

_____. "U.S. Army Enlisted Cap Insignia, 1905-1918." XXIX *Military Collector and Historian* No. 1. Spring 1977: 22-29.

Gero, Anthony. "The Elusive Pillbox Cap, 1870-1900." XIX *Military Images* No. 3. November-December 1997: 24-26.

Hutchins, James S. "The Army Campaign Hat of 1872." XVI *Military Collector and Historian* No. 3. Fall 1968: 65-73.

Jacobsen, Jacques Noel, Jr. "The Uniform of the Indian Scouts." XXVI *Military Collector and Historian* No. 3. Fall 1974: 136-144.

Langellier, J. Phillip, and Lenahan, Jean. "U.S. Army Engineer Officers Dress Uniforms, 1902-1903." XXXV *Military Collector and Historian* No. 4. Winter 1993: 151-159.

Madaus, Howard Michael. "Dating the Earliest Use of the şPillbox Cap' in the United States Army." XXXII *Military Collector and Historian* No. 4. Winter 1980: 177-179.

Miller, Robert. "Military Funeral in the Philippines 1909." XV *Military Collector and Historian* No. 4. Winter 1963: 125.

Ross, Leroy E. and Emerson, William K. "Hat Cords of the U.S. Army." XXVII *Military Collector and Historian* No. 4. Winter 1976: 148-153.

Sperry, T.J. "1872 Insignia Expedient Attachment Devices." XLI *Military Collector and Historian* No. 1. Spring 1989: 43-45.

_____. "Winter Clothing on the Northern Plains." XLIV *Military Collector and Historian* No. 3. Fall 1992: 116-120.

INDEX

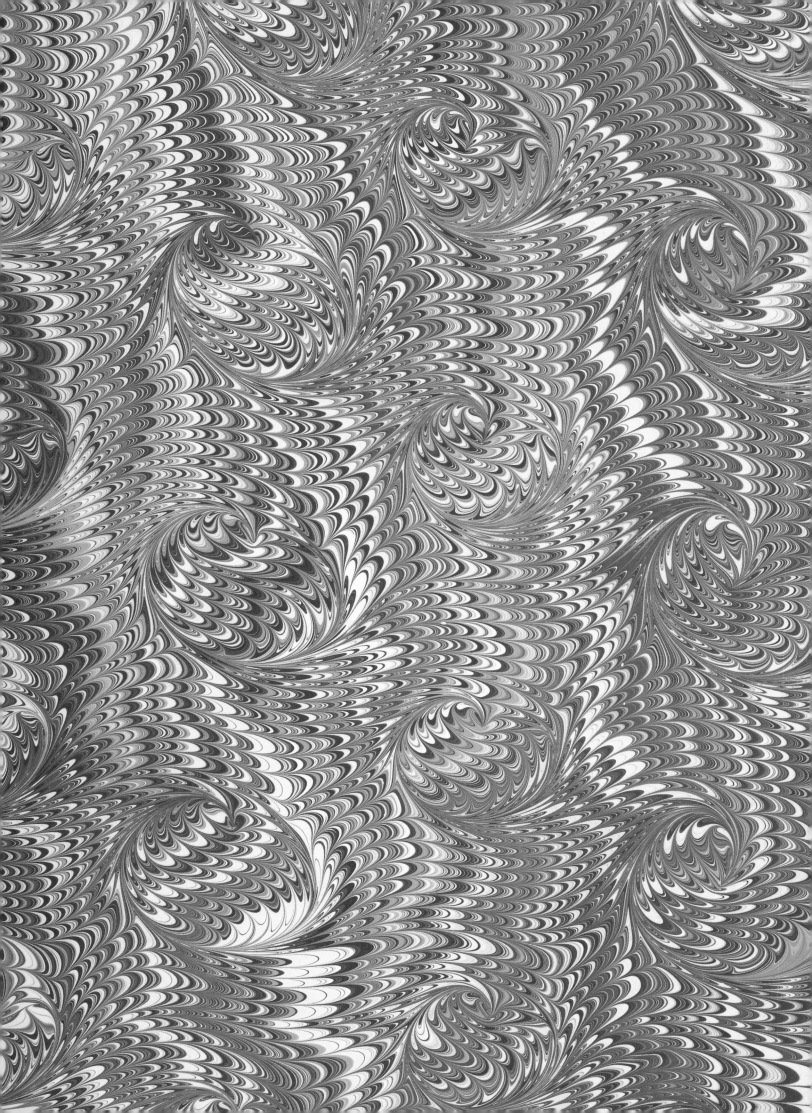